Date Loaned

APR 3 '38			
MAY 9 '38			
DEC 4 '38			
OCT 8 '53			
5/18/32			
OCT 11 1964			

Library Bureau Cat. no. 1138

HELEN KELLER'S JOURNAL

Books by
HELEN KELLER

HELEN KELLER'S JOURNAL
OPTIMISM (AN ESSAY)
OUT OF THE DARK
MIDSTREAM: MY LATER LIFE
MY RELIGION
THE SONG OF THE STONE WALL
THE STORY OF MY LIFE
THE WORLD I LIVE IN

HELEN KELLER'S
JOURNAL

1936—1937

MCMXXXVIII
DOUBLEDAY, DORAN & COMPANY, INC.
Garden City, New York

PRINTED AT THE *Country Life Press*, GARDEN CITY, N. Y., U. S. A.

COPYRIGHT, 1938
BY HELEN KELLER
ALL RIGHTS RESERVED

FIRST EDITION

FOREWORD

ON MARCH 3, 1887, *a young Miss Annie Sullivan, but lately graduated from the Perkins Institution for the Blind in Boston, arrived in Tuscumbia, Ala., to begin the education of a deaf and blind child, not quite seven years old, whose name was Helen Keller. "Teacher," the little girl called her on that miraculous day about a month later when she first discovered that things and people had names; "Teacher" she remained for nearly half a century.*

In Midstream, *published when they had been together forty-two years, Miss Keller wrote: "I have been frequently asked what I should do without her. I smile and answer cheerfully, 'God sent her, and if He takes her, His love will fill the void,' but it terrifies me to face the thought that this question brings to my mind. I peer with a heavy heart into the years to come. Hope's face is veiled, troubling fears awake and bruise me as they wing through the dark. I lift a tremulous prayer to God, for I should be blind and deaf in very truth if she were gone away."*

Anne Sullivan Macy died on October 20, 1936, leaving Miss Keller alone to answer the dread question. Yet not alone. She had Miss Polly Thomson, of Glasgow, Scotland, who for twenty-two years had been a devoted companion to her and her teacher. Miss Thomson immediately applied for American citizenship, and a few days later the two women sailed for Scotland to find a quiet time in which to readjust their lives. Miss Keller began this Journal

Foreword

on the ship. It is a record of her awakening from a great spiritual numbness into a renewed determination to make her life of service to others—to live so that on each third of March to come she can look back upon some achievement that has justified her teacher's faith in her. Miss Keller's whole philosophy is in these pages.

NELLA BRADDY

*Aboard the SS Deutschland, en route for England.
Midnight of November 4, 1936.*

The deepest sorrow knows no time—it seems an eternal night. Truly did Emerson say that when we travel we do not escape from ourselves, we carry with us the sadness which blurs all places and all days.

This is the first voyage Polly and I have had without Teacher, who was the life and the center of our journeyings by land and sea. Not until now have I realized that I shall not see her on earth. Our friends who came to bid us good-by brought flowers and fruits for only Polly and me. We have just one room with two beds and coffee served mornings for only two. Dear, brave Polly, who used to read aloud to Teacher constantly, now reads to me with her fingers when I can pay any attention. The anguish which makes me feel cut in two prevents me from writing another word about these life-wrecking changes.

Most of the time I appear to myself to be a somnambulist, impelled only by an intense faith. It is sweet because it helps me to cross halfway with Teacher into her new and infinitely richer life. It is terrible because it drives me relentlessly to think of others' sorrow before my own, to hold up the torch of hope for the blind when

Helen Keller's Journal

tears blot out all the stars for me, to perform one task after another when the joy of work is fled.

SS Deutschland. November 5th.

A day dreadful beyond words. I am beginning to come out of the stupor of grief, and every nerve is aquiver. It does not seem possible that the pain flooding through my heart can ever be stilled, but I know it is a sign of returning spiritual health.

Sometimes as Polly and I walk up and down the deck she describes to me the gulls dipping and circling about the ship and the tiny white sea swallows that fly incredible distances—from three to four thousand miles.

Are those sea swallows wise or foolish to go so far out to sea, defenseless, small, beyond rescue? At first I was inclined to think it was contrary to the laws of nature for them to risk such long flights, especially as great numbers perish from cold or fall prey to large fish as they sleep on the water.

On the other hand, many reach safely "lands that keep the sun", and return triumphantly North with the spring!

SS Deutschland. November 6th.

Even more amazing than the wonders of nature are the powers of the spirit. Instead of having dumb thoughts or conventional phrases about another world, why can we not take unto ourselves wings of imagination and traverse unafraid vast immensities of the unknown into the joyous, human yet divine warmth that is heaven?

Helen Keller's Journal

SS Deutschland. November 7th.

To my surprise I find that the sea swallows have waked in me fresh courage-thoughts. I am still weary, and every physical exertion is an effort, but gradually I am regaining my habit of "looking around." With emotion I feel the courtesy and good will of the Germans ministering to our comfort and their endeavors to divert our minds with pleasant talk. The atmosphere of the Deutschland is so homelike I have no sense of being a stranger. Everywhere the German love of beauty greets my fingers—chrysanthemums large and small, compact, curly petaled, round and slender like daisies, arranged in every corner and at each landing as we climb up and down the stairs, cozy rooms with every modern advantage crowded into the least compass possible.

SS Deutschland. November 8th.

What earthly consolation is there for one like me, whom fate has denied a husband and the joy of motherhood? At the moment my loneliness seems a void that will always be immense. Fortunately I have much work to do—more than ever before, in fact—and while doing it I shall have confidence as always that my unfulfilled longings will be gloriously satisfied in a world where eyes never grow dim nor ears dull.

This evening, after a brilliant day, Polly kept telling me how marvelous the sunset was. She said sky and sea were suffused with a rose tinge defying the power of

Helen Keller's Journal

the brush or the pen to capture. Often I had felt petals showered upon me by a passing breeze; so I could imagine the sunset as a vast rose garden from which the petals had been shaken and were drifting through the sky before sinking into the gray November night.

SS Deutschland. November 9th.

Today I had a lunch of frankfurters and sauerkraut—the first meal I have eaten with any relish for many weeks. (This happened to be the special German dish on the lunch menu, and a favorite one of mine.)

Little by little my delight in philosophy, poetry and travel is reviving. This morning I am in a mood to wander forever over the face of the waters. E. V. Lucas quotes from *Chinese Biographies* an anecdote which chimes in with this state of mind. A Chinese philosopher of the eighth century, Chang Chi Ho, spent his time angling but used no bait. His object was not to catch fish. When a friend asked him why he roamed about so purposelessly Chang's answer was swift:

"With the empyrean my home, the bright main my constant companion and the four seas my inseparable friends—what mean you by roaming?"

SS Deutschland. November 10th.

My first consciousness of time.

Captain Friedel invited me up to his cabin at noon. He entertained me pleasantly with anecdotes about the

Helen Keller's Journal

celebrated Hagenbeck Zoo in Hamburg. He told how one evening at another zoo in Nuremberg the door of the monkey house was left unlocked—a lapse of memory—and a hundred monkeys ran loose, spreading terror through the streets. The next morning a housewife, turning from the stove, saw a monkey standing in the doorway and rammed a saucepan down on his head, and the blacksmith had to be called in to remove it.

He said he had been at sea forty-two years and a captain thirty-two years, and he regretted the departed glory of the sailing ships. I was glad to meet such an able seaman, such a jovial personality and a captain so beloved by the crew that they call him "Papa Friedel."

Tonight I attended the farewell dinner of the Deutschland. The dining room had been transformed so as to represent the bottom of the ocean. I touched the fish supposed to be swimming about. The caviar was brought on a lump of ice shaped like a fish. Before dessert, in came the Loch Ness monster—a huge creature about thirty feet long, with one eye red and the other white—and lumbered around until he was killed by a waiter dressed up as a sailor. One of the cakes served was a model of the monster and gave me a vivid "picture" in my fingers.

SS Deutschland. November 11th.

Armistice Day. Sorrow has borne me far from earth, and as yet I sense happenings in the world only with the surface of my mind, but dimly I realize that this is Armistice Day. What a glorious homage we shall pay the dead of the Great War when we can call November 11th World Peace Day.

Helen Keller's Journal

Tonight Polly saw the Lizard Lighthouse, and we were homesick, remembering how when Teacher first saw Cornwall she was captivated by its beauty and its wealth of legends and ballads.

Old Neptune is true to form as we approach the rocky, dangerous Cornish coast.

The ship is listing; our trunks are falling all over the room. The table is almost on top of me as I lie upon my bed, and my hands can scarcely keep their balance on the keys of the sliding typewriter.

Park Lane Hotel, London, November 12th.

The storm raged through the night, and we slept badly. However, we were not a bit seasick. As we stumbled about the ship the stewards most kindly lent me a steadying hand.

The water had quieted down when we got on the tender, and it was a delight to sit out in the warm sun. So strongly did I feel Teacher's nearness, it was tantalizing almost beyond endurance. Several nights before Teacher had kissed me in a dream, and literally her face against mine breathed youth, sunshine and flower-sweet air. Since then I have had a sense of following, following, following her, and I keep expecting to find her somewhere—in London or up in the Scottish Highlands her Celtic soul loved.

Whenever I come to Southampton I am excited by the hugeness of the docks and the steamers from the seven seas loading and unloading. (I can feel the mighty cranes descending thunderously into the hold and ascending with their cargo.) This time I especially

Helen Keller's Journal

noticed how well ordered the docks are—no rush, no confusion. All who looked after our luggage showed us courtesy, and we got through the customs easily. Only a little way farther, and we found a small, swift, comfortable train waiting to take us to London.

The autumn wind had made us shiver; but after we left the Southampton Station tea was served, and we soon felt a delicious warmth tingling through us. Eagerly we drank four cups of English tea—the first we had tasted in two years—and ate four slices of excellent English bread and butter, then settled down to the latest news bulletin and a thoughtfully phrased editorial in the London *Times* about the arrest of many Germans in Soviet Russia. Such proceedings show the terror and suspicion that fall upon the guilty and the innocent alike when demoniac forces like Hitlerism are abroad.

From the Waterloo Station we took a taxi which, to my amazement, could carry our twelve pieces of baggage! I shall never forget the two trunks and three big cases of Braille notes I brought for literary work on the top of the taxi and the other seven stowed inside. I wondered if we should reach the Park Lane Hotel alive —I thought the trunks might fall through the roof—but soon I was convinced of our perfect safety. We drove through the usual London mist pierced by innumerable electric lights. With ripples of excitement in her fingers Polly enumerated the places we passed:

"Helen! The Houses of Parliament—you remember our dining there with Sir Ian Fraser when Teacher was here.

"Westminster! . . .

"The Mall! . . .

"Now we have come to Piccadilly. . . .

Helen Keller's Journal

"Oh, that's the Green Park opposite the Park Lane!"

A heartbreaking sense of emptiness swept over us because Teacher was not beside us to repeat those names in a voice full of happy memories and anticipation of another visit to the Park Lane where everything pleased and rested her.

Almost in tears I arrived at the hotel. Everyone there, even the clerks at the desk, the head porter and the doorman, welcomed me with such a friendly warmth it made me feel that I had come home, and I was less lonely. At the Park Lane we do always experience a deep sense of true English hospitality.

Park Lane Hotel, November 13th.

A good cry yesterday morning washed away some of the shadows from my soul, so that I am able to see more of life's brightness and to chat with a few people.

This morning I went to the U.S. Lines to say "How do you do" to my good friend Mr Moore and to make arrangements for our passage home. He said he would also arrange for me to fly to Paris to attend the unveiling of the Borglum statue of Thomas Paine on January 29, 1937.

From the office I walked along the Mall and Piccadilly. Polly's exceeding love of beauty found admirable objects in every window display she described to me—books such as rare illuminated Bibles and beautifully illustrated *Arabian Nights*, *The Hundred Years*, by Philip Guedalla, and *The Life of Lord Carson*, pictures like Watts's "River Scene", a boy with his arms round

Helen Keller's Journal

the neck of a swan, splendid animals and—"Oh, Helen! there's a handsome picture of a general on a black charger, and he looks so like Mr Migel!"[1]

I was glad Polly's eyes were so full of charming sights. With my own senses I perceived the odors of fresh bread, wineshops and passing motorbuses. A whiff of enchanting single English violets made my heart give a little jump, and we went into the florist's to buy some.

I knew when I entered the Green Park by the smell of grass and burning leaves. It was a blessed corner to commune with nature away from the street traffic— men, women and children walking just for the pleasure of it, dogs gamboling without leash or muzzle, pigeons and gulls. I touched the noble plane trees and oaks and enjoyed the softness of the grass. The sparrows were very cocky and so fearless we almost stepped on them. We inquired why the plane leaves were being burned, and the reply was that it takes them five years to rot! Their ashes make a fine dressing for the soil.

What endless fascination there is for me in a gentle city like London, where everything significant to the eye, the ear and the touch is within reach!

Charlie[2] and Jean lunched with us here at the hotel. We stayed so long in the dining room talking, I am sure even the English waiters grew impatient to have us leave and let them clear the table. Up in our room the flood of talk didn't abate a jot, and I began to wonder if the proverbial British taciturnity ever existed. After tea our friends left; and we rested an hour in obedience to our physician's peremptory orders.

[1] Mr M. C. Migel, president of the American Foundation for the Blind.
[2] Charles Augustus Muir, author of detective stories and of serious studies of Scottish history and romance.

Helen Keller's Journal

At seven o'clock Ned[1] came to see us. We had dinner served in our room so that we could talk quietly about Teacher's last days on earth. I felt the silent, throbbing sorrow in his handclasp as he listened and read the newspaper accounts we had brought of the funeral and the memorial services at the National Cathedral in Washington and the collection of beautiful, unique messages I had received.

As ever, Ned has a heart of oak which no obstacles can discourage nor reverses of fortune subdue. He did not leave until half-past eleven, and we had uttered but a tiny part of what we wanted to say.

Park Lane Hotel, November 14th.

Up early so that we could read *The Times*'s comments on the alarming state of European affairs. Tensely alive to an atmosphere charged with the lightning of coming events, I am wondering what will result from the new Nazi coup d'état (relative to German waterways).

It is devoutly to be wished that all statesmen should join Mr Baldwin in his warning that the world is moving towards war, but it is no news to me. For eighteen years I have tried to suppress a great fear of another world war and the yet worse misery it may entail, but I cannot escape facts. Have not all the European nations —except for a while Germany, Austria, Hungary and of course Great Britain—kept on arming at frantic speed ever since Armistice Day, 1918?

---

[1] Mr Edward L. Holmes, inventor of the Holmes Master Compass and an intimate friend of Miss Keller's since her seventeenth year.

Helen Keller's Journal

Full of earnest good wishes, I greet Britain in her once more taking the lead in attempts to secure the peace of Europe. But I cannot believe that the stronger Britain is in armaments, the greater will be "the certainty of peace." History teaches that fleets and armies are as provocative as weapons openly carried by private citizens, and that the innumerable treaties signed after wars have settled nothing.

It seems to me Mr Eden's courage must be remarkable, since he undertakes to prove in face of general disbelief that sneers against the League of Nations are unjustified.

The horror of civil war pierces me afresh as I read of the atrocious fighting in Spain. The worst of it is that no other solution appears possible in a country where for centuries the government has been founded on force, education confined to a small class, tolerance trampled upon, and the caste system as rigid as that of India, though veiled with poetry and romance. My heart bleeds for the defenders of Madrid, but it is proud tears I shed for the masses who are giving their lives to create a more enlightened and civilized nation. I shall not believe until the last that their superhuman heroism is to end in defeat.

With deep interest I note the message of Sir Kingsley Wood, minister of health, on "the comprehensive effort to improve the physical condition" of the people. I recall the anxious articles I have read at different times about the lack of proper nourishment and "the town blight" of Britain and the United States as well. I am glad that both Parliament and Congress are taking up more and more public welfare, which I consider the essence of government. Eagerly I follow the splendid work of

Helen Keller's Journal

abolishing the London slums and am glad it will be completed in two years. Memories still burn into my soul of the Mulberry Street slums in New York which I visited as a child with Teacher and Alexander Graham Bell, and the dreadful alleys of Washington, D.C., and Pittsburgh which I saw as a grown woman. It would be a blessed satisfaction if I might die knowing that the barbarity of slums was wiped out of civilization.

Round half-past eleven Mac[1] came for us in his car, and we motored out to his charming country house, Heatherwood, Pirbright, Surrey. The weather raw, with occasional bursts of sunshine. The drive so crammed with historic interest, Polly's flying fingers could scarcely keep pace with Mac's pithy comments—Hyde Park Corner with its overpowering Artillery Memorial, beautiful wide commons, Putney Heath where Dick Turpin so often performed the operation of separating rich travelers from their fat purses, Richmond Park with its gnarled oaks which I have felt, dating from Henry VIII's reign, Hampton Court which I visited four years ago, and always the Thames winding in and out through a changeful, sweet countryside. Remembering Queen Elizabeth's gorgeous progresses to and from London, I wondered what Henry VIII's journeys were like when he went to Hampton Court or hunted in Richmond Park.

When we reached Mac's house his wife welcomed us at the door most cordially. She had often expressed the wish that I should visit her out there and make the acquaintance of her beloved garden. For the first time I saw their bright, lovable little boy, Jimmy. There was also Mrs Eagar's sweet sister, Miss Heald. Mrs Eagar

[1] W. McG. Eagar, secretary-general of the National Institute for the Blind.

and Miss Heald are both deaf, and naturally there is a special bond between us three.

We warmed our hands at the fire a few minutes, then had a good old-fashioned English lunch, which we greatly enjoyed after the long drive. Afterwards we rambled through the garden and the rockery. There were few flowers left, but the chill air did not blunt the marvelous sweetness wafted from many shrubs, especially rosemary and box hedges. Polly reveled in the brilliant colors of rowan berries and foliage still clinging to the trees. Near the house I tried to embrace an immense old yew which proved to have a circumference of over thirty feet. Everywhere we were followed by two darling Lakeland terriers, Whiskey and her daughter Eggnog.

It was Mrs Eagar who gave me my precious Maida; so I felt quite at home with her two dogs scampering and rolling each other on the lawn. We inspected the apple house, which answered almost exactly to the descriptions, in Margaret Deland's *If This Be I*, of the fruit granaries in Pennsylvania. My fingers strayed delightedly over the carefully graded fruit, and the taste of the small sweet apples carried me in a flash back to the orchards of my childhood.

Mac showed me an out-of-door cage full of lovebirds; and when they heard my odd voice I could feel them fluttering about in agitation. There were many white pigeons around, and Mac caught one for me. The bird made me happy by resting on my breast confidently and refusing to go, even when we all petted him together. Finally, as he opened his soft wings, he left on my finger tips a fairylike impression of a snowy feather fan darting through the air. Then I knew it was a fantail pigeon, and with a tender thrill I remembered my little pigeon friends at home in Alabama that used to perch on my head and shoulders and knees, fighting for crumbs.

The biting air chilled me, but the fragrant tea we had that afternoon warmed the cockles of our hearts. I feel almost like Dr Johnson these days, drinking so many cups of tea. . . .

Regretfully we said our good-bys, and Mr Eagar and Jimmy took us to the train. As I cuddled down in the warm, comfortable compartment Jimmy put into my arms a bunch of odorous sprays almost as big as himself "to make us think we were really in the country while we stayed at the hotel."

Park Lane Hotel, Sunday, November 15th.

Lady Fairhaven, the daughter of my wonderful friend, H. H. Rogers, who helped me through college, invited us to lunch at her London house, 37 Park Street W. I wanted to walk over, but Polly feared that the endless twists and turns of London might lose us completely, and we took a taxi instead.

A handsome young manservant opened the door of the taxi and ushered us into a beautiful hall. Another manservant took us up in an elevator. As we stepped out I smelled the banks of flowers I have always found in Lady Fairhaven's home, in London and at Park Close. Lady Fairhaven herself came forward to embrace me, and in this tenderness I felt afresh her father's friendship and her own.

After some chitchat we went down to lunch. Lady

Helen Keller's Journal

Fairhaven insisted on our going in the elevator because it was easier. Every detail of the meal was delectable. My dear hostess kept putting choice tidbits and sweets on my plate, saying to Polly with that adorable chuckle of hers, "I am doing this in secret," but I detected what she was doing and told her I had a ruinous sweet tooth and shouldn't be led into temptation. But I enjoyed those tidbits all the same.

Before we re-entered the cozy drawing room Lady Fairhaven stopped in the hall to show me the splendid vegetables from Park Close for which she had just won a prize. I did not dream that England could raise such tremendous onions!

Sitting by the fire with her hand in mine, we talked intimately about Mr Rogers and how I still missed his counsel, and about Teacher and the appalling changes her passing had already wrought in my life. For a few minutes we fell silent; then to make me smile she drew out an intriguing jewel and laid it on my palm. Its shape was that of a bunch of grapes in pearls and diamonds, and it hung at the end of a necklace of colored pearls. As I looked she drew out of that jewel the daintiest spectacles imaginable!

These gems of artistry have no end! I nearly forgot to mention our drinking coffee out of exquisite Crown Derby cups with delicate gold spoons representing Mother Goose's rhymes, which Lady Fairhaven received in the long ago as a wedding present. The spoon I had was in the image of Tom, the piper's son.

Helen Keller's Journal

Park Lane Hotel, November 16th.

In the headlines of this morning's paper appears Prince Paul, senior regent of Yugoslavia, now visiting the Duke and Duchess of Kent. How the name of Yugoslavia inundates me with exciting memories of our visit to that country and our meeting with King Alexander a few summers ago!

I can recall that meeting so clearly. When we reached the palace gate the guards saluted, and so did the soldiers stationed at different points along the driveway. On either side of the palace steps were more guards, arrayed in white and scarlet, with gold epaulettes and a gold A in their caps.

The marshal, a middle-aged gentleman dressed in white, met us with the elegant manners of a courtier, assisted us to alight, kissed our hands and conducted us into the library—a beautiful and dignified room with a great French window opening on to a lawn, from which we could see the gardens stretching away in the distance like a Persian carpet. Near the center of the room was a huge globe of the earth hung in a great circle of wood. The doors of the bookcases were made of handsomely wrought iron. The summer palace is built like a peasant's cottage, but regal in its simplicity.

We had understood that the marshal would give us instructions as to the etiquette of meeting the king. We waited, expecting him every moment to enter and tell us what we were to do. Finally the door opened, and he asked us in French to follow him. He ushered us at once into the king's presence. We did not know who it was;

Helen Keller's Journal

we thought it might be another official who would instruct us; but when my teacher saw the man rise and come forward to greet us she knew it was His Majesty and spelled into my hand quickly, "The king!" He shook hands with us and bade us be seated.

A more gracious and friendly person it would have been hard to find anywhere. He was very interested in my visit to Yugoslavia, for his delegate to the World Congress for the Blind in New York had urged me to visit His Majesty's school for the sightless in Zemun. I expressed my gratitude to him for taking such a warm interest in the handicapped and said that what he did for the blind in Yugoslavia he did for the blind of the world by setting a kingly example. He assured me that my visit would inspire him to do more. I told him how delighted I was to find in his country such a friendly feeling towards the United States. "I am very glad you feel our good will," he replied. "It is very deep and sincere." I remarked that I was delighted His Majesty had received me in the summer palace, and I added laughingly that I had always felt a little sorry for kings: their burden was so great. He smiled, and I went on to say, "But here in this lovely country place Your Majesty can enjoy himself as much as the simplest of his subjects." After some talk about the remarkable way in which Belgrade had been built up since the war I said I had come from a democratic country, but that after seeing all that he had accomplished for his people in such a short time I was inclined to think that a good king was the best kind of government. He said he had known about me for many years and read my books, but he would very much like to see exactly how Miss Sullivan had begun to teach me and how I learned to speak and to read the lips. We gave a demonstration. Polly said the king was fascinated and never took his eyes from us during the narrative. He exclaimed several times, "C'est merveilleux!" There was a great bowl filled with exquisite roses on a table at his left, and afterwards he took one of the roses, carefully picked off the thorns and handed it to me. A sweet and tender climax to our long, interesting talk. Two days later, when we arrived in Ljubljana, the minister there formally presented me with the autographed photograph the king had sent me —beautifully framed in gold, surmounted by the crown and an initial A for Alexander. Afterwards I was decorated with the medal of St Sava. It is said that there is an empty throne in every country waiting for a bold man to seize it. There was no empty throne in Yugoslavia. King Alexander I filled it completely by the force of his personality, his decision, his courage and vision. He was a great man in a position to do great things. The shock with which I learned of his assassination at Marseilles is still poignant in my memory.

Later.

This afternoon some friends came for tea, and we talked for hours. Who ever heard of a woman who was too tired to talk? After our guests had gone I felt like a squeezed lemon, and I thought we should lie down, but Polly said a walk might do us more good. As we started we discovered it was raining, but we went out all the same. Through a mass of cars and taxis we walked to the Marble Arch and back. Polly had a fat black crow to pick with the weather because it was so dark she could hardly see anything to describe to me.

Helen Keller's Journal

We passed the house where the Duke and Duchess of York live and the dark old house which was presented to the Duke of Wellington after his victory at Waterloo. The gate facing Piccadilly must be about fifteen feet high. The elaborate ironwork I felt in it seemed to me the kind John Ruskin deplored. Going round, I touched the wooden wall surmounted by iron spikes—and barbed wire! I want to know more about that strange place.

Farther on we saw a man sitting on a bench in that raw wind, and I marveled. I could not help thinking of W. H. Davies' enlightening, elemental book, *The Autobiography of a Super-tramp*. Then came the brilliantly lighted Dorchester Hotel and Grosvenor House, and there were touches of splendor that reminded Polly of Radio City.

Sparks of delight flew in my mind as she mentioned that mighty epic of execution—that center of art whence radiate music and wireless waves to all lands. That enchantment wrought by machinery! Often I am asked if I do not think the machine is destroying the best attributes of man. I reply: "No, each machine is an extension of man's mind over matter. Rockefeller Center embodies a daring idealism. Shining and soaring, spangling the night with light, gracing the day with its hanging gardens, it gives wings to the imagination. It is a marvel of genius not only in architecture but in the organized labor that raised it. I believe the very sight of Rockefeller Center, even to those who do not enter its vast halls, tends to elevate their minds and foster a loftier conception of what a city should be. Some may say it was madness to rear such an extravagant entertainment center, but surely it is a prophecy of beauty that shall invade the darkest street canyons and humanize the harsh, crowded areas of existence with its celestial light."

Suddenly Polly spelled into my hand:

"A woman leaning against a lamppost ... Why, oh, why?"

Another of the mysteries that keep my imagination astir.

The drizzle had become a dense, sticky mist which was especially disagreeable because it held in suspension a volume of smells from motors and coal smoke. However, the lights and the cars dashing past, and speculations as to where so many people were speeding, rendered our walk a real adventure. The life of London is crowded with interest in all weathers.

Back at the hotel we took off one soaked garment after another—hats, coats, shoes and stockings. How a tramp in the rain doubles the dividend of pleasure to be derived from a hot tub! ...

Park Lane Hotel, November 17th.

Polly and I up at seven. The rain still heavy. A friend said yesterday he did not remember an autumn in London when it had rained so much.

With pleasure I read from *The Times* that at last Connelly's *Green Pastures* is to be shown on the screen in England. Several years ago I saw it as a play and was deeply moved. It seemed to me that through the ripples of humor and merriment I sensed the fervent faith of the plantation Negroes in the Southern part of the United States whom Archibald Rutledge calls

Helen Keller's Journal

"the kindliest race in America." While I wish every Negro to have the same rights and advantages that I have, I hope they will never sacrifice to the white man's world-idols their beautiful, Christlike neighborliness.

Just returned from the National Institute, where I spent three hours. What a place of comings and goings, receivings and sendings it is! Mac was constantly hurrying from one telephone to another, and naturally it was hard to get in a word with him. However, he managed to see that all my wishes were fulfilled.

Books I borrowed:

Kenneth Grahame's *The Wind in the Willows*.

Two books on London: *A Wanderer in London* by E. V. Lucas, and the other by H. V. Morton, which I hope may give me some sense of direction when different parts of the city are mentioned to me or I walk through them.

Omar Khayyam's *Rubaiyat*. A friend, Mr Lewis, president of the Thomas Paine Memorial Association, New York, sent me to the SS Deutschland before we sailed a beautifully bound copy of the *Rubaiyat*, and besides the pride of possessing it I want the pleasure of reading it in Braille.

"*Marie Bash* ——" Out like a candle goes my memory of that formidable Russian name. I have conscientiously tried to master this title of a world classic; and each time I have thought it was secure in my mind I have started to say, "Bash-that-chef!" Other people whom I know have the same difficulty, which saves my face.

Also I subscribed to the Braille edition of the *Daily Mail*, for I want to save Polly's hands untold hours reading me the long news bulletins and frequent fine editorials.

Helen Keller's Journal

The new Braille writer ordered. It is just what I need for rapid writing, "to my great content" as Pepys would say. Mr Ratcliffe, of the National Institute, showed me how to manipulate the machine. It combines all important requirements—interpointing, interlining, light pressure on the keys, a restful position for the arms when working and a case easy to carry. I shall be sorry to say good-by to my little old Stainsby Wayne which has traveled with me for years.

While there I was glad to see Sir Ian Fraser again. He is as handsome and cordial as ever. We were introduced to Mr Rowley, a charming personality who turned out to be the nephew of the poet, Walter de la Mare. He told me he had lived in the U.S. for some time, especially New York and Chicago. Everybody was talking at once, and Polly was interrupted continually, trying to tell me things, so that her sentences resembled broken bits of spaghetti.

Just now there is at the National Institute an exhibition of dolls in costumes of different countries. I could not stay to see much of it, but I fell in love with two of them. One is the favorite of Princess Elizabeth, Pamela, a darling with flaxen curls tied in tiny red bows, a soft winter suit and cap, leggings and shoes, all red. The other is Princess Margaret Rose's Bridget, lovely in a white summer silk dress with bare legs and dainty slippers. Mr Cockin, the publicity manager for the Institute, who was interviewing me, asked to have my picture taken hugging both royal dolls. He even wanted a picture of me at my new Braille writer! A verse popped up in my mind from the *Rubaiyat*, beginning, "Ever we move as in a show...." Another doll was picked out for me to look at. With delighted fingers I recognized the

Helen Keller's Journal

elegant headdress with a big comb, the mantilla and delicate flowing lace robe of a Spanish donna.

It evoked a picture in my touch of La Argentina, the dancer, whom I saw in New York several years ago and who invited me for a few minutes chat behind the scenes. An interpreter translated her Spanish and my English. She was very tender and appreciative. After a strenuous day she took pains to show me the costumes she wore as a princess, a peasant or a maiden about to be wedded. So I knew through my ten eyes how she wrought into her steps and gestures the tossing of lily buds in a breeze, the flutter of a dove or the lilt of sea waves. How fascinating and happy she was after performing before an enthusiastic audience! It is well for her that she did not have to live through the Spanish Revolution. With dramatic grace she put on a costume which was woven for her by grateful peasants to whom she had administered in bitter poverty and sickness, and she said it was the robe she felt happiest in when she danced.

This digression from the Institute symbolizes the incessant windings of life from one experience to another and the surprising flights of memory started by an object, even a bit of lace! . . .

Returning to our hotel, I observed that the new London taxis are a decided improvement upon the old ones, steadier, warmer and more comfortable. After all that activity we came back very hungry, and I had one of my favorite lunches—a mixed-green salad and biscuits with Camembert cheese. I eat salads a great deal, not only because I enjoy them, but also to keep my figure, which, alas! is difficult.

At four o'clock I went out to Ealing to dine with

Helen Keller's Journal

Major Leslie Barley and his wife, Muriel, a daughter of my lifelong friend, Dr James Kerr Love, the eminent aurist and the most warmhearted advocate of the deaf in Scotland. Dr Love was in our talk and our hearts, and after dinner I telephoned greetings to him and Mrs Love at West Kilbride. I hope he got all I said—it was the second time in my life I had summoned enough courage to try my imperfect speech over a telephone!

Dr Love's intellectual and physical powers are a constant wonder and inspiration. A short time ago he celebrated his seventy-ninth birthday, and his daughter said in one week he had performed forty-three operations! He has just written another book, *The Deaf and Common Sense*, which I especially welcome because it will help the general reader to a clearer understanding of deafness and its isolating consequences, and quicken his sympathy for those whose silent world many people shun.

Lack of hearing has always been a heavier handicap to me than blindness. Sealed ears render more difficult every path to knowledge. The deaf are as hungry for a word as the blind are for a book under their fingers, yet it is harder to find people who will talk with the deaf than people who will supply the sightless with embossed books. That has not been my individual experience, I am glad to say. Sympathy has sweetened my days with society; religion and philosophy have assuaged my sorrows; but I remain unsatisfied, thinking how many deaf persons are immured and lonely through others' neglect or impatience. Regretfully I perceive the impossibility of working for both the blind and the deaf as I have often longed to do. The effort to alleviate either misfortune more than fills a lifetime; and besides, these tasks are redoubled by the endeavor to safeguard human eyes and ears against disease, accident, ignorance. Reluctantly, therefore, I have confined my activities almost exclusively to the dwellers in the Dark Land.

Major Barley, Muriel's husband, talked to me very instructively about his work with chemicals. He believes that chemicals are the basis of all physical life and that as science advances they can be manufactured in sufficient quantities to supply everyone with food, clothing and shelter at less cost than is possible now. The subject is new and bewildering to me; I have no idea of the processes by which those tremendous results may be achieved. But I do know it is an audacious experiment, fostered by a glorious vision that is shedding light throughout a distracted, fear-darkened world, and I shall try to get a clearer idea of the details. Major Barley recommended to me what he considers a helpful book for the layman, *The Next Hundred Years*, and as soon as I obtain a copy I shall begin another thrilling adventure, looking into the civilization of the future.

I came back near midnight and found a business message which called for an immediate and quite long letter. Now it is half-past one, and my eyes refuse to open again. We must be up at half-past six to do our packing, as we leave for Glasgow on the Royal Scot. As always, I shall pack my own bags, so that I may know where everything is and be as independent as I may under the circumstances.

Helen Keller's Journal

Park Lane Hotel, November 18th.

In the Shakespearean phrase my eyes are still "seeled up" by drowsiness, but a cup of hot coffee has waked me sufficiently to write.

English bacon and eggs for breakfast—the first I have had since arriving in London, and how good they tasted! I have just said to Polly that I rather enjoy this hard work, and the English way of life enables me to do it in peace of mind and body. Yesterday the weather treated us to its worst usage, and I exclaimed, "Men may come and men may go, but the rain goes on forever." However, the air feels lighter today, and I think we shall have a pleasant journey.

En route to Scotland, November 18th.

An autumn day sweet with sunshine and the odor of fields still green and falling leaves that I smelled through the open window. The cattle grazing peacefully; the countryside changing from pastures to smoke-blackened towns; and then to grassy hills "atune with the wind", and streams playing hide-and-seek with the sunbeams among the trees and great moors.

Polly and I were alone in the compartment until lunchtime, and I could hardly believe it. Teacher had always journeyed with us through Britain, doubling with her passionate love of beauty our delight in what we saw and touched. She must be asleep, I thought, or she would be spelling into my hand the charm of light or color or flying cloud.

Helen Keller's Journal

The yearning for her companionship almost unnerved me; but despite her skepticism she had not challenged for nothing my faith that our spiritual nearness would outlast death, and I braced myself thinking of her blessedness in seeing without effort or pain and the joyous, unfettered use of her powers.

I pictured her, brilliant, animated, spreading charm and gaiety among her friends rediscovered. A sweet awareness came over me that the loveliness which she had cherished on earth was shining about her as an aura. Though beyond my reach, I knew she had not forgotten our sojourn together amid the shadows and that she wanted to share with me the infinitely higher knowledge and happiness of her unhandicapped life. For every thorn of poverty, every disappointment endured, every ache of loneliness and misunderstanding, and the sight she vainly strove to keep to the end, there was without doubt a splendid recompense.

No; perhaps I should not say recompense, but rather the unfolding of her own inner personality with undreamed power to quicken the eye and make the ear sensitive to loftier harmonies. Since teaching had been her work and her glory, I imagined her tenderly receiving the sensorially crippled, passing from this world to the next, and so instructing them that they need not grope nor be buried in silence nor stumble along desolate ways. Who knows? This may have been real news she whispered into my listening mind. Certainly my soul was so conscious of her presence I could not—I would not—say she was dead, and I do not now.

I still perceive, as it were, a lameness in my spirit. The wrench of separation from a beloved, unique, lifelong companion seems to have torn away an essential part of me. Deaf-blind a second time, I find any effort to speak cheerfully, to resume interest in a changed world, to work alone through substituted guides and minds different from Teacher's—all these I find as hampering as sharp pain-throbs.

Nevertheless, as the hours glided by fresh life pulsed through me; and my hold on present duties and opportunities grew stronger.

I turned to a book I had brought, André Maurois's *Life of Disraeli*. It appeals to me as an internationalist, written in French by a Frenchman about one of Britain's most eminent political leaders. It is vivid, instructive, generous as far as may be to all the actors in a fateful empire drama, balanced by a just regard for spiritual values and the large perspective of history.

I do not remember a more impressive word picture than Maurois's portrayal of Gladstone and Disraeli. Gladstone, robustly self-confident, exalted with rectitude, a dragon breathing fire against the archenemy of mankind in public, and at home felling mighty trees with the conviction that he was the divinely appointed woodsman who should clear away the dense, unhealthy vegetation of corrupt politics from the British Empire. Disraeli, always ill, old, struggling for breath, unable to walk, yet steering Britain with indomitable will out of a disastrous European conflict and planning the change of an empire based on force into a federation of self-governing peoples with an imperial parliament. Sixty years have elapsed, and only now has this statesmanlike policy won an advocate here and there! While recognizing the equal sincerity of the two titans, I prefer Disraeli because of his long views, his gentleness and tolerance to all races, his imagination and revealing humor. Never did he forget a moment his motto, "Life is too short to be little." Democracy that means freedom for all the people from oppression by one or many is the rock upon which I rest my hope for a saner, more finely organized society; but Gladstone's fierce partisanship blinded him to the ultimate good both of his own people and the nations at large.

Closing the book, I leaned back and marveled for the millionth time at the wealth and freedom literature has made mine.

Later—The Manse, Bothwell.

Today at lunch on the Scots Express I was agreeably surprised to be recognized by a waiter who had seen me three years before on my last trip to Scotland. He said I gave him some flowers which he took home to his mother. I could not recall the flowers, but it warmed my heart to know he had never forgotten me.

Tea was especially enjoyable this afternoon, because there was a cheery Scotswoman sitting by to share it with us. Polly liked her wholesome face, and I was glad of the sweet home talk that strikes a common chord in the souls of all travelers. I noticed she was knitting stockings, and I said I envied her that skill in handicraft. It had always been a joy for me to create a useful or attractive article, and I had rarely squeezed in time enough to gratify this instinct.

Suddenly Polly spelled, "Helen, here we are in Glasgow!"

Her brother, the minister, and his wife were waiting for us, and the warmth with which they embraced us both made me feel that I, too, had come home. As we

Helen Keller's Journal

walked along the platform a porter from the Central Hotel (where Teacher, Polly and I had often stayed) greeted me most kindly. It makes me proud to receive such cordial salutations from those who do the work of the world.

At the Manse the door was opened long before the minister turned the car into the driveway, and everybody crowded on the steps to welcome us—his oldest son David, who is studying at the University of Glasgow; Effie, the only daughter; and two younger boys, Robert and John; Jean, the soul of loyalty in household service; even the dog Skye. There was a general rush to bring in our baggage, the children guiding me with adorable solicitude upstairs to my room.

I have been here several hours, and the boys cannot yet realize that I can find my way about; they are so afraid I may fall or bump into something. I am happy to have two such dear little knights on the lookout for my safety and comfort.

Like the foolish city folk we have become, Polly and I were thinly dressed, and despite our fur coats we got chilled motoring through the heavy fog, but the fire in the minister's study and Jean's delicious Scotch broth warmed us up quickly. After supper we gathered round the fire to hear and tell the thousand and one little things which only a look, the tone of voice or a gesture can truly interpret. It was good to feel Polly's fingers less weighted with grief than they have been for months. Skye lay at my feet, his big paws on the fender, his nose almost in the fire, and did not seem to mind being roasted. He is quite as affectionate to me now as when he was a two-month-old puppy; I saw him first in August 1932, when the Thomsons, Teacher, Polly

Helen Keller's Journal

and I went on a fascinating trip to the island of Skye and on our way back to the mainland stopped at a hotel at Loch Alsh. Two puppies belonging to the hotel frisked about us while we sat in the sunshine, and Effie played with them. We negotiated one for her as a living souvenir of one of our happiest outings, and that is how he came to be called Skye. He was one with the heather-breathing hills, the sparkling loch and the rocks and moors. Heavier grown, he is still lovable—a fat, comical cross between a fox terrier and an Airedale or a spaniel —long ears and feet big enough for a Newfoundland.

The Manse, Bothwell, November 19th.

Eager to be up and working this morning, I could not wait for the announcement that my bath was ready, and decided to have a cold sponge-down in my bedroom. Thought it could not harm me by way of discipline! Shivering, I began and went through it as a nun performs a penance. It required long rubbing and toweling to thaw the frost out of my fingers and toes, besides three or four cups of hot tea and a bowl of Scots porridge.

Nothing starts a day so well as a cheerful family breakfast. With pleasure I watched the children enjoying their eggs and tea. Even in the bustle of getting ready for school they remembered to kiss me good-by, and I felt less reluctant to clear the decks for action.

Last night I found a mass of American mail in addition to the many unfinished tasks I brought over from New York. The pressure is such that at first I thought I would take rooms at some quiet hotel and live like a hermit, attending to this extra correspondence, but unexpectedly our problem was solved in a few minutes.

The minister and his wife have the dearest way imaginable of helping everyone. They had a deep love for Teacher and are anxious to ease our burden. They urged Polly and me to stay with them, ensuring us privacy and peace. It is wonderful to have understanding friends who do not object if, in the day's work, tables and chairs and floor are strewn with mail, a typewriter, a Braille machine, manuscripts and books. Already the drawing room looks as if a hurricane had swept through it, but at least we have made a beginning, and *ce n'est que le premier pas qui coute!* Surely there is no road of effort so steep but a loving deed may soften its harshness.

Another blessing at the Manse is the laughter and freshness of childhood which will keep at bay the melancholy that troubles me unless I am vigilant, and I need a serene mind to accomplish anything.

Letters of condolence were piled up about us. Polly had spelled them into my hand three hours. The reiterated words "loss", "death", "parting", dragged from page to page. Absent-mindedly I made a stupid remark, Polly got nervous, and sharp words flew between us. For several minutes we sat mute, with stinging tears in our eyes and a sense of frustration; then we broke down, remembering Teacher's prayer that we might be united. From four to five hundred letters and tributes have now been read, and cards of thanks for sympathy sent out, and we are still inundated.

This journal is a godsend. It is helping me to discipline my mind back to regular work. Telling what I have enjoyed doubles my pleasure; writing of "blues", disappointments and difficulties shrinks them to insignificance.

Tonight I went to see James Bridie's play, *The Black Eye*. Amusing, full of lively dialogue. Everyone enthusiastic over the splendid acting of the Scottish amateurs. I was sorry I could not hear George Windlestraw; his fine enunciation was so admired. That clean kind of play is especially refreshing to one who has often been disgusted with morbid sex plays in New York.

The Manse, November 20th.

A hard frost this morning. Roses still blooming in the garden. The holly trees round here are heavy with berries; but the blackbirds are eating them so fast there will be none left at Christmas time.

Polly and I read more letters that opened up the wound in my soul. This multitude is a measure of the affection and honor in which Teacher was held; my suffering is a measure of her preciousness to me. But to be reminded every moment that the most cherished part of one's life is gone is intolerable.

This evening we visited the Bothwell Castle colliery. I heard how modern machinery is used in this colliery and every precaution taken for the safety of the miners.

I was taken nine hundred feet down in a shaft. Eight of us at a time crowded into the cage; it was an exciting sensation, swaying from side to side. I felt drippings from the well as we descended. I touched the long lines of hutches filled with coal between which we walked, and the endless rope that propels them. Walls on both sides, some of solid rocks, others built of bricks; powerful girderings; the refuges, or manholes, into which the men run when they see the hutches coming.

"How can the men see those dark holes?" I asked. It was explained that the refuges are whitewashed so they can be easily distinguished from the blackness all around. Going through tunnels lighted only by safety lamps, I thought: "Airmen flying blind in a fog and miners quarrying in a deep pit are among the few who can imagine what blindness means."

Although I knew there was a circulating air current I had expected disagreeable odors and was surprised to smell scarcely anything except a little oil and coal gas occasionally. The miners kindly let me examine their lamps, overalls and instruments. They had drilled a hole four feet into the coal and were ready to dynamite it. They paid us a handsome compliment by asking if we would fire the shot, which we did. Polly's shot was a good one. I was clumsy and had to try three times. The loud report vibrated through every atom of my body when two tons of coal crashed to the ground. Then through my feet I perceived the crunching of the cutting machine as it cut through six feet of coal in five minutes. It is a blessing to have a companion like Polly in adventures like this. She is fearless, observant, eager to give me my share of educative, even hazardous, experiences.

Back at the surface, I visited the winding-engine room and the small power station from which electricity is supplied to the machinery and where are the dials that indicate the amount of power used in every part of the mine. In the lamp cabin I saw the safety lamps, which the men had been using, cleaned and filled with oil. Next I was shown a cage full of canaries—another safety measure. As soon as they detect white damp they fall off the perch, and that is a signal for the men to come out of the mine. I wish all mines everywhere were operated with as much intelligence and humanity, but I know otherwise.

The Manse, November 21st.

The children are at home today. I am glad, because I like them near while I work. The typewriter attracts them, and they watch me with curiosity; but they are so quiet I am not disturbed.

The minister is occupied every waking moment. I hardly see him except at meals and sometimes in the evening. He has a large parish, which often means traveling long distances to visit the sick or the bereaved. There seems to be no rest for him.

Today's Braille edition of the *Daily Mail* contains an item especially encouraging to me: President Roosevelt's efforts to promote peace with South America. The sooner the U.S. and South America realize that co-operation and intelligent evaluation of each other are vital to their welfare, the less chance there will be for commercial and financial interests to rend asunder the civilization of the Western Hemisphere.

The Manse, November 22nd.

Polly and I heard her brother's stirring sermon at the Church of St Bride's on the text, "Am I my brother's keeper?" Simply yet forcefully he urged his listeners to beware of indifference to the physical and intellectual needs of those among whom they live daily. The habit of routine tends to benumb the spirit and stiffen the mind, so that we forget our responsibilities towards the less fortunate, and they become objects of charity, not our brothers to keep safe in God's green pastures. As Polly interpreted I felt that the minister's own rich life of neighborliness preaches a sermon more potent than any words.

The church, which has been restored, is beautifully suggestive and symbolical. It was wrought by builders in whose faith religion and art were one.

I read all the afternoon Maria Bashkirtseff's *Journal* in French. Its weird, whimsical, rebellious spirit, from the cry of a temperamental child to the tears and ecstasies of an eighteen-year-old artist, held my fingers so that I could not lay down the book.

In her preface Maria says, "If this journal is not the exact, the strict, the absolute truth, there is no reason why it should have been written." What a naïve phrase! Everybody interprets words his own way, and consequently no two persons see anything with the same eyes. The truth of discourse zigzags like a ship. Only by sincerity of sentiment and veracity of purpose can we get its bearings.

What a pathetic prayer for a girl of twelve: "Oh, God, make me happy in this life, and I shall be grateful!"

Again, with premature sophistication, she writes that a wife should not be appearing before her husband in wrapper and boudoir cap, cold cream on her nose, demanding money to beautify herself. She expresses contempt for man as a fundamental egotist, full of intrigue, envy and humbug. At sixteen she declares that everything which is not sad is stupid, and everything which is not stupid is sad. But deep down she was singularly courageous, and her dream of becoming a great artist ennobled her tempestuous twenty-four years.

The Manse, November 23rd.

Up at half-past seven. From nine until one I wrote letters which did not soothe me. Weary and restless, I was glad when the children entered the room, like sunshine. Lay down awhile after lunch, wrote three hours more and an hour after dinner. Sometimes I am uneasy about my hands; I use them too constantly, writing, reading, listening to conversation and reading people's lips; but work is the only sure bulwark against despair.

West Kilbride, November 24th.

Up early because Mrs Love was coming in her car at eleven o'clock to take me to West Kilbride for a few days. Worked so long at letters I had only half an hour to pack and dress, but I forgot the scramble in the joy of seeing my dear friend again.

A thick yellow fog made the driving hazardous. Twice we were lost in Glasgow, and even on the right road no one felt sure a moment. People walked by carrying lamps, and the smell of petrol hung chokingly about my face during the six hours journey. On our arrival Dr Love hustled us into the firelit library, not even waiting for us to take off our coats and hats, so eager was he to make us at home and hear the news.

Helen Keller's Journal

After dinner he spoke of an article he had written on Teacher for the magazine for the deaf and wished to know if it satisfied us. How could we help being pleased when his style is so clear and his sympathy unusually perceptive? He, too, has given me a cozy corner where I can shut myself up for another struggle to finish my letters. . . .

As a step towards a federation of peoples replacing an empire founded on militarism, I welcome the news of the Anglo-Egyptian treaty ratified today. The fact that little criticism from any party was heard leads me to hope it may prove a genuine, lasting power for good. Naturally Egypt desires complete independence, but at least this treaty is supposed to enable that country in a practical manner to protect its own interests against invasion by another aggressor. With satisfaction I read that army recruiting is very difficult indeed. Here nobody discusses the likelihood of another great war with hostility to any nation, but with misgivings and sorrow for mankind. . . .

What a word picture to kindle the imagination! The assembled physicians and dons at Oxford University in their academic robes, speechless for a moment, witnessing a miracle of public-spirited generosity, then rising and cheering Lord Nuffield for five minutes. With his gift of two million pounds for medical research at Oxford he is another world benefactor. Like John D. Rockefeller, Jr, he looks centuries ahead and perceives that health in all lands is among the indispensable guarantees of human progress.

Helen Keller's Journal

West Kilbride, November 25th.

Dr Love alone at breakfast this morning. When I entered he jumped up, cut my bacon and eggs for me and patted my hand by way of coaxing an appetite. But with him I need no coaxing, the eggs are so good and the fire so warm; and his terse, penetrating comments on the news from the Glasgow *Herald* render breakfast an event in itself.

Start writing at half-past eight. The maid Agnes brings a cup of hot tea at eleven, and Mrs Love joins us—a welcome break. Just as we were finishing tea Polly, ever on the lookout for something significant to tell me, said that the fog had cleared, and out of the window she could see Goatfell, rugged and dominant— the monarch mountain of Arran. Instantly memory transported me to that island where Teacher went with us, June 1932, to visit the Duke and Duchess of Montrose at Brodick Castle. How delightful it all was—their cordial kindness and the duke's appreciation of my handicaps, going over the ancient castle, touching a huge oaken table with knife cuts dating from the fourteenth century when no plates were used, and the lovely rock garden which the duchess tends with her own hands. The duke in Highland costume was a picturesque figure as he led me about among trees and flower beds, while his sweet daughter, Lady Jean, gathered a great bouquet of fragrant pinks for me. I recall, too, how the duchess ran—yes, ran—up the hill to the castle to make sure of our having a cup of hot tea before we left, and how, when it was discovered that we were very late, the boat was held up until we hurried aboard.

More letters written until Dr Love came home. He made me laugh with good stories told in his inimitable manner, and now I am going to bed, sure of a peaceful sleep.

West Kilbride, November 26th.

Besides its own home sweetness, this house is associated with events I love to remember. Opposite is Dalveen, a rose-embowered cottage where, through Dr Love's kindness, we spent the month of June 1932 when I was invited to receive the LL.D. degree from the University of Glasgow. Wonderingly I live that day over again—Teacher's happiness in the honor conferred upon me, Bute Hall with its large stained-glass windows, like a church, Dr Love sitting beside me, my trepidation as Sir Robert Rait capped me and I listened to a Latin oration. That was but one day. If I should declare the beautiful kindnesses to us every day, every hour of that month, this record would never end.

Dr Love, who is at home today, invited James Bridie, the dramatist, to lunch. His real name is Dr Mavor. At first I thought I could not keep pace with his conversation. I imagined it was like the dialogues of his play, *The Black Eye*, which reminded me of "G.B.S." However, I was pleased to find that he was easy and delightful to talk with on a variety of subjects. *The Sleeping Clergyman* was discussed, and I regretted that I had not seen or read it, but I resolved to get the book, which is now in Braille. I asked him if he would explain its meaning to me, and with a laugh he replied: "I don't know myself. Perhaps after you read it you will be able to tell me!"

Out in the garden it is warm, as if there had never been a fog clinging icily about the land. Beyond the wall the cattle are lying in the sun, and Polly says the only sounds she hears are the chirps of blackbirds, thrushes, robins and starlings. Usually when I am here I walk back and forth beside the privet hedge, stepping aside every few minutes to caress the banks of flowers whose odors reach me, but I am still subject to the despotism of unfinished tasks.

West Kilbride, November 27th.

This is the fifth day of fog—heavy fog, serious delays by rail and at sea; and motor accidents. Dr Love has been talking about infra-red rays as a means of seeing in this liquid darkness. I should think the time would soon be here when fog-piercing lights are put on all cars and ships, so important are they to public safety. Before leaving for Bothwell Mrs Love gave us the cup of tea that warms and fortifies. In Scotland the tea-kettle always seems to be on the fire, that there may be "a cup of kindness" for everyone. Dined at the St Enoch Station Hotel with Somers.[1] He loved Teacher dearly. We talked about her most of the evening. There are no words for the tenderness with which he listened to what we told of her last days, or the appreciation with which he spoke of the books they read together, the long arguments concerning politics and social problems that kept them up until midnight. These reminis-

[1] Somers Mark, a Scot whom Miss Keller first knew in New York.

Helen Keller's Journal

cences are especially consoling because they renew my sense of her youth.

The Manse, November 28th. Morning.

Refreshing to have young life laughing and dancing about me. The children have all learned the manual alphabet, telling me what they do at school, asking questions for me and reporting the answers. I do not know which I enjoy more—John's chubby, labored spelling or Robert's gazelle fingers, gliding from letter to letter, occasionally giving the impression of a leap when he gets excited.

The persistent, incessant demands of my work have left me little time for children, and I feel young once more in their companionship.

Writing about hands recalls to my mind a poem by Robinson Jeffers about a painting on a rock so unique and mysterious I think of it very often.

HANDS

Inside a cave in a narrow canyon near Tassajara
The vault of a rock is painted with hands,
A multitude of hands in the twilight, a cloud of men's
 palms, no more,
No other picture. There's no one to say
Whether the brown shy quiet people who are dead intended
Religion or magic, or made their tracings
In the idleness of art; but over the division of years these
 careful
Signs-manual are now like a sealed message
Saying: "Look: we also were human; we had hands, not
 paws. All hail

Helen Keller's Journal

*You people with cleverer hands, our supplanters
In the beautiful country; enjoy her a season, her beauty,
   and come down
And be supplanted; for you also are human."*[1]

Later.

On the train to Dundee this afternoon to visit Polly's sister Margaret. Following the winding, forest-crowned, and in places hill-shadowed, river Tay. The sun setting. Polly's fingers racing with the changes of color: "Pink! ... Blue! ... Mauve! ... Green! ... Gold! ... Rose! ... Lavender! ... Oh, Helen! the water is one sheet of burnished gold! ... The sky is jade as far as my eye can reach!"

Down comes the dark—sudden, complete.

Dryburgh House, Dundee, Evening.

We have just met Mrs Scott, with whom Margaret stays as a companion—Margaret, whose responsive little hands are eloquent of home, brimming over with faith in others, no matter what disappointments she endures—hands that soothe sorrow and sweeten joy yet more. . . . Mrs Scott is handsome and intelligent. It is a pleasure to know she is the strong mother of ten children and beloved by twenty-two grandchildren. All her sons are married, except one who was killed in the World War, and her daughters, too, except one who lives with her.

[1] By Robinson Jeffers from *Dear Judas*. Reprinted by permission of Random House, Inc., N. Y.

Helen Keller's Journal

Dryburgh House, November 29th.

The sun rose at eight twenty-six and set at three forty-two. Breakfast at nine. I was amused at the wee china lady that covered my egg.

I brought my typewriter, as I do wherever I go. Mrs Scott has kindly turned over the old nursery to me to work in. The windows are eight feet high, all vitaglass, and I enjoy the warmth lingering so long in the room after the sun is gone.

I wrote without much spirit today. Wishing to capture a different mood, I went out and strolled about the grounds. Everything I touched sent a happy thought skipping up my mind—hedges of laurel, holly, beech and yew, the deep turf, roses and chrysanthemums still holding their own out of doors. Mrs Scott showed me her nine cocker spaniels, five of them puppies, over which she is as foolish as I am over my Dane and my two Shetland collies and Lakeland terrier. Everywhere I have been in England or Scotland I observe with gratification what a large part gardens play in the home life of the people.

Tonight we sat in the drawing room, listening to the service at the Chapel of St Andrew's over the radio, which Polly spelled into my hand. Worked at the typewriter until 11 P.M.

Dryburgh House, November 30th.

Wrote before breakfast, vainly hoping to catch up with a month's accumulated mail. Enjoyed the delicious melon and toast with Dundee marmalade which I always order at home in New York. The wonderful coffee Mrs Scott gives us at lunch and dinner is from her daughter's plantation in Nairobi, Kenya.

Mrs Scott and most of her family are great travelers, and it is like reading a fine book to hear her varied, colorful experiences. She had a number of people to tea this afternoon, among them her deaf sister, who, in spite of her handicap, spent five years visiting Japan, China, India and Africa alone. She fills me with admiring envy; I would sacrifice much for just such independence!

A letter full of sweetness just received from our friend, the Marchioness of Aberdeen, inviting Polly and me to lunch with her at Gordon House in Aberdeen. She has resigned from the presidency of the International Women's Council of Peace, and she sent me her beautiful farewell address. Her noble words must have energized the purpose of her listeners. Her faith that world peace will triumph over evils which appear insuperable today is a prop to my own. Sometimes my heart sinks when I hear that forty million gas masks are being prepared for Britain alone and that medical students in the University of Edinburgh are being trained to treat gas poisoning. The situation looks indeed hopeless when war and its increasing diabolical means of destruction are expected and prepared for.

Dryburgh House, December 1st.

Two hours more of writing this morning, then I caught the train for Aberdeen. Met at the station by

Helen Keller's Journal

Mr Baird, Lady Aberdeen's minister, and her secretary, Mrs Mackenzie. Mr Baird gives constant thought to international affairs and works zealously for peace and good will among the peoples. I wished I could feel as encouraged at the moment as he did regarding the prospect of a united, civilized mankind.

Lady Aberdeen met me in the hall, and I was impressed afresh by her regal beauty. At the table she guided the conversation with a rare union of stately grace and gentleness. Her idealism and her intellectual vigor shone forth as one subject after another came up —the latest news of peace, education, books, politics and gardens. I spoke of Maurois's life of Disraeli. She seemed surprised when I said I preferred Disraeli to Gladstone and stated my reasons. Quickly she said— and I could feel a twinkle of the eye in her hand on mine—"I will send you a book about Gladstone that will knock those heresies out of your head." She went on to say that both men were friends of her own family and that Disraeli was very gallant to her mother. She put my hand on a bust of Gladstone. Certainly his face was not that of a man who lets imagination or philosophy "blunt his sense of sin", or—I must add— humor correct his highly colored opinions!

Lady Aberdeen had asked me to plant a tree for her; so we went into the garden to set out a maple. A spade was put into my hand that the late King George V had used planting his tree at the House of Cromar. As I turned the soil and spread it over the roots my mind dwelt tenderly on the happy hours we had spent with her and Lord Aberdeen in their hospitable home each time we had visited Scotland, the flowers with which they had loaded us, the pictures they had sent us of each other and their favorite mountains, some painted by Lady Aberdeen herself. With these delicate bonds of affection and oneness in our vision of a happier human race it was hard for me to bid her good-by.

The Manse, December 3rd.

There was snow on the mountains when we left Dundee this morning. Mrs Scott's thoughtful hospitality followed us all the way to Bothwell. She lent us two fine rugs to keep us warm, and we were glad, especially when a chill wind penetrated the compartment. Now the wind has increased, and I actually feel it "ranting", tearing and howling down the chimney.

The Manse holds the sure charm against the melancholy that ever tracks me—the laughter of childhood, bracing simplicity, struggle and stimulating intelligence. How I appreciate this haven from interruptions too constant and jarring! I grow fretful remembering the thoughts put to flight by the thousands of autographs I have written and the pictures and books I have signed and interviews I have given during thirty years. What care and concentration must be put into letters, messages and articles reiterating endlessly the needs of the blind!

Yet few people realize this, and I seldom have the privacy supposed to be the writer's prerogative. A kind hostess says to me, "You shall be left by yourself this morning," and I become absorbed in a particularly difficult task which I should have a whole day to finish.

Helen Keller's Journal

The first thing I know I am asked please to come downstairs to tea just for five minutes. I find perhaps ten callers, who stay not five minutes but one, two, three hours! By the time they leave my last bit of patience has melted like "snaw off a dyke"; for I know I shall not be able to recapture either the writing mood or the idea I was pursuing. At such times I am ready to break off diplomatic relations and any other kind with the human race!

Another eruption of mail that means Trojan industry for weeks. And beside my typewriter is a reproachful stack of unread Braille letters. Two hands are too few—I should be a hundred-armed Briareus.

Out of a clear sky comes a cablegram inviting me to visit Japan in the spring and help to convince the Japanese that their blind can be lifted from misery to the rank of useful, self-respecting human beings. There are hard problems to be solved before Polly and I can enter upon a work of such scope and international significance, but we are resolved to accomplish it somehow.

Polly has just spelled a portent into my hand: it is announced in all the papers that the Cabinet is facing an extremely delicate, difficult situation created by King Edward VIII's intention to marry an American lady who has divorced two husbands. Unless he renounces her a constitutional crisis of the most serious kind may follow that will affect the empire. In awed silence I wonder whether the king, upon whom the people have bestowed a deep affection, and whose name is revered throughout the dominions, will take a step which runs counter to their principles. Or will he abdicate a throne which carries with it vast opportunities

Helen Keller's Journal

for constructive leadership of a federation of commonwealths, and live his own life?

> *The worldly hope men set their hearts upon*
> *Turns ashes—or it prospers; and anon,*
> *Like snow upon the desert's dusty face,*
> *Lighting a little hour or two—was gone.*

Customs in all lands are changing; new precedents are being established; free spirits will not submit to authority that would dictate the regulation of their domestic lives; but whichever way this empire-girdling question is settled, there must be an element of tragedy.

With tender sorrow my heart goes out to the Queen Mother, over whose head the thunder and lightning are sweeping. Proudly I remember the eighteenth of June 1932, when by royal command Teacher, Polly and I attended the garden party at Buckingham Palace.

It seemed like a dream as we stood in a crowd of eight thousand people amid the splendor of a world empire. At some distance were Queen Mary and the late King George V, under a gold-and-crimson canopy, greeting potentates from the East in gorgeous robes, brilliantly arrayed Parsi ladies and distinguished men from the ends of the earth. Finally an equerry came to inform us that their majesties would receive us, and we walked down the sloping lawn to the royal tent. They shook hands with us most kindly. King George asked Polly if I could understand everything he said. He expressed a wish to see how people communicated with me, and Teacher gave a short lip-reading demonstration. Their majesties showed great interest in our work and said how wonderful it was. The queen asked if I was enjoying my visit to England. I told her how charmed I was with the English gardens.

"How can you enjoy flowers when you cannot see them?" she inquired.

I explained that I smell their fragrance and feel their beauty of blossom, leaf and stem.

How approachable King George was! He impressed me as a symbol of the strong, simple, hard-working manhood the English people admire. And we liked Queen Mary too; she was so straightforward and gracious in her queenliness. Her hand was that of a mother into whose ear the unfortunate might pour their sorrows and perplexities.

The Manse, December 4th.

Last night the family was gathered about the fire like millions of other families in Britain—stunned by the news of the king's contemplated marriage—when David brought in the latest bulletin. Parliament was expected to assemble on Monday to discuss the subject, and the dominions would be consulted. All day the air had seemed weighted with the urgency of a swiftly approaching climax to one of the strangest dramas in British history. . . .

The *Braille Mail*, December 5th, contains a detailed account of the burning down of the Crystal Palace on November 30th. I am dismayed to think how the magnificent organ, the apparatus in the research laboratories of the Baird Television Company and all the works of art in the palace were destroyed. Now I shall never see a landmark of London that had a history and a romance all its own—a place upon which generations looked with pleasure as a center of entertainment and

Helen Keller's Journal

historic interest. Replacing it with a new building cannot compensate for the loss of a unique structure which housed an unparalleled exhibition in 1851—the arts and industries of all nations.

The first holiday home for the deaf-blind, Fellowship House, Trinity Road, Hoylake, Cheshire, England, has come into existence! My heart went through the whole gamut of joy as I read today how Fellowship House was established the end of last June and how it has made possible visits full of sunshine for one hundred and twenty-seven doubly handicapped persons, many of whom had never had a holiday. With tender pride I learned that the deaf-blind have themselves raised, over a number of years, four hundred pounds.

I wrote a letter to the London *Times* in the summer of 1932, requesting that people with leisure and a wish to do good should learn the hand alphabet, visit the deaf-blind, talk to them, take them out for walks and make their hearts glad in other ways, but I never dreamed that only four years later they would have Fellowship House—a blessed oasis in their desert of loneliness. The reason why God permitted me to lose both sight and hearing seems clear now—that through me He might cleave a rock unbroken before and let quickening streams flow through other lives desolate as my own once was. I am content.

How exquisitely these words of Emily Dickinson voice my feeling about Teacher's passing!

> *So much of Heaven has gone from Earth*
> *That there must be a Heaven,*
> *If only to enclose the saints*
> *To affidavit given.*

Helen Keller's Journal

This verse is in *Unpublished Poems* by the shyest, most spiritual poet of New England—one of the treasured gifts I have received from the American Printing House for the Blind. Another gift is Van Doren's *Anthology of World Prose* in twenty-six volumes, containing masterpieces from twenty nations.

The Manse, December 5th.

For the first time, I believe, in the annals of the British press there is no "Court News" in today's newspapers. It is reported that Mrs Simpson has disappeared. What does all this portend? This is a colossal drama beyond the art of language to encompass—a king shrouded in silence, an empire hanging on his next public act.

The Manse, December 6th.

At the Church of St Bride's this morning. Thankful for a shrine of true worship and beauty where we may escape the foolish turmoil of earth. Then we can erase material concerns from the book of our lives

> *that, like a palimpsest, is written o'er*
> *With trivial incidents of time and place,*
> *And lo! the Ideal, hidden beneath, revives.*

Polly and I stayed to see a baby baptized. It was adorable, the way he smiled and cooed through the ceremony. I remembered my godchild, whom I held half an hour in my arms on a similar occasion; the minister (supposed to be leading him to heaven) denounced the devil so long I wondered whether he gave more thought to the devil than to Him who said, "except ye be converted, and become as little children, ye shall not enter into the kingdom of heaven."

The air was crisp; I felt the crunch of the melting snow as we walked home. For a short time the sun poured in at the door with delectable warmth, then there was the east wind again, roaring down the chimney, and I felt Skye jerk up his wise head at each gust in searching wonderment. Never have I known two days alike in Britain; the weather is always doing something interesting.

With amazement I hear that Professor Gilbert Murray, of Oxford, has pronounced King John "the cleverest of the Plantagenets." It will take a good deal to convince me! I have always believed King John was extremely stupid and obstinate, both as a man and a ruler.

The Manse, December 7th.

Nothing has happened today outwardly; but for me there is never a dull day. There is in me an ego that observes, examines and philosophizes constantly. I cannot look out of the window or see the expression of a face or catch the tone of a voice; and yet what a wealth of experience is within my reach! Every gesture of the hand, every footfall, every joy is examined and weighed and noted in my mind. Only when I have said as clearly as I can the best I discern in human beings am I satisfied. While I am full of sympathy or indignation or delight that indefinable element seems uppermost. Perhaps that is the real me. So many different egos pass through my consciousness, though, that I hardly know what I am.

The minister has a charming way of saying grace at the table and having me read his lips. I wish more people said grace; it really sweetens the meal and helps us to remember that it is the Lord who satisfieth the desire of every living thing.

Still no "Court News." The three last days seem a period of dark silence.

Today I walked round the graveyard that leads to the church. I feel as Socrates did when his friends asked him where they should bury him, and he replied, "It matters not where you bury my body, since you cannot catch me." Touching the tombstones did not disconcert me as I passed and repassed them, but I kept thinking how many graves are being dug throughout the world for agelong institutions, kingships and beliefs. The birds were pecking away at holly berries. I wondered how they manage to keep warm at night. I have heard that sometimes their wings almost freeze against the bough where they find shelter, and they struggle in the morning to free themselves.

The Manse, December 8th.

We have just received four fine plump partridges from friends in Dingwall, Ross Shire, not far from South Arcan, where we spent our first long holiday—a sabbatical year with Teacher from June 1933 to September 1934. While grateful for the gift, I could not help the tears springing to my eyes when Polly opened the box and I touched the limp, still forms with soft silken feathers. No more, I thought, will they flutter those beautiful wings, beaded with dew, where the sun lies warm upon the fields of South Arcan or feed in the heather where we sat and dreamed.

Oh, the beauty of that year at the old farmhouse in the Highlands! How often memory throws open the door and I stand bathed in the sun's warmth! Bread crumbs drop from our hands for the partridges, pheasants and thrushes, which do not move when we step close to them. Again winding lengths of sweet turf stretch under my feet as I walk alone with a shepherd's crook to guide my steps, while spring rolls, wave upon wave, its odorous floods of gorse blossoms, golden broom, hawthorn and wild roses. That was liberty! For I had never been in a place where I could wander so far by myself.

The Manse, December 9th.

An unusually peaceful night's sleep. But the melancholy which so often spreads its raven wings over me returned as I read about the disaster of the Royal Dutch Air Liner at Croydon. With the same dreadful suddenness has crashed about me the life with her for whose presence I long, waking or sleeping.

Among the names of the victims I noted Señor de la Cierva, inventor of the autogiro. I recalled that he was at the White House in April 1931 when Teacher, Polly and I met President and Mrs Herbert Hoover. I received the delegates to the World Conference on work for the blind which was being held in New York, and after the reception, by special invitation, we lunched with the president. After talking about the blind I asked his opinion of the autogiro which we had seen in the grounds. He said he was greatly interested and thought it had wonderful possibilities; then he mentioned Señor de la Cierva. I remember the president's delightful cordiality and unassuming simplicity. He spoke hopefully of the political situation and renewed prosperity but listened indulgently when I told him of my fear that our economic problems would not be solved for many a year. When I spoke of his terrific labors he said quietly, "You don't meet such a dull man as I every day!" Teacher and I were impressed by his modesty. Certainly he had wisdom to perceive his limitations—a quality that much greater men often lack.

Today we lunched with Dr Love's daughter Marjorie and her husband, Dr Young. Dr and Mrs Love were there also, as dear and interested in all we do as ever. Naturally King Edward's marriage project was the main subject discussed. Everywhere I hear how vital affairs of the nation are being held up by his indecision, and I can see how impatient the people about me have grown. Somehow it seems likely to me that he may abdicate. Whatever he resolves to do, it is clear that his subjects have been deeply hurt and that the one link which holds the empire together—loyalty to the sovereign—will in time be broken. Of old it was prophesied that "all kingdoms, powers and principalities shall pass away", and the Lord alone shall reign, but that does not lessen the pain for those who have seen in King Edward a bright pledge of democratic leadership and in the British Empire a hopeful means of achieving world peace.

The latest report this evening is that Mrs Simpson is willing, if need be, "to withdraw from a situation that

Helen Keller's Journal

has been rendered both unhappy and untenable." However, I doubt if the king will accept this solution of the problem.

The Manse, December 10th.

While we were walking in the dingle near the churchyard I was surprised when Polly said, "The lamps are already lighted, and it's only two o'clock." I was interested to hear that in this neighborhood a man still goes the rounds before dark with a long stick, turns on a gas jet and kindles each lamp in turn seventy years after Stevenson wrote *A Plea for Gas Lamps*.

Wild rumors are pouring in thick and fast, but now it is certain that King Edward VIII has abdicated. Intense excitement prevails everywhere. I doubt whether His Majesty will reap from his decision the happiness he anticipates. There is a love of the people surpassing the love of woman.

Certainly I believe that God gave us life for happiness, not misery. Humanity, I am sure, will never be made lazy or indifferent by an excess of happiness. The order of nature will always necessitate pain, failure, separation, death; and these will probably become more menacing as the complexities and dangerous experiments of a vast world civilization increase. The delicate task will remain ours to ensure God's gift—joy—to His children. Many persons have a wrong idea of what constitutes true happiness. It is not attained through self-gratification but through fidelity to a worthy purpose. Happiness should be a means of accomplishment, like health, not an end in itself. Every human being has undeniable rights which, respected, render happiness possible—the right to live his own life as far as may be, to choose his own creed, to develop his capabilities; but no one has a right to consume happiness without producing it or to lay his burden upon other shoulders merely to fulfill a personal desire.

All of which is by way of saying that it seems to me King Edward will require extraordinary resources within himself if he is ever to have peace after the years he has devoted to the welfare of his subjects throughout a colossal empire. Any life assumes true nobility and significance only when one believes that one is born into the world for ends higher than any which can be reached within the narrow limits of earthly existence.

It seems as if Browning's poem, "The Lost Leader", had been written for this fateful day.

The Manse, December 11th.

This evening we were in Glasgow, seeing a motion picture, *San Francisco*, dramatizing the earthquake and fire that destroyed that city in 1906. The first part was one of the love stories for which I have no use in pictures depicting historic events, but the last part was gripping, overwhelming. It chilled and terrified me like the black flag of a beleaguered city. I could feel the rumbling of the earthquake, the collapse of buildings, the roaring of flames and the bursting of water mains. Again I was wrapped in grief as I recalled Ned's[1] forceful description of the harrowing scenes he witnessed. He used to live in San Francisco, where he worked as an architect, and he threw himself body and soul into the labor of

[1] Edward L. Holmes.

Helen Keller's Journal

reconstructing part of the city. Polly described for me the familiar Market Street, where we have often walked or motored during our visits to San Francisco on our lecture tours up and down the immensity of the United States. What I most loved in San Francisco was its magnificent bay with the old ferryboats and ships of all nations passing through the Golden Gate. If we journey thither again I wonder whether we shall find the view from the superb new bridge—said to be the longest in the world—as picturesque and romantic as ever? The tragic side of many architectural enterprises is that they destroy natural beauties which are a priceless possession and cannot be replaced.

The excitement over the king's abdication continues unabated. Sorrow, indignation, hurt pride are being expressed by all classes of people. And I feel there is an unanswerable challenge in the silent millions who carry their burdens, sick or well, safe or exposed to danger, and ask for no release.

The whole world has listened to the king's farewell broadcast from Windsor Castle tonight. I sensed a noble ring of veracity in his words and honored him for the frankness with which he spoke out his mind. More than ever I grieve with the Queen Mother in the tragedy that surrounds her son's departure, and marvel at her calm fortitude.

Looked at from every angle, Edward VIII's surrender of a power he could have wielded is hard to understand. No doubt he has encountered a mass of difficulties that require constant thought and ingenuity. So much greater would have been his triumph in solving them.

Impatient with frustration, we ask ourselves why terrible obstacles should be placed in our path! We cannot but wonder at times why we cannot have smooth sailing instead of being compelled always to fight against adverse winds and rough seas. No doubt the reason is that character cannot be developed in ease and quiet. Only through experiences of trial and suffering can the soul be strengthened, vision cleared, ambition inspired and success achieved. Most of the men and women honored in history for their service to mankind were acquainted with "the uses of adversity." They triumphed because they refused to be turned aside by difficulties or opposition. These obstructions called forth their latent energies and the determination that carried them far beyond any goal to which they would otherwise have aspired.

The Manse, December 12th.

Yesterday I wrote to my friend Alexander Woollcott. He had sent me a precious tribute to Teacher. He told how some high-school girls asked him a great many questions. One of the questions was: "Who, in your opinion, is the greatest living woman?" He said he didn't even need time for reflection; there was no doubt in his mind; and he replied, "Anne Sullivan Macy." He went on to speak of "her great work that lives after her as *A Christmas Carol* lives after Charles Dickens." Another reason why there is a special warmth in my heart for Alexander Woollcott is that he brightened dreary hours for Teacher with daily floral greetings while she was in hospital.

There is drama in everything he does and says. Once while calling on Teacher at the Doctors' Hospital in

Helen Keller's Journal

New York he said to her, "I shall not be surprised if King Edward VIII makes history." What eloquence may he not let loose with his tongue and pen on this stupendous chapter in the annals of man!

I cannot put into language the singular effect of King Edward's exit—self-dethroned, self-exiled, at the age of forty-two. In him were embodied all the finest aspirations of the English race. He absorbed into his personality the youth of the nation; he symbolized their new hope, their forward-looking movements. He was the friend and interpreter of the problems of many peoples. He was democracy on a throne. He was London, England, Youth, the world over. Now there is a vacancy which all must feel.

Of course it is the people who labor that hold the country together; but it is a rare gift to arouse enthusiasm and universal affection, to be a link in an empire struggling towards a higher status—a federation of commonwealths! I repeat, King Edward was a bright pledge of many beneficent changes. He was an age in action and speech, a dispenser of all that causes multitudes to expand with sympathy, or the will to serve, or the desire for self-improvement; and now he has gone.

A welcome diversion from these thoughts was a charming Chinese play, said to have been acted three thousand years ago, which we saw tonight in Glasgow. It was given without any modern equipment, so that a great deal was left to the imagination. The story on which it is based is of a Chinese emperor whose daughter, Lady Precious Stream, tried to marry his gardener. (In those days, despite their lowly rank, gardeners were honored as artists.) Her two proud sisters made life bitter for her, and he was banished. A beautiful white wild goose bore a token of constancy to him from Lady Precious Stream, and she followed him alone over long, perilous mountain roads and through hostile countries. Finally the emperor was moved by their noble loyalty to one another and dealt punishment to his prime minister, who had wrought them shame. The actors were clever amateurs. Polly described to me their fascinating costumes and the Chinese music. From beginning to end the play was a rainbow poem.

The Manse, December 13th.

How often the thought saddens me that my limitations prevent me from rendering larger service to the poor, the overladen, the ignorant! But why murmur over my bowl of longing, as the Japanese would say?

I realize that mortals are only tiny drops lost in an ocean of time. The most any race or individual can do is to enter a little more deeply into the purpose of the Divine Mind. That race, that individual, fulfills the highest destiny that is the best medium to transmit the current of good will through the ages.

There is another sustaining belief for me—that a watchful Providence guides equally the planet's course and the flight of the sparrow, marks human affairs and strengthens endeavor. This faith that God is "personally" interested in us gives a fairer aspect to the weary old world where we live as strangers and enemies. It imparts to those who can believe a consciousness of power. It lets them be sure that mankind *can* prevail against the snares, machinations and greed of the wicked. Knowing that the hosts of the Lord encamp

Helen Keller's Journal

about them, they fear not armies or navies or lines of defense. Confidently they tell themselves that one day all men *will* be lovers and human calamities will vanish in the sunshine of peace and good will upon earth.

I am aware that this conception of the Creator seems antiquated to many. Occasionally I fail to hear His voice within me, and doubts overwhelm my mind; but I cannot let this belief go; for then I should have no light through the darkness of the world.

Without some kind of God, even if only one benign deity among dark powers, man could not have survived toiling under crushing loads, pierced by glacial cold, scorched by desert suns, seeing his loved ones slain or ravished or dying of hunger! He remains primitive, as related to the unmeasured new forces he is discovering. Still handicapped by ignoble instincts and superstition, he needs increasingly an open-eyed faith in a beneficent Power with whom he may co-operate to overcome and to create. This force alone can prevent him from disappearing in a cataclysm, "annihilated by his own foolishness."

In *The Life of the Spider* Henri Fabre declares impressively that matters which seem trivial often point to the infinite pains with which that befriending Power preserves the least things. He dwells upon the superior Intelligence regulating the smallest details. He reminds us that the first man to rub a piece of amber and to find that thereupon it attracted bits of chaff did not envisage the electric marvels of our age. He was only amusing himself in a childish way, and he left no record. Yet this neglected experiment was somehow made good; it was repeated, tested and probed in every imaginable way until it has become a vital part of civilization.

Helen Keller's Journal

The Manse, December 14th.

Everyone is telling me how beautiful the Archbishop of Canterbury's voice was last night over the radio. His speech made me realize as I had not before how generous, forbearing and united the people throughout the empire had been during the division between the government and the Crown. Now, doubtless, the hand of fate will lift the curtain and let in the light upon a drama of the ages.

The question, What are the characteristics of modern man? has always interested me. I try to find an answer in my reading. Of course my opportunities of observation are limited; but I am constantly augmenting my criteria for judgment through others' experiences and my own.

One characteristic, it seems to me, is an intenser enjoyment of life—a love of swift movement as shown in dancing, travel, airplanes, high-speed machines. Another trait is an appreciation of beautiful, simple lines and symmetry, typified by new buildings and improved city planning. Then there is a keen sensitiveness to color, illustrated by fabrics and women's clothes. On the other hand, modern man, by his tolerance of jazz and the crash of machinery, evinces a curious dullness to harmonious sounds.

In conversation I notice frequently a hatred of extremes, impatience with decided views, dislike of fussiness and interferences with personal habits, an utter lack of reticence.

I also observe a strong repugnance in the young to

pretense and superfluity of dress. They are easily bored and find the exchange of ideas tiresome; but they like to tear tradition to pieces and shatter old customs. They have a quick perception of what is humorous or ridiculous, and they avoid serious discussion. However, I sense among them a growing spirit of service which augurs well for the future.

The first wavelets of Christmas have touched the Manse today. Holly is being cut from the trees close by for wreaths to be hung in the church hall. Not since I lived in Wrentham twenty years ago have I seen anyone cut holly and weave it into wreaths. I miss the sweet old-fashioned simplicities that in America once marked Christmas as the birthday of Him who was lowly born and lived always among the humblest folk.

The Manse, December 15th.

A very pleasant tea this afternoon with a miner's family up in the hills above the sweet, fruitful valley of the Clyde. We sat cozily eating scones and pancakes in the kitchen, which is as trig and trim as a parlor. "The Cotter's Saturday Night" kept singing through my mind as I touched everything—the teakettle on the hob beside the scrupulously polished oven, the handsome toddy bowl, the two big box beds set into the wall. I believe this family represents a type of character that is vanishing in Scotland.

On our way home we stopped for the Manse children as school was closing. I enjoyed hearing how they poured out from the gates, a thousand boys and girls at Hamilton Academy—a lovable waterfall of youth!

Helen Keller's Journal

Into the car piled the three children, laughing and filling my hand with bright chatter.

While we waited for them my thoughts wandered back to the two occasions when I met Dr Maria Montessori, the Italian educator. Her personality, blending intense earnestness and charming vivacity, thrilled me. She expressed much interest when she heard that Teacher and she had independently discovered that the child should not be taught things but rather encouraged to find them out for himself. I remembered how bitterly she commented on the fettering attitude of the Church in Italy towards intellectual freedom and the way in which childhood is marred by poverty. Again I met Mme Montessori in San Francisco at the Pan-American Exposition. A huge meeting was held to honor the great teachers of our time. I still glow as I recall Dr Montessori's eloquent tribute to Anne Sullivan Macy.

Polly tells me the Union Jack is flying from the church tower for King George VI's accession to the throne. With what mingled emotions he must be assuming his world role as king and emperor!

The Manse, December 16th.

A booming south wind, rain, hail, thunder this morning and piercing cold in the afternoon. . . .

This is one of the rare days when the onrushing stream of work permits my hungry fingers to snatch a morsel from a book. I secured a Braille copy of James Bridie's *A Sleeping Clergyman* from London, and by stealing hours from Morpheus I have finished this play. It seems a wholesome antidote to modern fatalism and

Helen Keller's Journal

smugness. With wit and courage it attacks the tendency of physicians, ministers and social workers to sink into a rut. The animation of the dialogue, the wind of scorn sweeping through shams and pharisaism, bring George Bernard Shaw to my mind.

That name! It evokes young memories of *Pygmalion*, which I "saw" in Chicago and which made me imagine G.B.S. would know the password of the silent dark if we ever spoke to each other. It happened one afternoon in July 1932 when Teacher, Polly and I were visiting at Lady Astor's, and she introduced us to him. As he greeted me I wondered if his hand, so unresponsive and cynical, could be the hand of him who had championed the deaf and the blind of mankind with such nobility. Ineptly I said how glad I was to meet him and that I had never felt more proud. Evidently Lady Astor thought he was not showing enough interest in me; for she laid her hand on his arm, shaking it a little and saying, "You know, Mr Shaw, Miss Keller is deaf and blind."

Teacher hesitated a few minutes before spelling his answer to me. From the silence which followed I knew something out of the common had happened. Then she repeated his words:

"Why, of course, all Americans are deaf and blind!"

I was amused by this remark, which I thought he had leveled at me especially. I have since been told that he did not intend it for me at all; but whether he did or not, I was far from offended—I had become so accustomed to his whimsical, incisive, in-and-out-of-season sayings.

At first I had no idea of writing an article on the interview with Mr Shaw; but the American newspapers

Helen Keller's Journal

insisted; and after thinking it over I decided that it could do no harm to repeat what he said, since he had taken every opportunity to censure or ridicule Americans. I never dreamed what harsh things would be said of him on my account, and I have regretted that article ever since.

My enthusiastic admiration for G.B.S. remains unquenched. Greatly has he wrought, mightiest among the Samsons tugging at the pillars of oppression and hypocrisy. The world is his debtor for the inhibiting fallacies he has destroyed, the idols he has broken and the mute lips his fire has kindled into brave speech.

The Manse, December 17th.

Again my desk and other furniture in this room are buried beneath letters, requests about the handicapped from both sides of the Atlantic. Polly spells them until her fingers wobble, and we seem as far from the end as ever.

I am sorry that a request, sent to America and forwarded here, for a Christmas message to the blind Boy Scouts of India has arrived too late for me to comply.

Another request is from Oswald Garrison Villard, who does not know I am away. He wished me to speak on December 12th at a mass meeting in celebration of Carl von Ossietzky's receiving the Nobel prize and on behalf of other prisoners. I regret that I could not be present at such an important demonstration for peace. The stupidity of the German government's attitude towards this seems unbelievable! But its machinations cannot check the splendid inspiration of Ossietzky's

Helen Keller's Journal

work for peace. He will go down in history as a martyr, a true lover of his country who refused his consent to a course which he believed would only plunge it deeper into strife and wretchedness.

A letter from the Roosevelt Memorial Association asking me to attend the annual dinner in October 1937. They postponed presenting the medals which Teacher and I were to have received last October. I accept with both gratitude and sadness. I am sure the distinguished compliment they wish to pay me will help spread the gospel of hope for shipwrecked lives. But no honor can ever be the same to me as when Teacher could share it. . . .

Out for a brisk walk to chase away mourning thoughts and regain poise for tasks which require steady nerves and careful thinking.

Haggis for dinner today. What a succulent, tasty, satisfying dish it is! No wonder Burns sang its praise:

> *Great chieftain o' the puddin' race!*
> *Aboon them a' ye tak your place,*
> *Painch, tripe, or thairm:*
> *Weel are ye wordy of a grace*
> *As lang's my arm.*

Back to work and kept at it steadily until I'm as full of impatience as a hedgehog of quills. Things have been spelled in my palm until it is almost raw. Gladly I escape to bed, where I shall read Kenneth Grahame's *The Wind in the Willows*.

Helen Keller's Journal

The Manse, December 18th.

An inquisitorial fate still keeps me a prisoner at the desk. One task after another comes jostling like the rhymes in "The House That Jack Built." . . .

With proud joy I learned from this morning's Glasgow *Herald* that Sir Ian Fraser had been appointed a governor of the British Broadcasting Corporation. Such a victory over limitations will shake to destruction the wall which stands between the sightless and life's richest achievements. What a unique opportunity he will have to inspire and educate the people through the tremendous power of radio!

Today I received a clipping from the New York *Times* about the bronze head of Mark Twain which is to be erected on the Thames Embankment. What a dramatic homage to a man who spent his happiest years on a great river! And what site could be more fitting than the Embankment, round which broods the darkness of submerged humanity! I keep thinking of the last time I saw Mark Twain at his home in Connecticut. In memory I feel his dear, sad face and read his lips—a face recording the infinite tragedy the world seemed to him and the relentless warfare against the brutalities, cagings and shams he witnessed. I never saw him laugh, even while he was gladdening others and arming them with mirth to strive and to conquer obstacles.

Hardly anyone else, except Alexander Graham Bell, saw as clearly as Mark Twain did how Teacher mended the broken lyre of my life and gave me mental concepts

Helen Keller's Journal

to replace sight and hearing. He declared that there was no God, yet his faith in the human will to renew marred lives and to pierce the deepest darkness with love was unbounded.

The Manse, December 19th.

Still raining. I wonder where all this rain comes from? But I captured a bit of sunshine in the few minutes we spent at the primary Sunday school party seeing four-year-old children round a Christmas tree. How flower-like they looked in their little party frocks!

The news has just come that a young deaf student, Mr R. Pitcher, has won the B.Sc. degree at the London University. He took this difficult course without any conditions whatever, thus proving his ability beyond all doubt. He has received warm congratulations from the Archbishop of Ripon and Lord Charnwood, whom I met in London at a luncheon given in my honor by the National College for Teachers of the Deaf three years ago. It interests me to read that a fellow student enabled Mr Pitcher to keep up with the lectures by taking concise notes of what the professors said.

How well I know this part of the steep height he has climbed! I could never have attended the classes at college had it not been for Teacher, who sat beside me during four years and spelled into my hand the lectures word by word. This illustrates impressively what the handicapped may accomplish if normal people co-operate with them in a spirit of comradeship.

Went this evening to a motion picture at Hamilton, *If I Had a Million*. The laughs it provoked refreshed me after a day of complaining winds, downpour and

Helen Keller's Journal

the clatter of typewriter keys. People sometimes express surprise that a deaf-blind person can get any pleasure in the cinema. Polly reads me the titles, spells the dialogue and describes the facial expressions and the costumes, which is pretty rapid work. She has an actress's faculty of conveying to me with her slender fingers the humor, pathos or beauty of the picture as it unfolds before her.

Every time I go to the cinema—and that is seldom—I am transported on the magic carpet of memory to Hollywood, where I had a motion picture made of the story of my life in 1918. Invariably people ask me how that is possible when I could not hear the director's orders. But George Foster Platt devised a signal system of taps for me to follow and allowed time for Polly to interpret his commands. The vibration *tap-tap-tap* reaching my feet told me when to act or stop. Despite my self-conscious clumsiness those rehearsals are a comedy I enjoy remembering.

Under the spell of that long ago Charlie Chaplin moves across my life stage with his shy manner and charming modesty. Smiles and tears alternate as he reels off for us *A Dog's Life* and *Shoulder Arms* and shows me his nondescript hat, trousers and shoes. I have a special affection for Charlie Chaplin because of his deep sympathy with the underdog of mankind.

Another change of scenery, and we are lunching with Mary Pickford at her studio bungalow, meeting Douglas Fairbanks as Don Q. in his handsome costume, watching her at her work making *Little Annie Rooney*. Vividly I recall her body, tense with exertion, her warm, sensitive face and hot, dirty little hands full of good will.

Helen Keller's Journal

An unruly southwest wind nearly bowled us over on our way to church and pelted us with big raindrops as we walked back. . . .

The minister preached a very helpful sermon based on the story that there was no room at the Bethlehem inn where Mary sought shelter before the birth of the Christ child. I especially liked what he said about the way that the pursuit of materialistic ends crowds out of our life-inn childlike receptivity, daily reading in the Bible, love of beauty and strong simplicity that safeguards health and interest in living. . . .

Kenneth Grahame's *The Wind in the Willows* has sped the rainy hours for me. It imparts a rich sense of countryside delights and the bonny, comfortable fireside ways in Britain. True, it does not appeal to me as a nature book. I have never been able to appreciate the fables of Aesop or La Fontaine or any others that put our thoughts into the mouths of dumb animals or make them ridiculous, wearing our clothes or rowing in boats or driving automobiles. Animals *as they are* have a far greater charm for me. However, my fingers tingle happily as Mr Grahame's exquisite descriptions of the river, the spring wild flowers and Pan with the baby otter in his bosom ripple and sing across the pages.

I have also looked into the splendors of Omar Khayyam's *Rubaiyat*, gathering here an opal, here a ruby, and roses everywhere, but I simply cannot read it through. Perhaps that is because grief has drenched me and "the new-washed earth my life shall be" can hold no more rain. Certainly the *Rubaiyat* keeps ever before me chaotic shadows, lurid light, storms, men in the clutches of fear or borne down by despair or drowning their torments in sensualisms, the desert and the grave. For that matter, it is a kind of grave that can never be fair with pure snow or green with spring's promise! There no light may reach the souls of the blind, nor understanding the deaf, nor speech the silent lips.

He who does not see that joy is an important force in the world misses the essence of life. Joy is a spiritual element that gives vicissitudes unity and significance. Belief in the triumph of good vitalizes a race; enlightened optimism fosters in man a constructive purpose and frees him from fears which fetter his thought. Pessimism or *passive* resignation weakens the spirit and topples society to ruin, while *determined* resignation is a force. The first is but a regret; the other is a possession, for it is faith, a motive power. Optimism is Jehovah's lightning, clearing a fate-befogged atmosphere.

The Manse, December 21st.

This is the shortest day of the terrestrial year, but in my soul's calendar it has been the longest.

> *The longest day's in June, they say;*
> *The shortest in December.*
> *They never came to me that way—*
> *The shortest I remember*
> *You came and stayed a day,*
> *You filled my heart with laughter.*
> *The longest day, you were away,*
> *It was the next day after.*

It seems years instead of two months since Teacher left, and I have experienced a sense of dying daily.

Every hour I long for the thousand bright signals

Helen Keller's Journal

from her vital, beautiful hand. That was life! The hand that with a little word touched the darkness of my mind, and I awoke to happiness and love; a hand swift to answer every need, to disentangle skeins of dark silence for a fairer pattern; a hand radiant with the light it retrieved that I might see, sweet with the music it transmitted to my inner ear. After fifty years I continue to feel her dear, communicative hand's warmth and urge in mine as, I am told, one maimed feels the life in a lost limb. Look as I will, it is not there, and this heavy day has ground over me as a glacier over a field once joyously green. More life has vanished in the Christmases which centered about Teacher, the festivities she graced, lighting all beauty's candles, the rare sparkle of her personality seeking out new ways to create delight.

But what is Christmas if it does not draw those we have lost closer with cords of human love and make our lives God-approved shrines for their memory to live in? It is a replanting of the seed that shall grow into a tree exuberant and fruitful. To think of Christmas and Teacher together braces me, as the sun lifts up the flowers on their stems after a frosty night. No doubt she was often disappointed in my shortcomings and work ill done. I cannot imagine what she saw worth while that kept her at my side half a century. I can only believe she was the medium of God's love. If she had cared less about me I tremble to guess what might have been; but because God sent her, richly endowed, into my empty world I am sure He will give her a second time to me this Christmas and to the handicapped of the world through the yet greater inspiration of her work. Certainly it shall not be said that I have surrendered to the intolerable fate from which she found bright exits for me through service, imagination and friendship.

The Manse, December 22nd.

If Santa Claus were to descend the chimney, reindeer, pack and all, there could not be more running to and fro here this morning. Round me are flowing two streams of Christmas cablegrams, letters and packages, one out to the post office, the other in at the holly-wreathed front door.

Six of us have been stirring the plum pudding, and now it is boiling, bubbling, sending a jolly odor through the house. . . .

Glasgow.

Polly and I have been visiting friends this afternoon, and here we are at the Central Hotel for the night in the very room where we used to stop with Teacher when we came to Glasgow.

Tonight I am thinking with tender sorrow of Albert Einstein's bereavement. Today's Glasgow *Herald* contained a notice of his wife's death. His gentle courage and lofty thoughts, leading on to fresh discoveries, will, I know, sustain him; but it hurts to remember how much he has already suffered—persecution as a Jew, the outrage of the German government's branding his humane pacifism as treason, banishment from a country he deeply loved, hostility shown by his fellow believers because he saw a more sublime image of God in their sanctuary and strove to reveal it to them. It seems too cruel that he should now lose the wise, faithful companion in exile who shared his hardships, labors and triumphs.

Among my most luminous memories are the too brief moments Teacher and I had with Professor Einstein at the St Moritz Hotel in New York before he sailed back to Germany in 1929. He said to her, "Your work, Mrs Macy, has interested me more than any other achievement in modern education. Not only did you impart language to Helen Keller, you unfolded her personality, and such work has in it an element of the superhuman." Two years later I saw him again at a peace meeting under the auspices of the New History Society.

How vividly I recall his sympathetic handclasp, his reserved, almost shy manner, the childlike simplicity with which he permitted me to touch his noble head. The marvel of being in a great man's presence eludes language. I can but say that as I stood beside him I suddenly felt as if earth's discords were muted in the large, fraternal aura of Einstein's personality, and a new world had filled this old one as the spring sun fills a winter sky.

Central Hotel, Glasgow, December 23rd.

This morning when I awoke my despondency had vanished, and only the sense of a happy dream lingered.

I dreamed that Polly and I landed alone somewhere on the shores of Scotland and got into an automobile. As we started I discovered Teacher seated beside me, glowing with young beauty and joy. We drove through

Helen Keller's Journal

a spring countryside much like South Arcan, Ross Shire, and how she looked and looked! "Oh, Teacher," I cried, "is it not lovely?" "Yes, dear," she answered and kept on gazing. Overjoyed, I knew her unclouded eyes were taking in the Highland glories of mountain, glen and loch she had not been able to enjoy in her pain and blindness. Sometimes Polly leaned over eagerly to describe the landscape, forgetting Teacher *could see!*

Teacher gave me an instrument covered with soft polished leather and containing coils of wire varying in thickness and sensitivity. "Observe this carefully, Helen," she said, "and it will help you keep your speech at its present level of excellence. It will also bring you different sounds from a distance just as we get them through the ear." I placed my hands on the instrument. To my astonishment each wire coil vibrated with a sound easily distinguishable from the rest—cars and teams going by, passing footsteps, birds singing, running water. I received all these impressions simultaneously, as I do the varied fragrances in a garden of many flowers. Overcome with wonder, I held Teacher's hand. Quietly she drew it back and caressed my cheek, and the next instant I found her place empty, but I was not troubled. I realized the caress was her sign that she had indeed been with me, and it was some time before I waked. Then a luminous peace spread through my heart such as I had not known. I am certain now she *was* there, but I have yet to find out whether the instrument she showed me is an encouragement or a prophecy of new victories over limitations. . . .

An editorial in the Glasgow *Herald* especially interested me on the Pan-American Conference which is

Helen Keller's Journal

about to adjourn after three weeks strenuous work. Its agreements seem to bristle with "ifs" and "buts." Still, I am glad it is felt that relations between North and South America are becoming more friendly and constructive. The Monroe Doctrine has always aroused my indignation since I realized its one-sidedness, and I welcome the new interpretation of mutual aid and co-operation for all the Americas. I note in some newspaper comments from home that Congress is weakening in its support of President Roosevelt, but I hope there may be a favorable public opinion formed which will enable him and the rulers of the other republics to start making the Western Hemisphere a haven of peace. In the long run we hit only what we aim at; therefore we Americans had better aim at this high purpose and every other that shall banish militarism from the earth.

Neither the League of Nations nor the World Court seems to me to have in it the seed of permanent peace. World peace will never come until the passion of supremacy is combated. Peoples must first be prepared for peace and be willing to make sacrifices for it, just as they now are prepared to deny themselves for war. That is why I await anxiously whatever the Pan-American congresses may accomplish in peace education.

It was a real pleasure to walk through the streets of Glasgow today while doing our Christmas shopping. The crowds were dense but good humored. Almost everyone was carrying parcels and holly, and I felt that the Christmas spirit truly reigned in the city as well as out in the quiet countryside. The assistants, too, though working early and late in packed shops, found time to be pleasant and full of good wishes for "a Merry Christmas." Happily I anticipate tomorrow with

Helen Keller's Journal

the children, free from desk work and the heartache it often brings.

The Manse, December 25th.

Yesterday I dropped a clamoring crowd of tasks so that the children and I might make merry together. They were decorating the house and kept stopping to show me a bit of mistletoe, declaring I should surely be caught, or a particularly bright sprig of holly berries. If I could not reach the festoons stretched across the hall they would put a stepladder in a convenient place and tell me to climb up for a look. Every time a package arrived we would bring it in and debate where to find space for it in the fast-filling drawing room. I laughed at the plump, beribboned, besprigged parcels that sat on this table exchanging compliments of the season with my Braille manuscripts and typewriter.

Now and then Robert would open the door of the bird cage and ask me to try to make friends with two exquisite lovebirds—his first Christmas gift. They were most coy and retiring, but to Robert's unbounded delight I succeeded in catching a finger glimpse of a downy breast, a tiny hooked bill and a wide-spreading tail. He told me he was going to tame them so that they would perch on my finger before I went back to America. I was able to picture them listening to the radio with their heads on one side, then drowning the carols with competitive chirping....

A jolly Christmas Eve dinner party with just the family. It was a joy to look at the table, so daintily decorated and festive. We had turkey and plum pudding. Between bites we laughed at the "quips and

Helen Keller's Journal

cranks and wanton wiles" evoked by Puck and Robin Goodfellow, pulled crackers and watched the children brimming over with curious, embarrassingly wise questions about the gifts they were to receive.

Back by the drawing-room fire all eight of us undid boxes and bundles until the room literally felt like a snowdrift of tinsel, ribbons, straw and delicate bits of wool. Surrounded by such gaiety and everybody's pleasure in his own and others' gifts, I found carols softly chiming in my loneliness. It is true, contentment cannot be with me, but it means much that the peace of remembrance and love are mine.

Today, I hear, is the warmest December 25th in seven years. Polly and I have had an hour's unforgettable walk, out among the fields and pastures where Christmas seems most true. A warm sun melted the hoarfrost as we stepped along, and up floated autumnal perfumes and spring prophecies from the grass so thick bladed, fresh, satisfying to hand and foot. Polly said the blackness of the bare hedges made the green herbage all the more beautiful. Sometimes she would stop to let me feel a moss-covered stone dike or a rhododendron bank or a gushing spring. Once we stopped to make friends with a little calf in a pasture. Gingerly he touched my finger tips with his nose and was off, evidently disappointed that I had nothing for him to eat.

Not a soul did we meet on the road except a farmer and his horse. Birds chirped quietly around us. A hymn chanted from a hospital in the distance scarcely broke the silence. Here indeed was the life-giving power—the strong, abiding foundation of simple, homely things. Here I heard, as it were, the mother tongue of my remote ancestors who wrestled with the elements—the

Helen Keller's Journal

language of the mold and the air I knew as a child. I realized that my delight in those fields and trees had endured because of the fields and trees I had taken delight in when young. Change may be the vitalizing wind blowing through the house of life, but it is not an abiding force. We need permanent things to soak peace into us as well as progress—the beauty of the earth, seedtime and harvest, the smiles of lovers, the joy of the young in being alive, pride in craftsmanship. Why, oh, why must we let ourselves forget these lasting treasures in an age of consuming ambition, speed madness and accumulated goods that leave us no chance to live? If we cannot be contented with a little no wealth will ever satisfy us. Only from simple beginnings can creation go on unchecked. . . .

The Whins, Stirling, December 26th.

Our friends, the Bains, invited us here for the Christmas week end. The Whins is a large, handsome, Georgian house, ivy covered without and full of warm Scottish hearts within. On the walls are deers' heads wreathed with holly. By the fire are four beautiful dogs—three Golden Labradors and a cairn. Lying on top of one other, Polly says, they shine like a pile of gold in the firelight.

The house is under the shadow of Stirling Castle and stands right where the ancient Caledonian Forest used to be. The garden rejoices my heart with its box hedges and mingled odors that no winter chill can subdue.

Last night a few guests came for dinner, among them a young niece of James McNeill Whistler. I had just been reading about Whistler in E. V. Lucas' *A Wanderer*

Helen Keller's Journal

in London and was greatly interested to know that he was the first artist to discover the loveliness concealed in London fogs. All through dinner there was animated talk about Newfoundland and Dr Grenfell's marvelous work among the fishermen. His book, *Forty Years in Labrador*, had already impressed me with his genius as an organizer and with the heroism and patience of the people among whom he lives.

The Whins, December 27th.

Breakfast in bed—a delicious luxury. Dear Elizabeth herself brought it to me—home-cured bacon, the best fried eggs I ever tasted, toast and marmalade and always the cup of good tea.

Under the shadow of Stirling Castle I have begun reading John Morley's *Life of Gladstone* in Braille. Lady Aberdeen, I remember, said she would try to knock the heresies out of my head when I told her I thought Disraeli was in some ways a greater statesman than Gladstone, and here is a book which I am sure she approves. I expect to learn much from this record of how he strove to apply the highest ethical principles both to national and international affairs. At the same time Mr Morley expresses what I tried to say to Lady Aberdeen. Gladstone did not possess the detachment, "often found among superior minds, which we honor for its disinterestedness"; and no one has, I believe, questioned Disraeli's mental superiority. Again, Gladstone wrote, "I know not why commerce in England should not have its old families." With their far-reaching tyranny over the plain people these old commercial families formed an institution which Disraeli feared in politics, and time seems to have justified his apprehensions. Commercial concerns have expanded from family business to corporate wealth which is self-perpetuating and which enlightened statesmen and economists now dread as the most potent oligarchy yet produced. However, I shall read on and keep a sharp lookout for new ideas.

The Whins, December 28th.

How pleasant the room I write in is! Drinah visits me every morning and puts her golden paws up on my knee to attract my attention. Evidently she understands by now that I cannot see or hear her.

While I am here I give the dogs their daily tidbit of roll. After lunch or dinner they are allowed in the dining room. They always take exactly the same position: Hamel, the mother, between her two daughters and Drinah at the end of the row. As I pass the tidbit from one to another I feel the ruffle on Carrie's neck, in fact a little golden mane, which I believe is rare among Labradors.

Today my head is buzzing with a letter that seems the call of destiny. Two years ago a blind man who champions the cause of the blind in Japan, Mr Iwahashi, called on me in New York. We quickly became friends; he was so understanding, full of the delicate Japanese imagination that blossoms in faith, art and philosophy. He communicated with me by writing in Braille what he wished to say; and my odd, halting speech did not seem to puzzle him after the first few sentences.

Helen Keller's Journal

When I said I hoped I might visit Japan his answer took away my breath:

"Will you come to Japan, please, Miss Keller, in the spring and open doors of help for our brothers and sisters shut out in a great darkness, if I arrange with the Japanese government to sponsor the trip?"

Hardly believing my fingers' report of his Braille invitation, I thanked him and explained that I could not leave Teacher, who was ill and rapidly becoming blind. In quaint English he replied: "God's miracles never stop. Perhaps by a way higher than earth's ways He will help your teacher to see, then she can come to Japan with you."

I thought the matter would rest there.

Several months later Mr Iwahashi sent a formal invitation, leaving the date open for my convenience either in the spring or autumn of 1936. Plans had been made by the Japanese government to provide hospitality for the three of us during the whole trip. He also informed me that all my books had been translated into Japanese, and he said that it would mean much to the cause if I would be present at the dedication of the new Lighthouse for the blind at Osaka during October 1936. Such a magnificent opportunity to kindle new hope for the handicapped, not only in Japan but throughout the Orient, dazzled my imagination. Nevertheless, I declined. Teacher's sight had not improved despite two operations, and her health was completely broken.

My Japanese friends' attitude towards this refusal did honor to their hearts. They invited us a second time last spring, not knowing that Teacher was growing worse. She was unhappy that I should let go another unique opportunity and almost overrode my objections.

Helen Keller's Journal

Still I said no and felt sure that would be the end.

Early this month, to my amazement, I had a cable begging me to visit Japan in the spring. Polly and I said yes to ourselves, but prudence dictated that we should consult Mr Migel. I wrote him at once, expressing a strong wish to obey the third summons, which I looked upon as a miracle. Mr Migel sent a letter warmly approving the plan; and now here I am with a long Braille letter from Mr Iwahashi entreating Polly and me to accept and declaring that everything is ready for us. He wishes us to be there the middle of April, travel through Japan, Korea and Manchukuo and finish our tour towards the end of June. While awaiting further developments my thoughts crowd and obliterate each other like fogs that hide landmarks. So swiftly are things happening, we must keep planning ahead every day now if we are to be prepared for any turn our affairs may take.

The Manse, December 28th.

This afternoon we motored to Edinburgh to do a little shopping and visit some friends. Going back to Bothwell in the evening, Polly gave a jump of delight. "Helen! there is Edinburgh Castle floodlighted. It looks like fairyland." From all accounts it must be a glorious sight, suspended in space, casting an enchanting spell of unreality upon the gray city.

Scarcely inside the Manse, we find another army of letters tumbling about our ears; but I am marching Polly and myself off to bed, foreseeing that we shall need all possible sleep to face the barrage tomorrow.

Helen Keller's Journal

The Manse, December 29th.

A letter from Mr Otto Schramm, the German publisher of my books, has excited a turmoil of mental insurrection in me. He has written me twice before, May 5, 1931, and April 18, 1933, trying to argue away at length my favorable views on Bolshevism. Now he says as a publisher he can no longer be responsible for such opinions and that the laws of Germany forbid the printing of such passages as I wrote, expressing a friendly feeling towards the great Russian experiment of economic democracy. Therefore he "must cut out of the German edition of *Midstream* the part about Lenin in the chapter 'Thoughts That Will Not Let Me Sleep.'" He goes on to say: "I must today emphasize that I hope you meantime have become convinced of your error of judgment, and therefore feel obliged to let me know that your attitude now towards Russian Bolshevism has entirely altered since you have learned about the evil and monstrous destruction to which this world-doctrine tends."

If, as Mr Schramm asserts, millions upon millions of Russia's people had been killed body and soul, that country would not now be emerging, as we know it is, stronger than ever from its agelong fight against hunger and ignorance.

No doubt Russia has committed blunders, grave ones; but so has National-Socialist Germany, and now it has reverted to the darkest of the Dark Ages, denying personal freedom to the young, suppressing all opinions different from those it prescribes, prohibiting all criticisms of drama, films, books, painting and sculpture except those which are handled from the Nazi point of view. . . .

Overslept this morning, which was perhaps just as well; for Polly and I have sat hunched over the mail all day. It was mostly Christmas—beautiful cards and tender messages and comforting thoughts for a New Year to whose strangeness I must close my mind if I am to keep my colors flying.

The Manse, December 30th.

Up early to wade through the first complete Braille copy I have had of the Economic Security Bill, including pensions for the blind, which became a law in the United States in the summer of 1935. Well do I remember how strenuously Polly and I worked to help get the pension law for the blind passed! I wrote letters supporting the measure; we flew to Washington to try to interest Secretary Frances Perkins, Mr Harry Hopkins and Mr Walker, of the Public Works Administration, and again to urge upon Senators Wagner, Harrison and Black the need to ease the burden of those doubly handicapped by blindness and poverty. It is gratifying to look back upon the passage of that bill and recall that all of us who had striven for it felt more encouraged than we had been for many years in our endeavors to reach the large majority of unemployable people without sight for whom the schools can do nothing. . . .

It is fortunate that I live in these days of Braille transcribing! That enables me to have countless letters

Helen Keller's Journal

copied so that I can read them over myself to save Polly; that is what absorbed me nearly all the morning.

After two years silence Mahatma Gandhi now says: "Show me the way, and I am prepared to go to jail again, and I am prepared to be hanged."

Is this his old energy blazing to a fateful conflagration, or is it a dying flame? More than ever I revere his sublime soul. There is another side equally fraught with tragic significance. The "untouchables" of India do not appear to desire national independence while their human rights are denied—and why should they?

Tremulously I read Sir Rabindranath Tagore's magnificent impeachment of caste which will go down the ages, *The Great Equality*. This is a cup of holy wrath prepared not only for the haughty of India but also the United States and every land where there is discrimination against a subject race or class.

I remember the gracious courtesy with which, during a visit to America, Dr Tagore accepted Teacher's and my invitation to a tea in his honor at our home in Forest Hills. How impressive he was as he entered the parlor, with his beautiful white hair, long billowing beard and stately draperies! After we had greeted each other he was silent for a few moments. I asked him if he would read one of his poems, and I placed my hand lightly on his noble face as he read aloud with a rich, deep voice "In My Garden" and "I Forget, I Forget."

The mystical beauty and timelessness of his verse stole like music into my soul. Not only as a poet did I sense his power; I realized that his mind was full of lamps of liberating courage. I said I wondered why India had not sooner won her independence. Dr Tagore replied:

Helen Keller's Journal

"We can wait for centuries as no other people can. Political freedom cannot truly benefit India. Only where love reigns in all classes, and the common good is the chief goal, can there be real freedom."

The memory of Dr Tagore's perceptive tenderness and royal presence is a benediction.

The Manse, December 31st.

Occupied the whole morning with my Braille notes.

I have been wrapped in a tempest of grieving thoughts. What had this old year brought that was new? To me, only the illness of her for whom I lived, and sorrow old as mortality. To the world, black clouds threatening Europe's peace hopes, wicked anti-Semitic persecutions and the sickening barbarities in Madrid. Had it not been for the children's presence (they begged permission to stay up with me to welcome the New Year), I could not have sat quietly in the circle round the fire while we talked about Teacher and the forty-nine years I had begun and ended under her inspiring leadership.

Suddenly Robert touched my arm, saying, "One minute to twelve!" David brought in his radio so that I could place my finger on the diaphragm of the loud-speaker and "hear" Big Ben striking its slow, sonorous notes. I dared not dwell on the happier circumstances under which I had listened to Big Ben by Teacher's side at home at the close of each year since 1925. As it was, I nearly burst into tears when we stood up, took hands and sang "Auld Lang Syne." Human reckonings do not give faith like the Divine Calendar in a second creation, a second life on earth after bereavement. But

Helen Keller's Journal

Use and Custom, kindly nurses of the child in our hearts, must have their due.

As we drank to the New Year I remembered: "Where the letter killeth, the Spirit multiplieth." Somehow I translated the letter of my pain into a prayer that during 1937 mankind may break away from an armed truce cruel with fear and bind themselves in a Holy Alliance of everlasting neighborliness and peace.

The Manse, January 1, 1937.

The sun is shining in all its strength, and we are just up, drinking cup after cup of tea to drive the leaden sleep out of our eyes.

Another hour with my notebooks. A fresh bouquet of New Year greetings and a very pleasant letter from Dr Mavor thanking me for a book, Walter Duranty's *I Write As I Please*, which I sent him at Christmas.

This brings back to my remembrance the eventful afternoon when I met Mr Duranty at the Hotel Chatham in New York last spring. His talk about world affairs was stimulating. When I asked him if he still thought the Soviet government was striving sincerely for the people's welfare he replied decidedly in the affirmative. He expressed the hope that there might not be another world conflict. From close observation he thought the working people of Germany might overturn Naziism and join Russia in a constructive effort for peace. His brave optimism caused me to feel more hopeful for Europe than I had in many a day.

Dr Mavor comments on the refreshing freedom from bias with which Mr Duranty writes about Russia's experiment with democracy and the correctness of his conclusions at times. He also pleases me by saying I am right in the guess I have made about the symbolism of *A Sleeping Clergyman*. With his letter he sent a new book, *Mr Bridie's Alphabet for Little Glasgow Highbrows*, in which I am sure I shall find many a laugh that leaves wisdom behind it.

Later. The Whins.

Here we are again at the Whins for a week. We had a ruinously delectable New Year dinner. Elizabeth's brother Andrew has a shoot on the estate of the Earl of Mar and Kellie near Stirling, and sent us some plump pheasants. We had black pudding that tastes a good deal like haggis, celery fresh from the garden, wine jellies, pies, glorious red apples. An hour later we walked along the golf course in King's Park under Stirling Castle. I could not open my lungs wide enough for the wind blowing off the Grampians and Ochil Hills to the north.

The Whins, January 2nd.

I read "Etiquette in China", an editorial from the *Morning Post*, and note a willingness to admit that few Westerners have the special intelligence for the refined entertainment of oriental etiquette. Who among us has acquired the exquisite courtesy of General Chiang Kai-shek and his kidnaper, Marshal Chang Hsueh-liang, one of his own subordinates? Chiang has been released, officially at least, without the vulgar chinking of coins.

Helen Keller's Journal

Neither he nor his late captor has uttered a harsh word. Instead Chiang has convinced Marshal Chang of his own sincere zeal for China, and Marshal Chang, repentant of his "impudent and criminal act", has followed him to Nanking "to await a befitting punishment."

The editorial goes on to say that if Chiang should go, to what lengths might "vociferous young China" not push his less adroit associates in the Nanking government? China may well be vociferous, with seven kinds of revolution going on at the same time—in the family, in economics, education, religion, woman's social status, caste and the grapple between long-entrenched individualism and public-spirited citizenship.

New eras usually come with turmoil and overthrow—witness early Christianity, Protestantism and the downfall of czarism. China is to be honored for shouting aloud words that have been only muttered and faiths that have been denied. It has gained the courage to be itself, to rebaptize its beliefs and ideals in the eternal fount of truth. Forward it must go. About the Chinese starvation, falsehood and greed are doing their fell work. Where they are there is no abiding!

I have serious doubts concerning Chiang Kai-shek's sincerity. Dr Sun Yat-sen commanded my warmest honor and respect. After his death I read conflicting reports about Chiang's policy. Some said he had pledged himself to Dr Sun Yat-sen's program of economic democracy, others contradicted this, but through all the rumors I noted an admission that he was not a radical. Nora Waln's *The House of Exile* was under my fingers last year, and I observed her tacit approval of Chiang as an aristocrat, a guardian of vested rights, finance and power. Vincent Sheean's autobiography told how Chiang gradually swerved from the principles laid down by Dr Sun Yat-sen until he caused or permitted a great many radicals and even moderates to be slaughtered. Apparently while professing zeal for uniting China he continues to give military protection to the very war lords that keep the nation divided and the officials preying upon the people. Time may yet reveal him as a farsighted statesman tragically misunderstood, but I cannot silence my suspicions; I can only pray wholeheartedly for China's deliverance.

The Whins, January 3rd.

This morning we attended the New Year service at the Church of the Holy Rude, or Cross—an epic in stone—where Mary Queen of Scots worshiped. Somehow I never think of her as a queen but as the ill-starred babe baptized in Scotland's spiritual travail, the pathetic young girl thrust into the vicissitudes of turbulent society before she could distinguish between right and wrong.

As we approached the church at the top of the hilly St John Street in warm sunshine I felt on my face what seemed a chrism of dew. On inquiry I found it was molten hoarfrost shaken in diamond drops from the ancient oaks surrounding the church. After the service we went into the choir where James VI of Scotland was crowned. He was only thirteen months old then; and the crown, I believe, was held above the royal baby's head by the Earl of Mar. During nearly three hundred years the great edifice of the Holy Rude was divided in two by a wall, and two separate congregations wor-

Helen Keller's Journal

shiped therein, one in the nave and the other in the choir; but now the church is being restored, and the dividing wall has been removed. That is as it should be; for the Bible is a shrine of beauty as well as righteousness.

After tea I dipped into the first three volumes of Morley's life of Gladstone. The whole work is in twenty-seven Braille volumes! Never did I realize that in youth Gladstone was the most conservative among the Conservatives. With amazement I learn that he opposed the emancipation of slaves in the British colonies, the admission of Jews to Parliament and dissenters to the universities without a test; that he voted against the ballot and the property tax, that he supported the worst clauses of the Irish coercion bill, including the court-martial clause. He lacked mental independence, a generous attitude towards others' opinions and curiosity regarding unexplored fields of human endeavor. He must have possessed miraculous will power and rare candor to shake himself free from tradition's many dull tyrannies and develop into the great legislator upon whose picture Disraeli gazed with benevolent, puzzled wonderment and said: "I have never hated Gladstone; the trouble is, I have never understood him." None of the old parties command my respect or allegiance on either side of the Atlantic, but there is a spellbinding fascination in the events Gladstone witnessed and out of which he and his generation made history.

The extracts Morley quotes from Gladstone's diaries indicate, I think, that he was too occupied with herculean tasks to keep a journal. Many of them are little more than calenders with such entries as "Breakfast", "Rode", "Wrote", "Lunch", "Tea", "House" (meaning time spent at Parliament), a list of books read or reread.

A moving service at St Cuthbert's, Edinburgh, broadcast this evening. The organ notes rolled in like mighty billows through the receiver as I rested my hand on the diaphragm. Polly repeated in the other hand as a glorious voice chanted "Comfort Ye My People", and an eloquent sermon was preached on that text—a call to the doubting, the discouraged and the sorrowing to return to the Lord their Shepherd and the life of the spirit.

The Whins, January 4th.

It has poured torrents all day, but I have the sun of the past week warm in my memory, and whatever the weather does here, the Highland air energizes my body.

The item which especially interests me in this morning's Glasgow *Bulletin* is about the Will Rogers Memorial which will be unveiled shortly in the cemetery above Colorado Springs. However splendid this memorial may be, it can only dimly suggest what Will Rogers was—a spirit of good will, laughing away foolishness or melancholy, softening hearts with his gentle wisdom, emphasizing the humanity in all races and throughout history. He was a friend to the handicapped. I never asked him in vain for help in my work for the blind. He either sent me money, saying, "Don't hesitate to ask for more," or he broadcast a message for me or wrote an eloquent paragraph calling nationwide attention to the sightless. It was a rare privilege to have had such a world-famed, richly gifted friend's support in a cause that the strong and the prosperous soon forget.

Helen Keller's Journal

Also I read that Andrew Mellon has offered an art collection worth two million pounds to the United States government, and it is understood that President Roosevelt will advise Congress to accept. I remember meeting Mr Mellon in Washington, when he was secretary of the treasury. We talked for some time about the enormous difficulty in raising money to help a hundred and twenty thousand blind persons. He said he was interested in my work and afterwards sent me one hundred dollars. The same day I met President and Mrs Coolidge at the White House. We had our pictures taken together. The president wore a very pleasant expression as I read his lips for the photographers. His interest in the blind was a constant encouragement to me during the hard first years of the existence of the American Foundation for the Blind. That morning I called on Robert M. Lansing, who had been secretary of state under President Wilson. I was impressed by Mr Lansing's quiet dignity and the sense that he had labored valiantly and endured great trials in service to his country.

The Whins, January 5th.

A crisp January morning. The winter wheat is already sown and will lie warm in the earth while the hard frosts keep it safe from the clawing north wind.

Out of a clear sky came the distressing news of my friend the Marchioness of Aberdeen's grave illness. A few hours later I learned that she had died.

In August 1934 Teacher, Polly and I were delightfully entertained at Haddo House, which dates from the sixteenth century. We lunched with the marquis and marchioness and a few other friends. Teacher and I sat in seats which had been occupied by Gladstone and Queen Victoria. I amused myself by trying to imagine an encounter between Anne Sullivan Macy, with her delicate Irish humor and sudden changes of subject, and Gladstone, with his sonorous, vague, involved periods and bulldog grip on an argument!

Lady Aberdeen was always very sweet to Teacher, whose work she praised with tender emotion. She led her about carefully while the rest of us were shown over the house. I remember we visited the library with its handsome Wedgwood fireplace, then a room which, by a marvelous fragrance, I knew was built of cedarwood. Out in the grounds we saw an imposing galaxy of trees set out by friends and guests of the family. One huge beech had grown from a sapling planted by Queen Victoria and the Prince Consort.

We went into the chapel, a shrine of peace where the late marquis, whom I knew so well, had often prayed and played his favorite hymns. Dr Reid, the musician, played for me. As the music enveloped me in its majesty Lord Aberdeen seemed to be at my side. With tears in my eyes I recalled visiting him and Lady Aberdeen at the House of Cromar the summer before he died. He took me into his study and, standing by the window, he spoke into my hand:

"That is Lochnagar up there—the mountain I look at first in the morning and last at night. Helen, Lochnagar with the golden sun on his head and the bright greenness below is like the hills of God unto which I lift my eyes and which I shall soon ascend."

I remember his soft speech and faraway look—and my presentiment that I should not see him again. Turn-

Helen Keller's Journal

ing from the window, he led me to his desk and said, "Here is your book, *Peace at Eventide,* in which I read every night before going to sleep."

What a soul-awing circle of deaths has been drawn across my days since then!

The Whins, January 6th.

A sunburst touched my face early this morning and actually coaxed me out of bed. I opened the window, and exuberant greetings floated up to me from the box hedges, just as in April. Polly said the crows were cawing lustily, the thrushes and tits twittering all around. Out in the garden I saw the yellow jasmine blooming, and they tell me snowdrops and other spring flowers will appear soon. How different Scotland, with its frost and snow melting at noonday and a happy imminence of spring throughout the winter, is from the Northern United States, with the sod frozen hard and not a sign of greenness or fragrance during four or five months!

Six long notes and two short written this morning, and there are still a dozen in the offing, but my hands demand a rest. Curiously enough a presentiment keeps knocking at my mind's door that I shall not much longer be able to keep at the typewriter as steadily as I have. Often my hands feel cramped or limp, which does not surprise me, as they have never been still, except in sleep, since I was two years old. They mean the world I live in—they are eyes, ears, channels of thought and good will. Sooner would I lose my health or even the ability to walk (and walking is among the few cherished bits of personal liberty I possess) than the use of these two hands. However, if I take proper care of them now and use other muscles not already overtasked I shall still have the joy of working in different ways. What these ways will be I am not certain, but I shall know when I begin experimenting.

The Manse.

Happy to be back with the children, whose lives are so far from the madding cares and griefs of the world.

Caught in a downpour hurrying from the cinema at Hamilton, and came home by starlight. The motion picture we saw was *Fury*, a powerful impeachment of lynching and of the citizens who perpetrate it in some parts of the United States. In my opinion their mob inhumanity is without excuse. Wendell Phillips, one of America's great antislavery champions, had wide experience with mobs and said they were usually "respectable", well dressed, with some education. Since childhood my heart has been hot against lynching, whether the victim is white or black. However horrible the crime, I would insist that no human being be denied a fair trial; and if the trial is delayed a mob—insanity let loose—is unthinkable for dealing justice. Revenge is given as the motive. Revenge indeed! Do not those who stoop to it place themselves on a level with the evil-doers they execute?

It is curious how thoughts behave. They elude me in a crowd. Like spirits, they must be spoken to in solitude before they will explain themselves.

Helen Keller's Journal

The Manse, January 7th.

A smiling day, a long walk and the relief of having dispatched eleven more letters yesterday have made my work especially pleasant.

John, the youngest member of the family, was sitting here, busy with his paints, and stopped to ask on his fingers: "Can you tell colors, Helen Keller?"

"Yes," I answered, "when I feel blue!"

He laughed and gave me a big pat on the shoulder, saying: "But really, can you tell colors?" I explained that I cannot distinguish them by touch, but I can imagine what they must be like from books and descriptions of scenery. His question reminded me how my audiences on lecturing tours used to ask everything under the sun:

"What is your favorite color?"

"What books do you like best?"

"Who is your favorite poet?"

"What is your idea of truth?"

"Do you like pretty clothes?"

"I believe you are a clairvoyant. Please tell me where to find my lost jewelry."

"What do you consider the hardest thing in the world?" And to this question I would reply: "To get Congress to do anything!"

"Do you close your eyes when you go to sleep?" was asked often; and I answered: "I never stayed awake to see!" . . .

Among my papers I happened to come across an article giving some curious objections that would be raised if George Washington were to run for the presidency today. It is said that the American Legion, the Daughters of the Revolution and the Liberty League would object because he was a representative of revolutionary tendencies; also because he was born an Englishman. President Roosevelt and the New Deal would oppose Washington because he believed in the Constitution and in "rugged individualism." Bishop Cannon and the Methodist Board of Prohibition, Temperance and Public Morals would say no because he believed in life, liberty and the pursuit of happiness and kept the best cellar in Virginia. The Roman Catholics and the Missouri Lutheran Synod would shake their heads over Washington's being a Mason. The Atheist Society would frown upon him because he was a churchman, and the Negroes and the Civil Liberties Union (I happen to be a member) because he kept slaves. The League of Nations Association would not want him because he warned against entangling alliances. The isolationists and "hundred per cent Americans" would fight because he was an ally of France and welcomed Lafayette, von Steuben and Kosciusko as his friends. Last but not least would come the United Amalgamated Fruit Growers of America—because Washington cut down the cherry tree!

The Manse, January 8th.

A keen, frosty morning. But at eleven, when Polly and I took our walk, the sun was warm enough for the cattle to be brought out to pasture. A herd of eight or ten came up so close that we stepped into deep wet grass to let them pass. It is always good to come home

Helen Keller's Journal

and see the cathedral-like Church of St Bride's gray and benign in that Scottish landscape.

Today I replied at length to Mr Schramm's letter:

>The Manse,
>Bothwell,
>Scotland

Mr Otto Schramm,
Stuttgart, Germany

Dear Mr Schramm,

I thank you for your letter, which was forwarded to me here in Scotland. I appreciate your kind expressions of sympathy in my sorrow. The precious flowers planted among my limitations by her whose friendship was summer sunshine to me seem withered at present, but Anne Sullivan Macy's courage, remembered, will keep me strong, and I shall hold fast to the free spirit which I consider my richest dower in the silent dark.

In order to avoid misstatements I have had your letter transcribed into Braille, and I have read it many times. I can see the yoke which the despotic censorship laws of Germany have put round your neck as a publisher. I would rather you did not continue publishing *Midstream* or any other book by me if in so doing you must omit or falsify my views on Lenin or whatever subject I choose to discuss.

By the way, I have *Midstream* under my fingers, and I find you are mistaken in speaking of my "sentence" about Lenin and Trotsky. Trotsky's name does not appear in the chapter "Thoughts That Will Not Let Me Sleep" or indeed in any other part of the book. Lenin has a whole page—not a mere "mention" treatment.

Helen Keller's Journal

Your own words, Mr Schramm, implying a coercive authority over those at home and abroad whose opinions differ from your government, grieve but do not surprise me. They justify the feeling I have long had that fundamental liberties, without which a nation's soul is dead, have been suppressed in Germany—free speech, a free press and information as unbiased as may be on world affairs. With this conviction I ask you please to drop all my writings from your list of publications.

What I shall say further will make you realize that you ought to take this straightforward course.

I have never changed my attitude towards Bolshevism, and even if I had, I should not "feel obliged to let you know of it" as you are pleased to put it. Any person at all versed in history knows Bolshevism originated centuries before Lenin's birth. Anyone with business sense knows Bolshevism is not responsible for "the evil and monstrous destruction" by which Europe is menaced. Cutthroat economic competition including Germany, greed for markets in backward countries, empire interests linked with trade routes, are driving the nations to ever greater, madder expenditure in munitions and armaments.

If all the charges your letter launches against Bolshevism were even half true Russia would literally have been wiped off the earth before now, and so would any other country concerning which such statistics could be verified:

"Murder and Annihilation of Millions of Russia's Intelligentsia."

"Starving of Millions of Peasants."

"Destruction of the Peasantry and Frightful Diminution of Agricultural Products."

"Physical, Mental and Spiritual Destruction of the Masses—Workers and Peasants."

How dare you stigmatize as "a reign of terror" the Spanish people's superhuman heroism in efforts to win their rightful freedom? From whatever sources such ill-assorted, ill-digested information is collected, it is distributed by the ignorant, and ignorance is always abusive. The man who does not stand sure on his facts is full of loud affirmations and mean interpretations.

It is as inconceivable, Mr Schramm, that Germans and foreigners everywhere should be continually lying about Germany as it is that everybody should always tell the truth about Soviet Russia.

I am filled with sorrow by undeniable facts in regard to Germany. As I told you three years ago, I knew about Germany's anti-Semitic atrocities, fear-clamping state control over lives and homes, imprisonment of thousands without trial, the blackest crime against genius—the exiling of Albert Einstein, whom the world honors, and branding him as a traitor for his humane pacifism. Now here is a final proof that the charges brought against your country are not all false or malicious—the law inflicting death upon any German who "knowingly and unscrupulously, out of sheer selfishness or for other base motives, sends or leaves his money or other property abroad." Another law robs the young of personal freedom—hereafter every German boy and girl "without exception" to be trained physically, spiritually and morally must join the Hitler Youth. Baldur von Schirach, youth leader of the Reich, has declared that "the lives of all German youth belong solely to Adolf Hitler" and that "the Hitler Youth is not the Church, and the Church is not the Hitler Youth." What is all this, Mr

Schramm, but chattel slavery, idolatry and infringement upon Christian consciences?

In the false position which Hitler has built up he cannot save Europe even if it needs saving. Only by substituting magnanimity for hate can Germany place itself beyond the reach of hostile propaganda and the revenge whose brooding ferocity never slumbers.

I realize how hopeless it seems to write this letter to one who may have been browbeaten into closing his mind against investigation. But the Lord's voice is powerful. Surely someday it will rend asunder the prison where all of you suffer and let in upon you the good will you have misconstrued and the deep-down humanity to which you have for a while become deaf and blind.

With a sad good-by and with an unshakable affection for the German people,

I am,
Sincerely yours,
HELEN KELLER

The Manse, Bothwell, January 9th.

A day's work, unbroken except by meals, from 9 A.M. to 11 P.M. The last Christmas mail read—a good deal of it. Six letters written. More Braille notes that will be signposts guiding me through what promises to be a rushed as well as a memorable year. A speech, requiring much thought, to prepare for January 29th, when Polly and I are to attend the unveiling of Gutzon Borglum's statue of Thomas Paine in Paris.

What a miracle Thomas Paine was! The more I consider him, the more it seems that God, in whom he did not believe, or thought he did not, planned his life from beginning to end. For Thomas Paine dwelt apart, observing, developing his individuality where repression was almost inescapable, discovering his kindred in other nations where a narrow patriotism would have obscured his vision.

Lonely, misconstrued, amazingly ignorant, he yet became a fear-ruling, chain-breaking, throne-shaking genius. Oh, miraculous moments when Thomas Paine spoke to the humble folk of three nations—England, France and America—even as God sent His voice over a tempest-tossed chaos, "Let there be light"! With his book, *The Age of Reason*, and the pamphlet, "Common Sense", which laid the train for the American Revolution, Thomas Paine disclosed superstitions that were not faith but blindness, sheeplike submission to tyranny that destroys the soul instead of saving, a famine of knowledge as fatal as physical starvation. Where few could write English with clear directness, he made of it a trumpet call to a new civilization that is still ringing through the world for those who have ears to hear.

The longer I live, the more convinced I am that those whom the gods wish to destroy they first make mad. When the giant Intolerance grows blind in his fury, as is happening in Germany, even the people's material necessities are threatened. This week Isabel[1] bought oranges, paying $2\frac{1}{2}$d. each. A few days later there was another consignment at 1d. each. On inquiry it was learned that the penny oranges had been rejected by Germany because they had come from Palestine! Such straws indicate where a destructive wind is blowing.

[1] Mrs Thomson, mistress of the Manse.

Helen Keller's Journal

In the midst of this dreadful influenza epidemic I read with eager hopefulness the announcement that at the Hampstead Laboratories they hope soon to have a more effective vaccine against this insidious plague.

The Manse, January 10th.

A day so springlike I almost expected to smell daffodils in the garden....

I am sorry I shall not hear Bert preach again for a long time, as Polly and I shall be at West Kilbride next week end and then go to London the following Saturday. His sermon on faith this morning was very suggestive. He taught that true faith is doing, not committing to memory by rote or blindly obeying any particular dogma. He imparted that sense of the Lord's own words: "He that hath my commandments and keepeth them, he it is that loveth me." This is the only possible way to make Christianity prevail. The Old Testament throughout lays the same emphasis upon faith as acting upon the perception of what is good. It seems to me neither the French word *foi* nor the German word *Glauben* has the same deed-compelling significance. I should like to study this subject further sometime....

Coming home through the churchyard, Polly told me about the monument to Joanna Baillie, a distinguished poetess and playwright, who was born in 1762 at the Manse, where I am staying. Her father was minister of the parish. Leading actors and actresses of the time played roles in her dramas—Edmund Kean, John Kemble and his sister, Mrs Siddons. Walter Scott was among her admirers and bestowed enthusiastic praise upon her work.

There is another bit of personal history connected with the Manse of Bothwell. The present Archbishop of Canterbury, Cosmo Gordon Lang, used often to play around here as a small boy. His uncle was the minister of this parish. It is instructive to find how many men from the Scottish manse have won high distinction. Among them were Sir David Wilkie, the artist; Thomas Reid, founder of the School of Scottish Philosophy that exercised such a masterful influence over Europe during the eighteenth century; Lockhart, Walter Scott's biographer; Henry Duncan, the founder of savings banks. Sir John Reith, of the B.B.C., is also a son of the Manse. Another who especially interests me is John Witherspoon, an American who held a position in Revolutionary times as principal of the College of New Jersey.[1] He revised the draft of the Declaration of American Independence. At a meeting it was objected that the time was not ripe to sever political relations with England, and Witherspoon made a vigorous speech, declaring that "the time is not only ripe but rotting!" He also served on a committee of Congress which undertook the extremely difficult task of persuading the thirteen self-centered colonies to form one nation, known as the United States of America.

Still another son of the Manse whom it was my pleasure to meet in Boston while in college was Dr Watson. Under the name Ian Maclaren he wrote *Beside the Bonnie Briar Bush*. I had read the book not long before, and it gave me the same sense of Scottish generosity I have today. I told Dr Watson I knew I

[1]Princeton University.

should not feel like a stranger in Scotland if I ever went there. He replied, "Our climate may have its rigors, but our hearts are like our houses—always a welcoming fire on the hearth and a sheltering nook for the distressed or the friendless."

The Manse, January 11th.

Two hours steady reading of between twenty and thirty letters that had been transcribed into Braille for my perusal.

An appealing little book came today, *Music and Light in the Dark Silence*, by Mrs E. M. Taylor, editor of *The Rainbow*, a Braille magazine published in England for the deaf-blind. She saw and heard until she was fourteen years old. In the winter of eye and ear so inert and dark, she tells how the warm breezes of memory blow upon her, so that color burgeons again, the world has a voice, and life is altogether renewed. I imagine she derives as much joy from these memories as I do from pleasant odors. Mrs Taylor, by refashioning the world in her own way, helps the loneliest and least equipped of human beings to refashion it in their minds. She stirs their imagination and stimulates their artistic feelings. That is why her influence and writings are an art as gracious and delicate as weaving fairy tales to clothe a hard, monotonous existence in alluring dreams.

First snowdrops reported blooming in the grounds of Bothwell Castle. I hope they will not suffer for their venturesomeness in an icy wind tonight.

Helen Keller's Journal

The Manse, January 12th.

Another day of spring sunshine, too persuasive for the young grass and buds on the trees, I am afraid.

With dismay and indignation I read about the kidnaping and subsequent murder of the ten-year-old son of Dr Mattson at Tacoma, Wash. I wonder if it means a recrudescence of the enormities upon which the kidnaping of the Lindbergh baby threw such a lurid light.

This morning's Glasgow *Bulletin* contains the distressing news of a Finnish ship, the Johanna Thorden, on its maiden voyage from New York, going down in the Pentland Firth. Only two lives saved! And this tragedy of human life wasted and the anguish in many bereaved families might have been averted if some of the frantic energy being put at present into ways to make war still more horrible was devoted to the discovery of effective fog-piercing devices. Such negligence even in the face of threatened war is a reproach to science, a blot upon civilization.

How well I remember passing the Pentland skerries when Teacher, Polly and I sailed to the Orkneys and the Shetlands, July 1933! I had expected a great shake-up in "the boiling cauldron"—the encounter between wild surges from the Atlantic Ocean, the North Sea and the Firth, but I was pleasantly disappointed. Siren-like, the water caressed the ship with rippling friendliness. Bert, who was with us on that voyage, told me, however, such a calm was extremely rare even in summer, and he described the treacherous coast bris-

Helen Keller's Journal

tling with crags and the fogs which frequently obscure it at all seasons.

The voyage to the Orkneys was one of Teacher's few last pleasures, and that is why it is peculiarly sweet for me to dwell upon. Almost the first thing which arrested our attention on disembarking at Orkney were the clover fields, the fragrance of which literally followed us like a heavenly flood from one end of the island to the other. I had always loved clover but never dreamed what ecstasy there was in leagues upon leagues of clover blossoms.

Another sensation new to me was feeling the air warm with sun until 11 P.M.—we were very close to the midnight sun! It seemed absurd to go to bed while life was in full swing, the streets crowded with cars and teams, all shops open, ships loading and unloading right under our hotel windows, birds singing everywhere.

While at Orkney we explored a good deal. I climbed with assistance one of the strange mounds that indicate early Norse occupation of the islands. Underneath was an ancient sepulcher which I entered. I touched the curious runic inscriptions on the walls and wondered how human beings without machinery could have dragged those stones, nine feet high and six feet wide, over long distances and hoisted them into position with such unerring accuracy. We also visited Scara Brae, a prehistoric village on the coast. Cautiously we crawled down jagged steps into—the Stone Age. Zigzagging between, and nearly getting stuck in narrow, winding passages, we entered rooms built half underground, with a stone fireplace in the center and only a hole in the roof to let the smoke out. The furniture was actually hewn in the rock—beds, cupboards and boxes which

Helen Keller's Journal

once held fish in salt water. Afterwards I was told that the inhabitants constructed their subterranean houses in this manner to protect themselves against tidal waves—and also to prevent their creditors from carrying off the furniture when debts were unpaid!

The days we spent at Lerwick were exciting. Everything suggested valorous living, storm and tumult—the grim cliffs which now and then succumb to the pounding of the ocean and topple below, the flat, wind-swept land where trees can seldom if ever grow and the snug fishermen's cottages. Lerwick fascinated me, with its tortuous streets quite as packed with gulls as with people, and the cargo boats coming and going. We were fortunate in having clear weather and water sufficiently smooth for a sail in a little boat round several of the Shetland isles, including Bressay, where we visited the celebrated bird sanctuary of the north.

No sooner had we arrived there than the air became aquiver with wings as millions of birds rose from their perches—gulls, terns, puffins, sea swallows and cliff skuas. Their shrill clamor came vibrating through the water to the boat, and I was as startled as the others, who heard it. Never in our lives had we been surrounded by such dense masses of feather clouds shimmering in the morning light. As we went by the precipitous cliffs the billows shook the boat, and I shivered in chill gusts bursting out of deep caverns mined by the sea. A fishing fleet passed us, with girls aboard who were following the herring round the Scottish coast, and we were told that a minister and a doctor accompanied them. The doctor certainly is necessary on those wanderings, as the girls are apt to injure themselves preparing and packing the fish.

Helen Keller's Journal

Always the gulls were in sight and earshot from the moment we landed at Lerwick to our departure. I obtained plenty of fish and amused myself holding a morsel high for a gull to catch on the wing. Polly kept saying, "Ready!" as the gulls overtook the boat, and my fingers tingled as a powerful beak jerked the fish away. Each success was the signal for a fight between those ravenous creatures; and while they fell upon each other another gull carried off the next prize. Everybody said that the gulls, flying so swiftly after the ship, poising with such grace to feed from my hand, were a delight to behold.

The Manse, January 13th.

This morning was sunny, but there were flurries of snow in the afternoon.

I walked from Bothwell to the place at the old Shuttle Row, Low Blantyre, where David Livingstone was born, and which is now a museum and memorial shrine. On the way we crossed a suspension bridge over the Clyde. I was able to walk the whole length alone, guided by the railing. My imagination was excited at every step. Had I not known it was a bridge twenty-five feet above the water I should have thought from the swaying, vibrating motion that it was a boat. We paid a halfpenny toll, and it interested me to hear that the miners and other workers who constantly use the bridge do not have any toll to pay. Snow fell as we climbed the hill leading to the museum.

I had always supposed that, though very poor, Livingstone's family had a separate cottage. To my surprise I found a high tenement containing twenty one-roomed dwellings. As we went up one of the two projecting spiral stairways I stopped to "look at" the cast-iron jaw-box where stale water was emptied; a hundred and fifty years ago it represented the only sanitary arrangement in the building! I saw the one-room home where Mr and Mrs Livingstone and their five children slept, cooked, ate and spent the evenings round the fire. It was considered a better-class domicile in their day. How pathetic the teakettle was to my touch on the cold hearth! It seemed waiting for somebody that never came, just as the old father waited for the noble son whom he never saw again after they parted in Glasgow.

The caretaker allowed me to touch everything I wished to—the spinning jenny at which Livingstone toiled, the fragment from the almond tree under which he was married at Kuruman, the vessels of baptism, the statuary symbolizing the stages of his terrific journey through darkest Africa. Wonderingly I listened as the amazing narrative unfolded itself in written records, the sextant which was his only guide through jungle after jungle, the instruments with which he healed and saved thousands of lives, and the "burning glass" through which he beheld the Victoria Falls and Lake Nyasa. With tears I touched a plaster cast of the shoulder bone the lion crushed when Livingstone was almost overcome, a model of the rude hut where he lay during his last illness, and the worn Bible he held in his hand when his eyes closed in death. There was also a heartbreaking sculpture of the faithful Negroes who carried his body for nine months over fifteen hundred miles to the seaport from which it was safely shipped to England. Often I had read of Livingstone's dauntless faith and endurance, but the shrine brought home the miracle he had wrought. Alone, unarmed, handicapped by languages difficult to learn, he yet made even hostile tribes aware of the immense love that was his personality. Polly spelled two sentences he uttered which stamp upon his brow an unwavering discipleship to Him who came upon earth that all men might have life and have it more abundantly:

"I shall attach no value to anything I have or possess, except in relation to the Kingdom of Christ"; and the protest with his last breath against Negro enslavement, "I can only add, may God's richest blessing come down upon everyone, American or Englishman or Turk, who will help to heal this open sore of the world."

The Livingstone Gallery is unique. It was made out of four small rooms, and the eight bed recesses were put to a poetic use by F. C. Mears, the architect whose work on the National War Memorial in Edinburgh Castle is widely known, and Pilkington Jackson, the sculptor. They filled the recesses with statuary imaging the qualities which rendered Livingstone's achievement possible.

Outside I saw a fountain, a massive globe of the world and sculptures suggesting the Twenty-fourth Psalm—"The earth is the Lord's, and the fulness thereof." Into them was wrought the wish that progress and light, plenty and peace might come to the African natives. Sadly I reflected how this high goal has been lost sight of in commercialism and Europe's greed for empire over the magnificent continent Livingstone gave his life to win for God. As we stood in the light of the setting sun Polly described to me the surrounding land which had been converted into playing fields for children, the

Helen Keller's Journal

woods, the Clyde underneath, and on the opposite side Bothwell Castle, grimly reminiscent of bloody feuds far from the spirit of the peaceful countryside where Livingstone incarnated the gospel of peace on earth and good will to men.

The Manse, January 14th.

There is a heavy frost this morning which makes me glad to hug the fire and warm my fingers while writing. The winters in the south and west of Scotland, however, are seldom severe and seem very short because of the many mild days that break them up and preserve an unsubduable greenness in sheltered lanes and copses.

It is never dull here at dinner or supper. The children come home full of school doings and send remarks flying across the table like fireworks. Their father listens to them as if he, too, were a boy while they detail items that arouse their curiosity in history or geography or languages. They ask the hardest questions they can think of, and he is quite as hot as they are in pursuit of an intelligent answer. Robert, who is fourteen, and John, who is twelve, show a wide-awake interest in world happenings, and at times we are rather taken aback to observe how much they know about the seriousness of the political and even the economic problems in different countries. Today John entertained us by telling how, when there is a little free time, his teacher allows him and the other boys to discuss international affairs and the probable effects of another great war. Occasionally the teacher puts in a question, not for the sake of having it answered, but to stimulate thought. For instance they were talking about the volunteers on both sides taking part in the Spanish civil war.

"Suppose Germany and Britain should fight," he suggested, "what would happen if the Germans attacked Gibraltar or Aden?"

John saw and pointed out the dangers against which Britain must safeguard itself and strengthen its navy as rapidly as possible. Incidentally, he said his teacher talked much about the Spanish question and seemed to show a decided bias in favor of the present government. While I am a sympathizer, it seems to me a teacher or professor should aim at impartiality in presenting a controversial subject to his students. That is the only way he can lead them to mental independence. More is gained by the mistakes of those who honestly try to think for themselves than by the correct opinions of those who hold them simply because they have not heard the other side.

Experiences in my own life have impressed me with this need of an open mind. At Radcliffe College I studied economics and government according to "approved", "progressive" and "up-to-date" theories. Not once in either course was Karl Marx mentioned nor his history-making book, *Das Kapital*, although party minorities were frequently referred to in France, Germany and Russia where socialism was playing a conspicuous role. My quarrel is not with the right of our professors to form their own opinions, but with their failure to give an account that is dignified and as truthful as may be of opposite views which are important enough to have advocates. Stevenson was justified in his sarcastic attitude towards "lying impartialists." He said we

Helen Keller's Journal

oftener learn the truth from partisans—at least we find out why they really pursue this or that policy. The fact remains, however, that sincere effort to be fair to opponents in a controversy is regrettably rare.

The Manse, January 15th.

This morning I received an urgent invitation to attend, in January 1938, a meeting in London to honor Emanuel Swedenborg on the two hundred and fiftieth anniversary of his birth. If it were possible I should accept with the greatest pleasure. For Swedenborg's religious writings have brought down to me truths from heaven that have given my spirit a thousand wings to defy the restraints of a sense-fettered body, but I shall not be in England at that time. The claims of the work for the blind are unintermittent, and winter is always the time when demands upon my energies are greatest. It was the compelling need of a long rest that induced Teacher and me to spend 1933 in Scotland; and I have come here again in winter time because I saw no other way to accomplish a task of extreme difficulty and delicacy—reintegrating my life, so shaken and lacerated by Teacher's going.

As it is hard to interest those who have everything in those who have nothing, so it requires incessant labor to win champions among the seeing for the sightless. There are moments when, like a mother with babies ever tugging at her skirts, I get rebellious because I may not go to all meetings that enlist my sympathy or listen long to instructive conversation in some nook of the infinite. Certainly there is magic in personal contacts

Helen Keller's Journal

which clarifies the mists of preconceived ideas that each of us carries about him or her like a private atmosphere. But these moods of murmuring flee with the other shadows as the good cause marches on.

Later. West Kilbride.

Polly and I are paying a good-by visit to Dr and Mrs Love this week end, before we start on our way back to America. They cannot do enough for us. It is touching how they long to wrap us with warm layers of affection against the trials and hurts of the world.

This house is well named Sunnyside. Dr Love never fails to turn to the sunny side, however dark the clouds in his spiritual sky may be. His cheerful courage inspires others to find an opportunity in every difficulty. Even while admonishing Polly and me to beware of age's inroads upon our bodies, he opens my soul still wider to youth's energizing power.

West Kilbride, January 16th.

The air this morning, Polly says, was vocal with birds heralding early spring. The yellow jasmine here has put forth blossoms as if to reconnoiter winter's movements, and before long hyacinths and jonquils and tulips adorn his trenches with victorious beauty.

The "good gigantic smile o' the brown old earth" in the afternoon sun tempted us all out for a drive by the river Clyde. Polly could not see Arran for the clouds that veiled it; but the quiet brown furrows in the

Helen Keller's Journal

plowed fields, the gulls following the plow in search of a meal and the beech hedges were restful to look upon. At Wemyss Bay we got out and walked to the end of the pier where people come from Glasgow and vicinity during the summer to sail down the firth. There is romance in the Clyde—the drama of cities and ships, great estates on the banks and wild mountains farther away that makes me want to sail the entire length of the river, and someday I shall. Rivers, like woods, with their varied smells and atmospheric changes, are books easy for me to read. . . .

Dr Love has John Gunther's *Inside Europe*, in which Polly and I find graphic descriptions of Hitler, Goebbels and Goering. Personalities more grimly antagonistic could not be combined in a government, and it is not likely that even the fear of Hitler and of each other will long prove sufficient to hold them together. That is the one hope for Germany, Dr Love says. A clash of ambitious wills is bound to send the Third Reich to limbo sooner or later.

It is a matter of daily wonder to me how the German nation can live so despicably, submitting like fishes to every inhumanity which statesmanship and civilization have combated since the first recorded cry of oppression —large numbers beheaded for political offenses to which no other modern country would attach the death penalty; forty-nine thousand people sent to concentration camps; criticism of art, drama, films; and books prohibited unless they be according to the Nazi point of view; Baldur von Schirach's proclamation that all German youth belongs body and soul to Adolf Hitler and that "the Hitler Youth is not the Church, and the Church is not the Hitler Youth." Then there are vast war preparations being pushed at an insane rate while the people are rationed on foods that do not build up resistance to disease or exposure.

Now this cumulative violation of human life has apparently reached the climax. The editor of the *Berliner Tageblatt*, Paul Scheffer, who strove to keep liberalism alive in one German newspaper, has resigned. Death and vengeance await anyone who shows hostility or indifference to Germany or lives abroad. In the *Nation* I read an article by Thomas Mann's son, who says that his father, who lives in Switzerland, is under the ban and that his novels can no longer be purchased in Germany. Even czarist Russia did not dare insult Leo Tolstoy or suppress the sale of his works, and here is Germany menacing a novelist admired by both conservatives and liberals the world over.

Gerhart Hauptmann's name, too, is mentioned in the article among those whom the German autocracy may succeed in silencing. Germany was seething with political excitement when I was introduced to Hauptmann during his visit to America. We met at a luncheon given in New York by a friend of Frazier Hunt, the world traveler, author, journalist and radio speaker.

Herr Hauptmann sat on my right at the table, and I felt indeed honored. He could not speak a word of English, and my German was rusty from long disuse. However, Herr Hauptmann showed quick friendliness when he heard me pronounce the name "Goethe" (the Goethe centennial was being celebrated just then), and gestures and quotations helped to elucidate our meaning. I repeated something from *Hermann und Dorothea*, and he nodded as if he understood. I spoke of the universality of Goethe's genius: "He was not only an inspired German but also a far-seeing citizen of the world."

Herr Hauptmann replied: "It is a tragedy how far Goethe's serene spirit still outstrides our age of militarism, suspicion and rabid nationalism. As Faust said, 'All life for all men shall be within my body tested,' and"—he paused—"Germany is enacting that mighty drama. All things are being tested within its body, and so far the outcome is hidden in darkness."

I perceived a slight uneasiness in his manner at which I did not wonder later on when I learned that he was trying to find out the result of the elections in Germany.

The next day Hitler was in office as Mephistopheles.

West Kilbride, January 17th.

Wind, rain and sleet the livelong day, but Sunnyside has worn the firelit smile that gets into the heart and keeps it sweet.

It is a pleasure to notice how the days are lengthening into spring. The *Braille Mail*, January 16th, said the sun would rise today at 7.58 A. M. and set at 4.23 P. M.

This paper also says that Mr Eden's remark at the Press Association dinner—Britain "definitely prefers butter to guns"—has irritated German Nazi leaders. Both Dr Goebbels and General Goering insisted a while ago on the necessity of sacrificing butter for guns, and now this statement is denied. The Moscow Broadcasting Station is accused of misrepresentation, since it tells the world that famine reigns in Germany, that there is no more butter, and Germany is manufacturing guns instead. So it goes on: nations, like individuals, are loud in blaming one another when their guilty secrets are found out.

I have always thought the Russian people would not really surrender their religion to any earthly power, and now I am sure of it. The old Russian Christmas was celebrated January 7th, and it is reported that the "few surviving churches in Moscow were more densely packed than ever before."

After dinner we all stretched out for a rest. Dr Love believes that everyone should, if possible, take a nap every day after lunch; he says it lengthens life. Longevity does not matter much to me personally, since I have eternity to live in and earth-time seems too long waiting to rejoin my loved ones who have gone first; but to relax for a short time has helped me to finish a hard task when nothing else would.

I have just been reading an article, "Anne Sullivan Macy", which Dr Love wrote for *The Volta Review*. Every sentence is warm with his understanding friendship for us both and enthusiasm for the faith and courage with which Teacher, alone, almost unguided, broke a trail through my desert of silent darkness and loosened the clutch of misfortune upon my life. The word picture he draws of her in our sweet home at Wrentham, Mass., could not be more tender or truer to the happy memories I cherish.

Dr Love received a grant in 1906 from the Carnegie trustees for the study of deaf-mutism, and it was on his consequent visit to the Eastern United States that we first met him. Thus out of the multitudinous seeds of blessing sown through Andrew Carnegie's generosity sprang a helpful friendship that is woven into the warp and woof of my last thirty years. After I met Mr and

Helen Keller's Journal

Mrs Carnegie at their home in New York City, 1913, they contributed to my work for the blind, and their wonderful kindness removed many obstacles.

How swift memory is! From the visit with the Carnegies in New York my mind flies to the three summers when we saw Mrs Carnegie in Scotland. Each time she invited Teacher, Polly and me to luncheon at Skibo Castle. What a glorious view as we approached the castle—the Moray Firth at some distance, and the surrounding hills "whence cometh our help", as Mrs Carnegie often said. Long waves of golden August light billowed from summit to summit and one emerald field to another. Then came the noble driveway with evergreens on both sides. We were told that in springtime it is like fairyland with seas of Scottish broom. I wonder how many people outside of Britain have any conception how ravishing this flower is in masses or how divine its fragrance is in the May sun. On the top of the castle waved the Union Jack and the American flag combined —Mr Carnegie's felicitous idea of reminding everyone that there should be eternal friendship between Great Britain and America. A piper in Highland costume gave us a spirited welcome as we entered. Our hostess herself led me into her husband's library and the music room where he had entertained King Edward VII. The rooms made me feel rather lost in their immensity, but the flowers filling every corner breathed home and peace. Mrs Carnegie took me out on her arm into the garden and showed me its monarch—a holly tree said to have been planted by St Gilbert, eight hundred years ago. She gathered me a great bouquet of carnations and the sweet verbena leaves which Mr Carnegie had especially loved. I always think of her as I saw her that day, tender

Helen Keller's Journal

and serene, surrounded by a beautiful family—her daughter with her husband and their four delightful children who brought me a great bunch of white heather.

West Kilbride, January 18th.

Last night Dr Love had been reading a book by Lord Melchett on the resettlement of Palestine by the Jews. I have long felt that their problem can be solved only if they have a home land where they can develop unmolested their peculiar genius in religion, art and social justice. Curiously enough Dr Love made an observation which has occurred to me several times while reading the *Jewish Braille Review for the Blind*. In the disputes between Jews and Arabs over the occupation of Palestine the argument is seldom if ever advanced that the Jews held the land long before an Arab invader appeared. One would think such an argument would be employed with telling effect. What have the Arabs done to develop Palestine? Have they not remained stationary in their customs, often laying waste their days with strife and brigandage, while the Jews, handicapped by agelong persecution and incredible calumny, have enriched incalculably the world's heritage of constructive statesmanship, philosophy and collective neighborliness? I am aware that some Arab thinkers in past centuries have towered above their countrymen; but as a race they have not kindled, as the Jews have, a steady light leading on to higher living.

This morning I hear the call of the sun, but I shall not budge. Dragons in the shape of letters have planted themselves on the desk. If I am to have peace I must

Helen Keller's Journal

keep at the typewriter until this afternoon, when Polly and I go to Glasgow to dine with a friend and return to Bothwell.

The Manse, January 19th.

Four solid hours reading—about a hundred answers to my annual appeals for the blind. (Mercifully Brailled!) I smiled and cried by turns as I went through them; they overflowed in kindly words bracing me to carry on until I rejoin Teacher. . . .

At 2 P.M. we drove over to the ancient Bothwell Castle, built during the second half of the thirteenth century and now being repointed by government workmen. Visitors are not allowed to go inside at present, but we walked around a long distance so that I might feel the foundation stones of the tremendous towers at every angle and the enormous strength of the walls—much like cliffs, in places eleven feet thick. How huge the grounds must once have been if during a siege it was feasible to shelter the people of the district and their flocks and herds! An airplane passed overhead as I was hearing how Edward I won his victory over the stronghold with the aid of engines that hurled missiles weighing from two to three hundredweight. Six centuries between that cumbersome, earthbound engine and the modern air-conquering war plane and we seem no nearer universal peace than the world was in Edward I's reign.

As we stood at one of the loopholes from which the arrows were fired I tried to imagine the shout, "An enemy coming up the Clyde!" and a Douglas at my side. But the picture would not form itself; I could think only of the tranquil river and bird songs floating through the soft air. Walking along a sandy path far below the great castle, I bent down and touched the water, and that made me feel that I really could count the Clyde among my river friends. I saw the snowdrops; Polly said the banks were literally white as if there had been a heavy snowfall. Among the trees I greeted a superb beech; it looked as ancient as the castle, with mighty gnarled trunk and roots that seemed ribs of the earth. It must be thirty feet in circumference. To my vexation I noticed a great many initials irreverently carved in the venerable bark. Why should men who seldom live to be a hundred years old make incisions to gratify a moment's vanity in a tree not of their creating that has survived countless human generations?

Isabel was with us, and we walked home over the Bothwell golf course. She plays there sometimes, and Polly says she is a very skillful golfer. She showed me how a tee is made and how with a well-calculated swing of the arm the ball is sent on its way. We had fun pretending to follow the ball stroke by stroke until, alas! it got into a bunker, but with a good shot we were on the green and finished the hole. Isabel is the only person I ever knew who talked golf so interestingly that I wished I might learn to play it!

The Manse, January 20th.

Bitter cold this morning; the ground all whitened by hoarfrost. The snowdrops at Bothwell Castle must wish they had not bloomed so early.

Polly and I gave a good-by luncheon at St Enoch's

Helen Keller's Journal

Hotel in Glasgow to some of our Scottish friends. The time we have left here is sad with sweet things ending for a while. It seems as if my courage would fail me on leaving Scotland, where I have found quiet and equilibrium to hold up a heavy-laden soul. "Alas! those fresh green days of life's fair spring" are sped, and in later years a great bereavement leaves a breach that does not entirely heal, even though faith remains steadfast. However, love and work will restore to me the peace which the world can neither impart nor destroy.

Today Franklin D. Roosevelt was inaugurated. About five-thirty the whole family listened over the radio to his speech. A pang shot through me as I thought of the last fourth of March in American history when a president entered office. At that time Teacher, Polly and I were together in Georgia, and at the hotel where we were stopping we listened to Roosevelt's first inaugural speech. Now we have heard him, here in Scotland, without her who found in high politics a subject of absorbing interest. It is a pity that the weather in Washington was so wet and horrid, but the applause and shouts when the President appeared on the platform were thrilling. Since I was twenty-one I have read every speech of a newly elected president; and none, except Woodrow Wilson's, has given me reasonable hope of achievement as this one has. There is a genuine ring in Roosevelt's declaration that he is "determined to make every American citizen's welfare his country's interest and concern." More than any other president, I believe, since Lincoln, has he stressed the need to find in government a means to promote the economic security and well-being of all the people. For the world to hear, he has condemned the injustice under which millions live in ignorance and one third of the nation face hardships, ill housed, ill clad, ill nourished. If only Congress and the people would stand solidly behind Roosevelt new vitality would quicken our democracy, and "the new materials of social justice" would strengthen the oft-shaken republic our forefathers founded. As a student of government and economics I realize to some extent the difficulties rising like a wall about President Roosevelt. He is terribly handicapped by the predominance of politics over administration in the United States. Politics once meant the public or common good as an end; now it suggests office seeking rather than service to the country. The goal for which Lincoln labored—a government of the people, for the people and by the people—remains unattained because politics is largely a tool in the hands of the powerful for their own purposes. Supposedly the majority of Americans share in the making of laws because they vote, but really they do not. Instead of taking the initiative they leave their problems to others to solve for them. Many vote blindly under the influence of big business, which brings pressure upon Congress, and the vast bulk of workers have not been active in politics because they have had no vigorous labor party to represent their interests. That is why I fear President Roosevelt may not find Congress sufficiently amenable to his far-reaching projects. The most I dare to expect is that he may impart a nobler tone to political ideals in the United States.

Ideas—constructive ideas such as Roosevelt seeks to embody—are lighthouses erected on the misty coast of futurity. Yet many Americans avoid them in conversation, and talking politics with a purpose of betterment

Helen Keller's Journal

is an idea. They forget that their strongest traditions were once new ideas "threatening" to religion and to the Constitution. This tendency to ignore ideas is another difficulty Roosevelt has to contend with in carrying out his policies for the public welfare. There are too few men whom the people have put into office really to look after their interests for him to count on for co-operation.

The Manse, January 21st.

Weather much warmer today. The children, coming back from school, said that the cattle were out sunning themselves in the fields.

Wrote this morning. After lunch I packed my cases while Polly worked on the trunks. We also posted Braille books I had borrowed from London, and many packages which we are sending home. Then Polly "made me up" for a film which David is producing. His idea is to show some of our doings during my visit here.

The first "shot" was taken while I was sitting at my typewriter; the second at tea, after following Robert through the dining-room doorway. That is as far as we got—so much time is needed to work out details in a film—but there will be more "shooting" tomorrow night. It is killingly funny to feel the children bustling about, calling to each other to watch the lights while David does his best to make his directions heard. I bless this picture taking, both for our general merriment and for the pleasure I have in living over my days as a would-be star in Hollywood. How solemn and clumsy I was! Once I was trying to write in pencil at a rehearsal,

Helen Keller's Journal

and the requirements of the camera were puzzling. Up rushed Polly, spelling, "Why are you pouting and looking as if you would bite somebody's head off?" I never dreamed I was. Thus each day I committed offenses against my best intentions in that other world of dreams and vagaries, Filmland.

The Manse, January 22nd.

More picture taking last night and more laughter. It was really pretty, the way Robert took me into the dining room and showed me the lovebirds, which are growing tame. They watched the camera intently and forgot their shyness long enough for me actually to look them over. I hope the picture will be as intriguing as those bewitching wee feathered sprites. We gathered round the table as if for a meal, and as usual I read Bert's lips while he said grace. Effie went through the motions of serving tea and handing cake around. Robert led me back to the drawing room with roguish comments under the rose on the facial expressions of the party. In the next scene John was at the piano playing very well his favorite piece, "Sound the Pibroch", and I was standing beside him, keeping time. I wonder when I shall again spend such happy hours in the society of children.

More packing today. The approaching departure almost chokes utterance even in a diary. Perhaps while one's soul is still torn with a recent calamity it is harder than at other times to part from persons and places one dearly loves.

We have just had our last supper together. I could

Helen Keller's Journal

hardly talk. This is the last night I shall be here in the body until 1938, but I shall often return in the spirit. Peace be multiplied unto the Manse of Bothwell, the Manse of my affections! ...

*En route from Glasgow to London.
Afternoon, January 23rd.*

A springlike morning which made it even harder to say good-by to the Manse. All the family accompanied us to Glasgow.

Robert kept spelling to me whatever he saw—pleasant old houses, grass where it was greenest, lorries going to the city loaded with milk, eggs, flour and vegetables, the big parade marching through the streets: for this is Charities Day, which comes every year, and to help raise Glasgow's quota of funds for hospitals the university students hold a parade dressed up in bright red gowns, ridiculous masks and costumes. But I was not in a mood to laugh. Hardly a word was spoken when we got on the train. Before I realized it the guard was waving his green flag and we were speeding away from six precious friends, big and little, waving on the platform. As if we did not feel sad enough already, we must needs pass Bothwell! Polly and I shed tears as she saw the Church of St Bride's, with its tower like a gentle spirit brooding over the neighborhood and the road where we had so often walked to nature's music undiscouraged by death or ravages of wind and flood.

The news in *The Times* did not serve to brighten my thoughts—the rising floods in West Virginia, Ohio,

Kentucky and Mississippi, and the crisis in Japan created by the fierce struggle between the military and the civil authorities for supremacy. Hirota, the prime minister, and Terauchi, the minister of war, typify vividly the opposing forces that have for a hundred years jeopardized the stability and well-being of the Japanese Empire. Running into such a disturbing atmosphere when we visit Japan will be a weird adventure. . . .

I was interested to know that the first part of the new English and American Dictionary has been published. It seems to me one does not begin to understand a people until one knows something about the peculiar words and phrases that denote their customs, ways of thinking and events in their history. I am glad the English people will now have access to a dictionary correctly defining key words which open doors into a new world—the pioneer days of America, the vast territorial expansions, a society roughhewn amid forests, unbridged rivers, untamed prairies and trackless mountains, inventions and industries that are changing the face of the Western Hemisphere.

With satisfaction—and a little envy—I read in the *Braille Mail* how efforts are being made to enable the greatest number possible in all classes to enjoy the Coronation ceremonies and the gaieties. There are now so many "vanished pomps" laid to rest, I wish I might catch a glimpse of this, perhaps the last coronation in Britain.

The item about secret interviews between Hitler and Mussolini seemed to point to some conspiracy alarmingly imminent. I hope they may be foiled in their efforts to isolate France from its allies and reinforce the

Helen Keller's Journal

nationalists in Spain. Such personalities are as terrible as natural forces that may cause a devastating earthquake or volcano any moment....

The Royal Scot swayed mile after mile at such a speed that Polly could scarcely spell, and the lurching motion rendered it difficult to follow her fingers. By the law of contrast the memory of an August day, 1930, floated into my mind when we traveled on the Flying Scotsman from Edinburgh to London. On that trip the engineer guided me to the engine. I sat on the seat where the Prince of Wales had sat; I shoveled in some coal to feed the fiery dragon. I marveled to hear how the brass shone, and I observed how free it was from dust or grime. And how smooth and rhythmic the vibration was! I reached out my hand for the air current as we literally shot through Berwick-on-Tweed. (We were then going over seventy miles an hour.) I shall ever remember the Flying Scotsman as a wonder of consummate workmanship.

From slumberland I fairly tumbled into Euston Station, where Jean Muir met us with an expansive welcome that only the beautiful Scottish word "couthy" fittingly describes. She brought us out to Berden, Essex, and here we are spending the week end with her and Charlie at their charming home, the Old Cottage. It was built in 1650, with a handsome thatch, stout oak rafters, diamond windowpanes, iron-studded doors with old knockers, and the soul of every English home—the garden! Two rough-haired terriers, Byng and Sandy, greeted us on our arrival. Byng, who is now deaf, has not left me all the evening. He lays his head on my feet as much as to say, "There is fellow feeling between us."

After dinner Charlie and I had a long argument as

to which is more tyrannical, the Hitler regime or the Russian Soviet. He wondered why I am more harsh in my attitude towards Germany than towards Russia. I told him it seems to me that, considering its abysmal misery during a thousand years, Russia is making wonderful progress under a benevolent if paternalistic government and that its Asiatic modes of thought and self-expression are fundamentally different from what Germany or any other Western country has experienced. I am afraid he thinks I am a heathen. When he deplored the anti-Christian campaign I said I was glad the Russian Church is overthrown. The fact is, we who live in countries not priest-ridden have no conception how completely that church possessed the souls and bodies of an ignorant, childlike, primitive people—how it imposed upon them countless superstitions according to which they sowed and reaped crops, contracted marriages that were really slavery, buried the dead and paid any rent the overlord might name. The godlessness now being preached, which certainly horrifies me, is not a result of Bolshevism, which originated long before the church became all powerful and which was often taught by mystics. As Carlyle thundered in his anathemas upon church degeneracy, godlessness is a consequence of faith long mocked, petitions and cries to heaven answered only by heavier taxation, evictions, floggings and cruel executions. The anti-Christ has been there all the thousand years.

If the Soviet is godless, at least it has not committed "enlightened" Germany's deadly sin against the genius of Einstein—a stain which, as I wrote to Mr Schramm, a thousand years of achievement cannot wash out. Even czarist Russia did not dare punish Tolstoy, and

Britain has not gone the length of banishing or killing Gandhi.

Another circumstance which I cannot overlook is that Germany was the aggressor in the World War and Russia was not. Posterity will judge without leniency the coldness with which the Germans trampled upon starving Russia's splendid endeavors for world peace and the hunger blockade with which fourteen foreign nations tried to crush the new Soviet Republic in 1919. As Lenin said afterwards, Russia must build up a large defensive army, and now this dictum seems justified. There is a possibility, nay, a probability that sometime Germany, Italy and Japan may combine in a supreme effort to subjugate Russia.

Berden, Essex, January 24th.

The sun and Jean came into our room together this morning. The thrushes were singing love songs, spring and romance were in every breeze fluttering through the casement. Jean told us to stay comfortably in bed and served our breakfast herself. She fixed my fish and egg, buttered the toast, poured the tea, so that Polly had nothing to do but eat, drink and rest.

When we had shaken off our laziness sufficiently to get dressed it was raining hard. We sat around waiting for a chance to get out in the garden, but the sky showed no inclination to clear up. Charlie came in after a while, and for a moment I could not credit my fingers' testimony when he put beside my typewriter a bowl of the loveliest pink primroses with yellow centers, which he had just picked in the garden. Primroses on January

24th! I understood then why Shakespeare and other poets keep saying "the rathe primrose" ... "the primrose early and wan." But they cannot be very "wan" when they sturdily hold up their fragile grace almost in the clutch of hoarfrost.

This evening we sat discussing literature, and Charlie read aloud "The Hollow Men", by T. S. Eliot, ranked as a great modern poem. It is powerful; the mind recoils before its tomblike finality as it does before James Thompson's "City of Dreadful Night." However, I am perplexed as to the real meaning of "The Hollow Men." Does it image those who strive for wealth or position but not for bread that nourishes the spirit? Or does it symbolize the present-day toiler robbed, by long hours at the machine, of his ancestral instinctive joy in creative craftsmanship?

When I suggested this Charlie seemed interested. He said: "Do you not think, Helen, the day will come when it will be possible for every worker to produce just so much in three hours at the machine and spend the rest of the time developing his own powers, providing his children with wholesome surroundings, the best education, a right start in life?" It was indeed gratifying to me that we so completely agreed on this principle essential to social justice.

After dinner it stormed; but the rain was soft, redolent of waking earth and sprouting herbs. Earlier Polly and I went out to inspect a small Elizabethan cottage which is for sale and to which Teacher took a fancy when we saw it from the outside in 1930. She hoped sometime it might be our holiday nook on this side. The owner of the place had an idea of selling it, but he did not make a decision until last summer. During her last days Teacher said to Polly and me, "I want you to have that little place in Essex; it would mean the beauty and seclusion you love, Helen, and it would help you to feel me near." But I am afraid it is out of the question, for the changes required to make it suitable for me would be too complicated.

This evening is a memorable one. Jean introduced me to Meum Stewart, who lives in a sixteenth-century cottage built on the site of a Roman fort; then to Clifford Bax, the distinguished playwright, brother of Arnold Bax, the composer. I do not remember when I have met such a romantic personage as Mr Bax. Tall, elegant, gallant, polished in manner and speech, he resembles a courier of old Versailles. I was surprised to hear that he knew about me when I was fifteen years old and he was eighteen. (At the time he was studying in Germany.) I asked him to tell something about his plays, *The Rose without a Thorn*—the tragedy of Henry VIII's third wife, Catherine Howard—and *Socrates*. He thought they would appear in New York before long; and I said if they did I should be sure to go to see them. When I spoke of the probability of my visiting Japan in April he related some experiences he had when he was there years ago. He went into many Buddhist temples and was profoundly impressed by the serenity of the priests. In Nagasaki, when it was raining, he saw the people carrying their little blossoming cherry trees indoors.

Someone referred to "The Hollow Men", and I asked Mr Bax how he interpreted it. He thought it describes the hopeless attitude of the unphilosophical when disillusion and indifference blight their faith and take the bloom off the world. I talked about Æ., whose poetry had often brought to Teacher and me moments as lovely as roses bright with morning dew. Mr Bax said he, too, read it with delight and quoted from memory the first lines of his favorite poem, "In Ancient Babylon":

The blue dusk ran between the streets: my love was winged within my mind,
  It left today and yesterday and thrice a thousand years behind.

As I had not read it, he promised to send me a copy. We also discussed Buddhism, which is his faith, and the teachings of Emanuel Swedenborg. Mr Bax's confidence in a future life was stimulating. It was a rare pleasure to converse with a man of such romantic personality and mind so richly stored.

Berden, January 25th.

A morning radiant with sun, glad with bird songs. MacGregor, the gorgeous parrot, peppered the chorus with profanity. His upbringing was evidently far from exemplary. He stays with Charlie all day in his study in a distant corner of the garden, and accompanies him on his afternoon walks. He flies overhead from tree to tree, and when he comes home he flutters in and quite amiably says "Hello!" to Jean. A hawk has tried to capture him, but MacGregor, with a strategy worthy of his clan, escaped by dodging behind the trees until he reached the sheltering precincts of the house.

I cannot put through language the expansive, revivifying atmosphere of the Old Cottage, surrounded

Helen Keller's Journal

by romantic lanes, green pastures which God surely made us to lie down in, the elms which are Berden's glory, and quiet farms dowered with the fruitfulness of centuries.

Still less can I measure the preciousness of friends like Charlie and Jean. If they were my own brother and sister they could not be more responsive to each joy and sorrow I confide, nor could they take more thought for my future. Many beautiful things have happened to me, but nothing quite like their spontaneous effort to buoy up my sorely tried courage amid new problems and responsibilities. It is a rare experience to lay bare one's mind as I do with them and be so quickly understood. Their talk is like water poured into a dry pump —it starts the stream of thought flowing afresh. They realize—like Teacher, John Macy and Dr Alexander Graham Bell—how much I miss in not being able to follow good conversation on account of its sudden turns and quirks, the subtle meanings which only a look or a tone conveys. How like John is Charlie in his eagerness to catch a flying comment or anecdote or a person's reaction to something said and let me enjoy it too! When Teacher and I lived at Wrentham we had a group of friends who were refreshing both as talkers and listeners. There was always a fresh idea, a book worth discussing in a leisurely manner, a bit of choice verse repeated with a felicitous effect, discoveries in nature and science interestingly presented. There was also willingness to extract the kernel from the talk of a voluble person or an argument long drawn out—a quality I seldom find in Americans nowadays. I sometimes think, as many writers do, that conversation is indeed a lost art. But perhaps absorption in my work

Helen Keller's Journal

the past twenty years or lack of skill in drawing out others of a kindred spirit is the reason why loneliness often walks at my side. However,

> *There's nothing in the world I know*
> *That can escape from love,*
> *For every depth it goes below,*
> *And every height above.*
> *It waits, as waits the sky,*
> *Until the clouds go by,*
> *Yet shines serenely on*
> *With an eternal day.*

It has waited in Scotland and England and is blessing me again in friendships doubly beautiful with noble thinking and generous emotion. . . .

Park Lane Hotel, evening of January 26th.

Sadly I pulled myself this morning out of another nest round which my thoughts will long linger. Charlie drove us to the station at Bishop's Stortford; and we passed the home of Lady Victoria Gosling, a daughter of the late Marquis of Lothian. She is a relative of the Lady John Scott who wrote "Annie Laurie." How many voices have tenderly sung that world-loved song for me since my childhood, at home, in Britain and in Yugoslavia!

Every mile I have traveled in Essex is packed with history, mystery, romance. With a shiver I have at times moved through the lanes, trying to conjure up in fancy the six or more buried civilizations upon which,

Helen Keller's Journal

for aught I knew, I might be treading. The very odor of antiquity has come off on my fingers as I touched the Roman walls, the ruin of St Botolph's Abbey in Colchester, the trenches where Queen Boadicea's army was defeated. Essex is dear to me also because it holds little pastoral Wendens Ambo where the people live just as they did centuries ago, though only thirty-nine miles from London, and where Teacher was happy when we stayed there from July to September 1930. Our retreat was a four-hundred-year-old house with a walled garden where I found long and diversified walks which I was able to manage alone. The place was called Trout Hall—why I could not imagine, as there was not a trout in the tiny river at the end of the garden. The ache at my heart does not slacken as we revisit spots that delighted Teacher, but it is a cross I can kiss and rejoice in the last vivid scenes that met her failing sight.

Jean came to London with us, and together we lunched at the Ivy Restaurant, which is frequented by prominent actors and actresses, writers and artists. While we ate sole and aubergine fit for the gods it was pleasant to watch lovely girls and men with interesting faces drop in, exchange greetings, get a bite or two of a favorite dish and hurry back to their work. Jean pointed out Lillian Braithwaite and James Agate, London's redoubtable literary critic, author of *Ego* and *Ego 2*. I hope we shall return to the Ivy when we are next in England; it offers alluring opportunities to study character. . . . From there we went on to Bradley's, where Polly and I ordered new suits. Mine is black and white, quite heavy, and I am glad, as I shall feel the chill winds of America especially after the equable climate on this side.

Helen Keller's Journal

A disappointing telegram awaited us at the Park Lane—the Thomas Paine statue is not to be unveiled on the twenty-ninth. It seems that sufficient time has not been allowed for the preparations, and the ceremony has been postponed until April. By then we shall probably be in Japan. My first impulse was to give up the trip to Paris, as a few days hurried visit there without the principal purpose I had in view seemed like *Hamlet* without the prince. Thinking the matter over, Polly and I are agreed that we may just as well carry out our plan; there is no telling what that ever-enchanting city, Paris, may have in store for us. I have always wanted to visit Domremy where my beloved heroine, Joan of Arc, was born; and if it is not too far a trip there will be a thrilling equivalent to the impressive occasion I expected to attend next Friday.

Park Lane Hotel, January 26th.

The morning chill and damp but not foggy. I was afraid we might be caught in the black fogs which have recently tied up London traffic, but they say that danger is passing, and a new one appearing—floods at Eton, Windsor and other places along the Thames.

The Times has terrifying news of floods in the United States which I have not succeeded in getting out of my head all day. Heavy rains have raised the levels of the Mississippi and Ohio rivers, and many cities and towns are inundated. A million gallons of oil near Cincinnati blazed up in flames as the deluge swept through the city, and the burning oil is being borne on the waves towards other flooded sections. The chief police com-

Helen Keller's Journal

missioner of Cincinnati describes the scene tersely as "hell let loose." Five hundred thousand people are homeless. Harry Hopkins is rushing over twenty-five hundred Works Progress Administration men to aid the sufferers in ten states, and it is predicted that the situation will be still worse shortly.

The Times also has an editorial on the sickening Zinovieff-Kameneff "purge" in Moscow. Seventeen more men, some of whom have occupied high positions in the Soviet government, are to be tried for their lives on a charge of taking part in a Trotskyist conspiracy against Stalin. What a spectacle—the downfall of distinguished, highly honored persons such as Karl Radek, the journalist who for many years elucidated with keen insight the meaning of international events, and Sokolnikoff, former ambassador to Britain, who until recently was praised for his services in reorganizing the Soviet finances! Those trials are utterly incomprehensible to me in a country so progressive as modern Russia. They read exactly like a repetition with different names of the hysterical witchcraft trials once held in Puritan New England. Apparently there is the same frenzied fear among the Soviet leaders and the same determination to force the prisoners to admit crimes they have never committed. No doubt Radek is guilty of attempts to overthrow the present government; but if he has a spark of manhood, why should he turn upon his past splendid work, blackening it and "confessing" that he has sold his country to Germany and Japan? No profounder student of human nature ever lived than Mark Twain, and he frequently said that when cornered, hunted offenders will tell any lie to shield their accomplices. Even so, why should Radek further degrade himself and his achievements with contemptible, crawling hypocrisy? In the history of every land humble folk put to torture have displayed more self-respect and nobility than this man equipped with magnificent intellectual powers and pledged to a mighty mission.

Went to the United States Lines this morning. Polly and I learned that we could not sail on the SS President Roosevelt from Havre because it is not carrying passengers on account of the American seamen's strike. I told him no strike had ever kept us from going anywhere! I was bothered about some cases we had previously sent to the Roosevelt. Mr Moore said he could easily have them transferred when he found another boat for us. We shall probably hear from him tomorrow morning. So there goes another plan we laid months ago with solemnly repeated assurances to our friends at home of our arrival on the Roosevelt February 12th. Sometimes the way circumstances put their heads together to bring mortals to grief is positively impish. An article I read years ago converted me to a belief in "the total depravity of inanimate things"; and the longer I live, the more I am confirmed in this faith by the perversity of objects and events. It is comfortable to lay the blame upon things instead of upon poor mankind!

Eagerly I await the details on my home-coming of the seamen's strike and the epoch-making struggle between the American Federation of Labor and the Committee on Industrial Organization. For years I have thought some leader or group would attempt a transfusion of fresh blood into the A.F. of L. Only in that way can the movement be hastened to form a genuine American labor party.

Helen Keller's Journal

Before lunch Polly and I looked over letters and business papers which never end. I realized overpoweringly what I was spared when Teacher listened patiently to this mass of routine mail and conveyed necessary information to me with skillful brevity.

Polly telephoned a good many people, inviting some to tea and others to dinner, as I knew we should not see them again until our next visit to Britain. Then we had our first fitting at Bradley's and got back to the hotel just in time to receive our callers, among them Sir Ian Fraser. I expressed regret that he was no longer in Parliament, and I hoped he would return sometime to lift up his voice for the blind. "Well," he replied, "the merit in being an M.P. is saying nothing. Being one of six hundred, I had no chance to accomplish what I wanted. It is my hope that as a governor of the B.B.C. I may render effective service to the blinded veterans of the United Kingdom."

Later Mac and Belle Eagar, Charlie and Jean Muir and Ned Holmes came to dinner. The Eagars had not met Ned or Charlie before, and it was a pleasure to see how quickly they became friends. Politics monopolized the conversation. The effects of the abdication upon the empire were quite a rich field for conjecture. There were comments upon the ability and firmness with which Baldwin had met an unprecedented crisis and the self-restraint of the people during those fateful days. The countless speeches in Parliament regarding the ex-king's matrimonial project were referred to, also James Maxton's dictum that the time had come to overthrow monarchy and set up a republic based on equality and public control of the means of life for all the people. Ned thought Maxton's remark was the only sentence out of those massive debates that would become historical.

Someone mentioned Mr Schramm's letter and my reply. Mac told about the inhuman attitude of a German newspaper, *Der Sturmer*, towards a Jew whom he employs. This Jew, a simple, kindly, transparent character, is a retired businessman who left Germany six years ago. He approached the National Institute for the Blind, asking for something worth doing. Not knowing the man's capacity or how long he would stay, Mac assigned him to the clerical department, where he is still rendering faithful service. Not long ago *Der Sturmer* sent a note to the Institute saying, "Kick out the Jew in your employ. Unless you do the same thing will happen in England as in Spain." Mac dispatched a stinging reply to *Der Sturmer* and wrote a noble protest to *The Times* against the spread of anti-Semitic prejudice. Since Germany is desirous of being on friendly terms with England, he said, it is incumbent upon the British government to warn the Reich that it is an offense against good relations between the two countries to permit the circulation of writings hostile to the Jews outside its borders. I hope this letter may carry weight, written as it is by the director of an institute widely honored for its beneficence to the blind of all faiths and nationalities.

The dictatorships in Germany, Italy and Russia were compared and characterized thus: the Germans worship Hitler, the Italians the war god, and the Russians the machine. Ned praised warmly the young Soviet engineers whose prodigious feats are astonishing the world.

"Yes," Charlie and Mac assented, "the Russian

ideals are wonderful, but how can they have lasting results with no religion, no freedom?"

"At least they have freedom to develop their special talents," I said, "which is impossible in present-day Germany, where art, literature, education are being reduced to a dead level and science turned into a pan-Aryan mania." As the guests were leaving Charlie asked me, "Why has Russia been piling up armaments instead of more tractors?" His question rather took me aback, as every article I had read by friend and foe alike describing Russia had mentioned tractors without end plowing the land. I must find out what I can on this subject.

Park Lane Hotel, January 27th.

One problem was solved this morning to our satisfaction. Mr Moore informed us that we could sail from Havre on the SS Champlain February 2nd. That pleased me especially because Andrea[1] had spoken of it with enthusiasm. She wanted us to go on the Champlain from New York last November, but we wanted a ship leaving earlier and went on the Deutschland instead.

Another problem which has caused my blood to tingle with dismay these last three days remains unsolved. By a strange accident an envelope containing part of my journal and other private papers disappeared. Polly and I carried it with us to town Monday. Several hours later, to our consternation, we discovered that the envelope was gone. Polly made diligent inquiries at the Ivy Restaurant and Bradley's without result. Doormen

[1] Mrs Conrad Berens, wife of the distinguished New York oculist through whose tireless efforts a modicum of sight was preserved to Mrs Macy almost to the end.

Helen Keller's Journal

and taxi drivers who took us to and from these places were questioned to no purpose. Finally we called in Scotland Yard, and they are still searching. I had read thrilling accounts of Scotland Yard's exploits, but I never thought I should have occasion to be a personage in a detective story!

I shall be very sorry indeed if those pages are not recovered. There are experiences in them, the recording of which has lifted a little the pall of grief from my mind and let in some life-giving thoughts. However, this trouble sinks into utter insignificance before the misfortune of authors who lost priceless manuscripts. There was Isaac Newton, whose precious treatise was destroyed when his little dog overturned a lighted candle on the desk. Broken in health and weary, Newton only exclaimed, "Oh, Diamond, thou little knowest what thou hast done!" I am impressed also by the fortitude of Robert Ainsworth, a seventeenth-century scholar whose wife, in a shrewish rage, flung into the fire the Latin dictionary he had just completed. Doggedly he went to work and rewrote the entire dictionary. To cite a modern example, Lawrence of Arabia lost his manuscript, *Seven Pillars of Wisdom*, in a railway station, and it was never found, but he rewrote it, and I am sure the book was richer because of the disaster that had overtaken him. Through such trials we become aware of resources within us that we might not otherwise discover.

Another reality that absorbed me was this morning's report of the flood crisis in the Ohio Valley—traffic at a standstill, drinking water polluted, fires breaking out, epidemics starting, soldiers and civilians desperately trying to strengthen with sandbags and gumbo mud the

Helen Keller's Journal

dikes along three hundred miles. Red Cross and other agencies taxed to the utmost to provide for the seven hundred and fifty thousand people driven from their homes. There is no estimating the damage wrought by the most destructive flood in American history. I fear it will be a terrific drain upon the government and philanthropic societies for years to come.

We were to have lunched with Lady Fairhaven today; but she fell ill suddenly, and the engagement was canceled. I was writing her a note of sympathy when Clifford Bax called with his friend, Sir John Squire, whom I thought very pleasant. Sir John said he had known about me for many years, and I liked his ease and charm. We talked about greater London and Sir Kingsley Wood's plans for reconstructing it. I wondered if many historic places would be demolished, as Mr Lucas thinks they will. Sir John Squire said no, the work would be mostly widening streets and facilitating traffic. I regretted that I had not had opportunity to see more of a city with such a fascinating history, the center of a mighty literature. Both Clifford Bax and Sir John said they would be most happy to show me London on my next visit to England. What a prospect—two handsome cavaliers with rich minds helping me to explore London!

Tea with Mr and Mrs James Maxton this afternoon at the House of Commons. Curiously enough, it was Sir Ian and Lady Fraser with whom Teacher, Polly and I dined there in July 1932. Then I could hardly believe I was bodily in that ancient building which is Britain's history embodied—the signing of the Magna Carta, the empire that has extended over a quarter of the globe, changing dynasties, a hundred years leap from

Helen Keller's Journal

one civilization to another! The enchantment deepened, I remember, as we went out and sat on the terrace with the beauty of a summer evening filling the sky, the Thames flowing as it had flowed for ages near by, the London Bridge and the Tower in the distance.

Now we have been to the House of Commons a second time, and there is yet another splendor—daring dreams, a day in which war shall be abolished, service worshiped as the only kingship, brotherhood the only rule and peace the sole empire.

Mr and Mrs Maxton greeted us cordially. As we went down the long hall to tea Polly's eager fingers positively hummed with interest in all she saw.

I told Mr Maxton how I admired him as a lone voice speaking fearlessly in a wilderness of prejudice and ignorance. I repeated what was said last night—that his remark on the crisis the government had faced was the only one out of all the speeches which would become historical.

"I must have American blood in my veins," he said. "I am a republican."

"Do you think monarchy in England will last much longer?" I asked.

He did not believe it would.

"I do," I answered. "The people are as ardent as ever in their loyalty to the throne."

"But you saw how quickly they transferred their allegiance from one man to another," he reminded me. "Is it not the crown rather than the individual they respect?"

I wondered. "And do they not like to be dazzled by the pomp surrounding it more, perhaps, than any other people in Europe?"

Helen Keller's Journal

"That is true," he assented. "Nevertheless, I can tell you that the English workers know there is something far wrong with the old order and that tremendous changes are needed. What holds them back is dread of experiments that may cause frightful tragedies such as have been enacted in Germany, Italy and Russia."

"If only their self-restraint proves equal to the struggle," I suggested, "then their new commonwealth will be a worthy climax to the wise leadership and noble traditions whose light shines through English history, despite its many betrayals."

"I sincerely hope so," he said, and I asked how he felt about parliamentary routine. "When a man enters Parliament," he replied, "he becomes accustomed to the slowness of things. It may irritate him, but it does not break his spirit."

I inquired if he did not get discouraged at the obtuseness and apathy of the workers in questions which concern them vitally. His answer was a rebuke to my occasional impatience with the workers in America: "So far I have never had the blues. You see, I'm an optimist!"

"What do you predict will happen in Europe?"

"The collapse of dictatorship in Germany, Italy and Russia. One man cannot carry the burdens of sole dictatorship indefinitely. He is subjected to an increasing strain, and if he calls in others to help him they are likely to overthrow him."

I blush to say I had not a moment to chat with Mrs Maxton. She was sweet and forgiving. "That is what happens when my husband is the center of any group!" Indeed, I almost forgot my tea. Mr Maxton turned to Polly and said, "You tell Miss Keller I have had tea with ladies often in the House of Commons, but this is the first time I have had two ladies who ate nothing! I'm too much of a canny Scot to want to pay for what isn't eaten or drunk!" As we were saying good-by at the door two other members of the House came up, and I was introduced to Mr Atlee, leader of the opposition, and to Mr Lovat-Fraser, descended from the turbulent clan that figures so picturesquely in the Scottish tales I read as a child.

"The clan was driven back in those old feuds," he said, "but now behold its peaceful invasion of Parliament."

I told Mr Atlee the Labour party would be a mighty power in the nation's destiny.

"That will be a slow process, very slow," he answered. "You know nature and human nature refuse to be hurried."

"I am teaching him politics and how to go faster!" laughed Mr Maxton.

How Teacher would have enjoyed a talk with Mr Maxton! She would have sparkled, and he would have had a happy reply for her whimsical sallies and penetrating arguments. I do not wonder he is a great favorite in the House. . . .

I have only begun to climb my calvary of love. In the empty house in New York where all I hold dearest was enshrined I shall not cease yearning for that other sacred place where God has led me beside the still waters and restored my soul. Too well I know how often Teacher will seem to die again as I go from room to room, object to object, and find her not. I shall need every mental picture I have of heaven, every beauty of God's Word, all the high examples Teacher and I contemplated to

Helen Keller's Journal

lift my soul up to hers above such an immeasurable, down-dragging loneliness. People write and speak to me as if they thought deafness and blindness monstrous afflictions. I wonder if that is because they have not experienced a noble friendship and then suffered the mortal wound of separation. I seldom am conscious of physical limitations, and they never sadden me, but there is no test so pitiless and searching as this sorrow. . . .

And now—to Paris!

Hotel Lancaster, Paris, January 28th.

The happenings of yesterday, pleasant and painful, are unforgettable. The morning was raw and misty, and somehow I doubted whether we should fly across the Channel, but I hoped against hope that the weather might clear. Polly and I up at six-thirty packing, telephoning and doing the hundred and one last-minute things that departure on a voyage entails. After breakfast we rushed off to Bradley's for a final fitting; and to save time the kind headwaiter, who takes interest in our comfort like a friend every time we stop at the Park Lane, labeled all our luggage for us.

While at Bradley's I received news that sent little rills of joy dancing through my body—the lost pages of the diary had been found at the store in a telephone booth! After such a mental relief I felt a still keener zest in whatever adventures might be in store for us.

At eleven o'clock we said our good-bys and thank-yous and left for Victoria Station, where we were to take the bus to the airport at Croydon. At the station we

Helen Keller's Journal

learned that the flight had been canceled on account of bad weather conditions. Mortified at the way our plans, so full of interest and novelty, had gone agley, we changed tickets, secured seats on the one-fifty boat train for Dover and waited two hours at the Grosvenor Hotel. When finally we got on the train we found it packed to the utmost with people bound for Paris, Marseilles, many going to the winter sports in Switzerland, others on cruises through the Mediterranean and as far as India and Australia.

Unfortunately the mist shut out the landscape until we had gone more than halfway. Then Polly was able to see the valleys of Kent, whose smiling loveliness in spring I had so often read of, the hop country and fine orchards. Much excitement at Dover, everybody rushing about to collect luggage. Polly and I had difficulty in threading our way through thousands of bags and cases destined for the Orient.

The weather continued dark and dreary, a chill wind had risen, and Polly said the sea looked cruel. We stepped aboard a cockleshell of a boat with misgivings that proved too well founded. Scarcely had the boat shot out from the pier than it gave a terrible lurch, and we were soaked as huge billows swept the deck. Two deck hands helped us downstairs. I shudder as I recall how we stumbled over people lying on mattresses, in the clutches of seasickness. Dizzy and ill ourselves, we sat huddled in chairs for what seemed an eternity. Pitilessly the boat listed, pitched, dived and shook us until I thought the breath would be torn out of our bodies. Every moment I had a sensation as if the Channel were crashing down upon the boat with the purpose of submerging it beyond hope of rescue.

Helen Keller's Journal

How we managed to find our seats on the train at Calais and endure five more hours travel I do not know. Under the circumstances we were indifferent to everything that would otherwise have fascinated us: Calais, a town round which the Anglo-French wars raged for a hundred years and which now binds two countries with fraternal ties never to be broken, a kindly, fruitful countryside much like Kent, the pines and dunes around Abbeville where the sons of two nations slain in the Great War were buried, and Amiens. However, the eternal magic of Paris and its bewitching lights roused us as we neared the station.

M. Wolf[1] met us with his car, and his hospitable welcome made us feel better at once. This morning I awoke quite a different person. I enjoyed my cup of excellent Hotel Lancaster coffee and the flaky roll that melts in one's mouth. The wonder of being really in Paris again after five years possessed my spirit.

But my good cheer faded as we looked at the colossal tragedy described in the Paris edition of the New York *Herald*. A million people now homeless; the Ohio River still rising; dikes giving way in many places. My only comfort was the news that the U.S. army has been empowered to save life by all possible methods. That is the only kind of defense that really protects in the long run and conserves to the nation what is won.

Hotel Lancaster, January 29th.

Attended a reception at 11 A.M., given at the George V Hotel in honor of Gutzon Borglum, sculptor of the Thomas Paine statue I was to have unveiled. Of course

[1]Proprietor of the Hotel Lancaster.

it was my wish to appear in a manner befitting such an important occasion. What was my concern, then, on finding that the case containing our dresses had been sent to the ship at Southampton by mistake! However, we wore our traveling clothes on the principle that any commissions and omissions in the social dress code are more easily forgiven than a sulky disposition which will not face the music with lifted head and smiling good will.

Polly had hardly a moment to glance round the handsome reception room or I to caress the roses when the handshaking began. Among the most interesting persons I met first were Jules Romaine, the novelist who is influencing French thought on social problems. He told me about the new series he is now writing, called "Men of Good Will." Then came Mme Marcelle Kraemer-Bach, *avocate à la cour de Paris*, a woman of penetrating intelligence. Mrs Hamilton, of the American embassy, told me she was of the same family tree as Thomas Paine. I began to wonder where Mr Borglum was when in he walked, and all eyes were turned to him.

In his firm, vital hand I recognized the fearless sculptor I had imagined. He gave me a sense of extraordinary perceptiveness and independence. After our first words of greeting I said or tried to say, in my awe before genius, "Meeting you is like a visit from the gods. I admire you not only because you are a great artist, but also because you think greatly through your marbles. When skill and daring imagination meet a masterpiece is born. In your statue of Thomas Paine you are preaching anew the liberty that shall reshape civilization."

"That is my struggle," he said, "to embody in art the elemental forces that have molded man's mind."

Helen Keller's Journal

As usual there were newspapermen, questions both in French and English, and pictures taken. After standing two hours Polly and I were glad of M. Wolf's ever-watchful kindness in taking us back to the Hotel Lancaster.

Later he took us to a milliner's shop to try our luck in hats. We succeeded as one succeeds only in Paris. Back to the hotel we rushed, in time to meet an American reporter from the *Herald-Tribune* whom the confusion of tongues at the reception had prevented from interviewing me. No sooner had she departed than it was announced that Mr Nelson Cromwell[1] had called. As he saluted us with his big, affectionate gesture it was as if great wings enfolded me protectingly—and that is the way I always think of his beneficence to the blind throughout the world. He reminded me how he and I had been friends without my knowing it during forty years. He used to see me walking with Nina[2] on the upper veranda of Mr Rhoades's house at Seabright. How strangely the present vanished, and I smelled that quaint little fishing village, the long boardwalk, the bulkheads lashed with spray, the ropes where we young people clung, surf bathing with a salutary wariness of the undertow!

We talked for two hours about many things. In a beautiful spirit he exhorted me to identify myself with the blind of every religion, race and tongue. It pleased him that I was probably going to Japan in April and might proceed from there to China with a message of

---

[1] New York lawyer, grand officer of the Légion d'Honneur, generous friend of the blind in the United States and France.

[2] Nina Rhoades, blind author, daughter of the late New York banker, John Harsen Rhoades.

encouragement for uncounted blind persons still neglected, untaught.

"Yes, Helen, try to say in their own way, 'Let there be light,' and even if some of them learn more slowly than others because of a dark religion there will be light for them all someday."

Mr Cromwell told me about the talking-books for the blind of France which he has had perfected and turned over free to the French government. He invited Polly and me to lunch with him at his house Monday and suggested that afterwards I speak into a record a greeting for all who struggle against the handicap of blindness, also to express my gratitude to the French government for including the supply of talking-books among its state functions.

More than ever I realized from Mr Cromwell's talk how masterful, generous, public spirited and far seeing he is in building up enterprises or co-operating in those already undertaken.

When my knight-errant (as he likes to have me call him) bade us good night we found to our chagrin that we were very late to a dinner which Mr Lewis had arranged for Mr Borglum at the George V Hotel. However, they received our apologies most kindly and made us quite at home. During dinner the conversation turned on art. Mr Borglum said to me, "I always have felt that only by approaching the unseen can the artist achieve anything worthy of immortality."

"How true that is!" I agreed. "Not until we look long behind the arras of matter and fear can we even half comprehend the soul that informs the body. That is the born teacher's art too."

"Well do I realize," he said earnestly, "that if your

Helen Keller's Journal

Teacher had not approached the unseen forces in you she could not have been your Praxiteles, breathing life into your sense-shut faculties." He commented on Jo Davidson's work, saying he had gained much from it but that he thought it was hampered by a too materialistic attitude towards art.

To my expressed regret that I was to be in Paris such a short time and could see little, Mr Borglum told me I should visit Napoleon's tomb: there was nothing like it in the world. Believing that the truth is the highest compliment one person can pay another, I said Napoleon, the warrior, had never aroused my esteem. "You must read Emil Ludwig's biography," Mr Borglum quickly replied; "it reveals a new Napoleon." I was glad to hear this, as I had pictured Napoleon as the utterly ruthless conqueror whose words Emerson quoted: "Friendship is a name only. I love no one, not even my brother." Yet somehow I could never give full credence to that dictum. As soon as I get hold of Ludwig's book, which is in Braille, I shall try to penetrate this strange character enigma.

Yielding to a sudden impulse, I uttered a long-cherished wish that it were possible for me to touch the Rodin masterpieces. Mr Borglum's swift question took me by surprise. "Would you like to see them tomorrow if it can be arranged?" It was as if "a moth yearning towards a star" should have its desire fulfilled.

"I knew Rodin well," he went on, "and his work has a very intimate significance for me. I will go to the museum and show the masterpieces to you." I was so thrilled I wondered if my fingers had misreported his words. As I write this I expect to wake any moment and find it all a dream—an artist who "with many a stroke,

[*161*]

many a sharp incision" catches angel visions in marble leading me to the shrine of another inspired sculptor in beautiful, fascinating Paris, the City of the Thinking Mind!

There were two other delightful guests at the dinner, M. and Mme de la Nux. M. de la Nux has been engaged in work with the League of Nations for ten years. His talk was philosophical, sympathetic. A remark about French character was volunteered.

"The Frenchman," M. de la Nux replied, "is too much of an individualist. He wants to work according to his own ideas, regardless of the common good. He cultivates his garden in his own way, and consequently the result is not as abundant or useful as it would be if he worked with others in disciplined co-operation."

I suggested that the Frenchman was rendering a precious service to society by not surrendering his individuality to the uniformity of modern civilization.

M. de la Nux assented but added:

"I should like to see the French adopt the give-and-take spirit which is conspicuous in the English and Americans."

"We have much to learn from the French," I answered. "For instance, their skill and their joy in creative handicrafts, which I fear we have lost."

"No," he said warmly, "I feel encouraged about America. Years ago I thought mechanism would quite destroy its native craftsmanship. But the financial depression has wakened the American people to a sense of their inner resources. Traveling through their towns, I observed an increasing wealth of constructive hobbies and beautiful articles made by hand in leisure moments. . . ."

Helen Keller's Journal

In this unexpected manner I glimpsed how international minds, like the Gulf Stream, circulate vitality —fresh appreciation of excellence in one's own and other countries.

Mme de la Nux reminded me of Teacher in her fine sensibilities. Like Teacher, she feels ugliness almost as physical pain, and her faith is a religion of beauty. With Keats she can say:

> *Beauty is truth, truth beauty,—that is all*
> *Ye know on earth, and all ye need to know.*

This wonder never grows less for me that people who were strangers but yesterday suddenly meet, smile, clasp hands, and something different is indelibly registered in their social consciousness.

A man from *Le Soir de Paris* was waiting to interview me when we got back to the Hotel Lancaster. As he could not speak English, his wife translated his questions while Polly repeated my answers. I hope the result won't sound like the confusion of tongues at the Tower of Babel. It was good to sit quietly a few minutes in the elegant, homelike lounge with jardinieres full of lilacs. M. Wolf has an artist's eye in the choice of flowers and their arrangement. He told me that they are no longer brought from Holland by airplane because florists in France have demanded protection.

Hotel Lancaster, January 30th.

It was quite raw this morning, but there was not the proverbial Paris *brouillard*. It seems as if I should move forever in a show. A photographer from *Le Soir* appeared after breakfast. Polly and I walked out with him and he took pictures of us on the Champs-Elysées beside a shopwindow resplendent with Paris hats and gowns.

Next the milliner came to try on our hats, which took some time. Seeing everybody here in the pink of fashion doesn't tend to lull my feminine vanity, and we have been doing our best to get hold of the missing suitcase ever since yesterday morning.

Mrs MacDonald lunched with us—a strong, warm-hearted, intelligent woman. I never see her without remembering her helpfulness five years ago. She happened to be at Cherbourg when Teacher, Polly and I landed. A veritable good fairy, she piloted us through bustling porters and piled-up baggage, recommended the Hotel Lancaster where we first sensed the soul of la belle France.

Mrs MacDonald gave us her news, especially about the publicity work she does for Mme Schiaparelli, the miracle-working couturière. Last summer they went to Russia on a business trip, and she learned much which she believes is true about conditions there. Everywhere she saw industry and progressive farming well organized.

At three o'clock Mr Borglum came with the gratifying news that permission had been obtained through the American embassy for me to touch Rodin's works. Just as we were starting two deaf-mutes who live at Le Foyer des Sourd-meuts asked to see us. They were accompanied by their wives. With moving warmth they saluted me in French, using the manual alphabet employed a hundred years ago by the Abbé de l'Épée in teaching deaf children. Happy that I could spell better than I speak in French, I expressed my love for De l'Épée, one of the most self-sacrificing liberators of captive souls God ever sent. They inquired if I knew about the deaf-blind of Larnay with whom they occasionally exchange greetings. I told them enthusiastically what I had learned from *Aidons-nous*, published by the Association Fraternelle pour les Aveugles-Sourds, and *Le Rayon de Soleil*, edited by Yvonne Pitrois, about what beautiful friends the sisters in many convents are to the deaf-blind of France. I was sorry to leave my friends with what I wished to say only half said. At best the hand alphabet is a slow mode of communication.

On our way to the museum we crossed the Alexander III Bridge, which in Mr Borglum's opinion is surely the most artistic bridge in the world. Mr Borglum dwelt on the skillful hands that had wrought its grace and strength. "Louis XIV was an ingenious locksmith," he said, "and it was his influence that stamped upon France the beauty of handicraft."

The first sculptures shown in the museum were "Victor Hugo" and "Grief." A chair was placed against the base so that I might reach the mighty figure of the Liberator, gazing with divine compassion upon anguish-bowed Grief, extending his hand, entreating her to be quiet and hear Freedom's trumpet call ringing from land to land. There, too, were the spirits, Night and Ignorance, hushed in their mortal combat at his dawn-heralding gesture.

"That is France," I thought, "with healing in her hands for poverty, treading upon the darkness that once doomed the blind and the deaf and the mentally weak to despair."

Mr Borglum led me to where "The Thinker" sat, primal, tense, his chin resting on a toilworn hand. In every limb I felt the throes of emerging mind. As I said to Mr Borglum, I recognized the force that shook me when Teacher spelled "water", and I discovered that everything has a name and that the finger motions were the way to whatever I wanted. Often before had my deliverance caused me to wonder, but not until then had I perceived clearly how Teacher hewed my life bit by bit out of the formless silent dark as Rodin hewed that mind-genesis out of the rock. What loneliness enveloped the first thinker as he reached towards the unknown. God within and the outer world lying at his feet with no power except his brawn, no motive save his will!

"Few people have understood the elemental meaning of Rodin's symbol as you do," was Mr Borglum's comment. "You have seen the struggle for existence in which the body goes as far as it can, and conscious thinking begins. Now come and behold the heights to which the mind has climbed."

Again I got on a chair, and lo! the magnificent dome of Balzac's forehead met my touch. It was the noble head I had pictured—that of one who had explored all religions and philosophies, observed the angelic and the diabolical in human nature, multiplied books holding up for scrutiny the loftiest and the humblest impartially. The cloak he wore seemed to me the majesty in which he had walked among his fellow creatures—a majesty above kings.

My heart contracted in the presence of the masterpiece "Calais." In that one face, with tears streaming through the hands which cover it, all suffering seems tangible. The haggard cheeks are marked by ceaseless toil, fighting, defeat. It is a work sadder to touch than a grave, because it is a conquered city typified, and also because of mankind's folly in waging wars. As the peasants with halters round their necks gaze on the ground you feel that inhuman drudgery and endurance without avail have beaten hope out of their souls. But one, who has a light of purpose in his somber countenance, is telling them that Calais's rescue may be wrought through their self-sacrifice!

Other statues I saw were what Mr Borglum called a faithful likeness of Clemenceau, grim, aloof, with an eye piercing through all shams, I fancied. Then came the patient, Penelope-like face of Mme Rodin; and two children whose darling grace made me think of flowers molded into features; and joyous Apollo bursting in triumphant splendor from his cloud prison.

"What a strange contrast between Michelangelo's wretched end and Rodin's glorious old age!" Mr Borglum ejaculated. "Michelangelo started with heavenly visions irradiating his art and descended to hell, blind, self-abased, hate filled. Rodin, on the other hand, began with repellent figures—evidently the disorderly impulses of his youth—climbed heavenward to serene, creative years."

With what laborious perseverance, I remarked, everything had been hewn into forms.

"Even so did Rodin achieve power to clothe his thoughts in words! He could not write until he was seventy—he hewed noble messages out of the rock of his sincerity" Mr Borglum presented me with a book of Rodin sayings I shall treasure among my choicest possessions.

"Here is another mystery," he continued, showing me three contemporaries: "de Chavannes", "Jean-

Paul Laurens" with apostolic benignity and "Dalou"—a modern Apollo. "Rodin wrought an immortal bust of Dalou, who won great financial success and whose works have not lived! Beset by grinding poverty to the last, Rodin toiled here in Paris, and behold, he is the only French artist to whom the honor has been accorded of two palaces to house his sculptures."

My mind needed solitude to make room for the grandeur which had inundated it during two hours. We rested at the hotel before dinner. Later we changed from evening clothes into walking suits and went alone for a stroll along the Champs-Elysées. The air was soft, the moon was snowing its loveliness upon the city. The traffic was at a low ebb. We went as far as Rue Royale, passing Maxim's, looking in the shopwindows which are the undoing of unwary mortals, Polly noting especially the jewelry, rare antiques and Lalique glass. Everywhere I recognized the odor peculiar to Paris—perfumes, powders, wines and tobacco agreeably blended. Polly wished we had a French cavalier to tell us about the historic buildings and streets. "Oh no," I protested, "I'm as dead to the world as a nun tonight." Since our youth "the night life of Paris" had been held up to us as an exciting, colorful spectacle, and we thought we might catch a glimpse or two by the way. We did pass three cocottes in one place awaiting their paramours. A few people were sitting at tables in the street, sipping liqueurs. Inside the cafés were many people dining, laughing and chatting, and over all shone the reposeful moonlight. This is the real Paris in winter, and the more I see of it, the better it pleases me. . . .

This is one of Hitler's famous Saturdays, instituted, no doubt, to allow hot heads to cool over the week end after his provocative decrees. We saw everyone buying evening papers. From their manner it was evident something had occurred that was good news. On returning to the hotel we learned that Hitler had declared he had "no point of difference with France" and that his chief concern was to co-operate in fighting Bolshevism.

Our mail for today unread. My heart quails as I wonder how I can work in bewitching Paris. I cannot write longer on my machine without bringing down upon my head the wrath of disturbed sleepers.

Hotel Lancaster, January 31st.

Polly and I rested late this morning and awoke to find Paris bathed in sunshine. We dressed hurriedly so that we might be in time for the service at the Madeleine. M. Wolf went with us. The church was crowded. It was a keen disappointment to me that the organ music did not reach my feet on account of the marble floor; I had hoped to revel in its rich vibrations; but by placing my hand on the chair I captured some chords, especially towards the end. The priest talked a few minutes in French about the Paris Exposition which is to open next May and the duty of the Church to raise funds for it. We saw people going up to the altar, kneeling and receiving the sacrament. It was a poem—the choir boys with candles, a melodious bell that kept ringing, the incense floating over the church, the responses of the organ. I could not follow the Latin, but that did not prevent me from worshiping in the universal language of the heart. It was touching when an old man, bent double, managed to get to the altar, go down on

Helen Keller's Journal

his poor knees, rise to his feet with a radiant expression and totter back to his seat. A woman with white hair and a black velvet bow took my hand in hers tenderly, saying she had long known about me.

After service I said to M. Wolf that I should be happy if I might see a few sculptures near the door or on the outside. I was surprised and delighted when I was permitted to touch anything I could reach, even the altar! Reverently I examined the loveliest altar I had ever approached—white marble, the cloth with Milanese lace; and I reached up to the angels' hands on either side and the tips of their wings. How delicately yet distinctly the feathers were marked in the stone! I walked round the superb Corinthian columns, and I sensed the grace of a Greek temple. The Napoleon mural was far above my head, but Polly kept gazing at it in wonderment. On the outside she showed me the heart-piercing Crucifixion and other representations from the Bible while the people looked at us curiously.

From the church we drove out to the Bois de Boulogne. The crowds *prenant l'air* in that sweet sanctuary of nature—walking or driving or sitting on benches—were the real Parisians I had always wished to see, with their beautiful family life and sane pleasures, a happy blend of vivacity and seriousness.

I had invited Mr Borglum to lunch at the Lancaster today, and he came. He said he was going to New York this week on another ship, arriving two days before the Champlain, and hoped he might see us. I enjoyed hearing about his travels. He is a Jutlander; and he told how when he visited Denmark the king heard of it and sent for him within two hours! His fame certainly goes swiftly before him. He was in America during the

Helen Keller's Journal

Mississippi flood six years ago. I spoke out my pent-up indignation as he reviewed the present disaster; it could have been prevented to a large extent if proper measures had been taken six years ago.

Mr Cromwell had placed his car at my disposal for this afternoon. Mr Borglum had hardly left when Miss Slade[1] appeared and took us out to Versailles. It was still raining when we alighted at the Trianon. However, from what we saw it was easy to guess the loveliness in springtime, with green slopes mirrored in the water and long vistas of blossoming gardens and woods on every side.

My pleasure in that trip was mingled with pain. As our loved ones depart from this world we live on old memories, which return with each new experience. From the Trianon my thoughts sped back to the September day in 1931 when Teacher visited Fontainebleau with us. She was quite as excited as I was, walking through the stately halls, inspecting the gorgeous tapestries, Marie Antoinette's room, resplendent with mirrors and the golden bed on which the Czar of Russia slept. Beyond the window was the Court of Love. Teacher used to tell me emphatically that traveling in foreign countries did not particularly appeal to her. Nevertheless, when she was once started she made things hum and our hearts glow with her appreciative outbursts, quick sallies, instructive glances at history and literature. No matter how others' love surrounds me, a glory is gone from my wanderings.

Mr Menten, a high dignitary from Holland who makes the Lancaster his headquarters whenever he comes to Paris, arrived this evening, and M. Wolf

[1] Mr Cromwell's secretary, from Boston, Mass.

Helen Keller's Journal

introduced us to him. He invited us out to Maxim's for dinner—Maxim's, that sometime gay, naughty café which has mended its ways, I believe, and is patronized by good Paris society. Mr Menten ordered a choice dinner which would have caused me to tremble for my embonpoint had not the conversation been a feast in itself. Mr Menten talked about Holland. I was enthusiastic over the role it has in the past played as a bulwark of liberal thought and respect for others' beliefs, which is finer than mere tolerance.

"It still plays that role," he replied. "The people of the Netherlands are fortunate in their geographical position and their willingness to learn from experience. They are not blind as they once were to the evils of war and empire. That is why their influence thrown on the side of peace is likely to count." He spoke of his peace work at The Hague.

"Not much has been accomplished there," I said regretfully.

"No," he agreed, "but I have accomplished something else—a happy marriage. My wife's home was very near there, and I take off my hat to The Hague whenever I pass it."

I hoped I might meet her someday. "Holland will receive you warmly if you will come," he assured me gallantly. "Then you can really get the spirit and the local color of the country."

I mentioned Queen Wilhelmina and how I had read all I could lay my hands on about her since we were both eight years old. He gave me another thrill with his invitation: "If you visit Holland I will introduce you to Her Majesty. She will welcome you most graciously. She has been interested in you for years." I thanked him as best I could for his genuine cordial gesture and left the date open for 1938, when I plan another visit to Britain and France. Who knows? I thought to myself; such an opportunity is a tide that may carry me into other seas of service and friendship to the handicapped.

We commented on European affairs. I was relieved to hear an authoritative statement from Mr Menten that immediate war had been averted between Germany and France, and he hopes and believes that another world conflict may be prevented. While Germany is the chief source of danger, he thinks it can be forced by peaceful means to adopt a saner policy. Hitler, he said, was not prepared for the decisive promptness with which other nations are arming, and he finds himself slipping into deep waters.

The orchestra music kept pulsing through our talk. By different tactile vibrations I perceived the low tones of the harp, the high, delicate notes of the violin, the mechanical beat of the piano. Also I caught the rhythm, and the dancing instinct in me responded to the lively mood of the music.

At eleven o'clock we took a taxi back to the Lancaster. M. Wolf told us about the driver, an old man well known and much liked in Paris. Instead of blowing a horn this driver whistles! Thus ends a day that seems "like an avenue of light and velvet" leading I know not whither.

Helen Keller's Journal

Hotel Lancaster, February 1st.

This morning I was in such a rush to do some work before interruptions started, I had only a cup of coffee for breakfast. There was an important gift to my work for the blind to be acknowledged. I had promised Mr Cromwell that I would speak into a record for the blind of France at Montevideo Building this afternoon, and I had not given a thought to what I wished to say. The telephone took that precious moment to ring, and that meant hushing the click of the typewriter keys while Polly listened and answered the message. I had only a few sentences to prepare, it is true, but I take special pains with these utterances lest an inept phrase should spoil the whole. I was halfway through when the inexorable telephone rang again, and I was called downstairs for an interview with a Rumanian reporter.

He could not speak English at all. M. Wolf again stepped into the breach, interpreting for us both while Polly spelled the somewhat halting results. I asked about Rumania, and after a wait due to translation the reporter described the beautiful mountains and natural wealth of the country. He asked me for a message to his people. The accounts of Rumania I had received were garbled, and our slowness in communicating ideas rendered it difficult to speak intelligently. I said I realized what harassing obstacles the Rumanians must be encountering in their political and economic development; I expressed the hope that the struggle would make their hearts tender towards the blind and that they would co-operate with workers who show the seeing how

Helen Keller's Journal

to be friends to the sightless. I talked about Carmen Sylva and the letters she had sent me in Braille thirty years ago, just as one woman to another, about her work for the blind, her longing to lay down the burdens of royalty and dwell in forest solitudes, painting, writing, communing with the unseen.

At long last I finished the paragraph left in my typewriter. I wanted badly to practice. On account of my halting delivery it is necessary for me to say my speeches over countless times before I can feel at ease or be sure that a few people will understand. Remembering how the microphone embarrasses me, I was anxious to get my voice as smooth as possible for the talking record, but there was no time. We had an appointment which it was too late to cancel. Like the old Puritan in the days of pen quills who said, "Trust God and keep thy finger dry," I admonished myself, "Trust God and keep thy voice soft."

Mrs MacDonald had arranged for us to meet Mme Schiaparelli at 11 A.M. Once again the telephone delayed us, another fifteen minutes elapsed, but when finally we arrived, word was carried to Mme Schiaparelli, who left her dress miracles to greet me with the dearest smile.

"It is a pleasure to have you here, mademoiselle," she said, taking my hand. "We all know about you and the wonderful Teacher whose work lives on in you."

I told her it was an honor to salute an artist beloved of everyone who works with her.

"Working together in sympathy is the secret of the highest art," she replied. "I am glad you are friendly to Russia. I have been there, and I know there is a struggling light of progress in that much misrepresented country." I told her I was leaving for America tomorrow

Helen Keller's Journal

but that on my next visit to Paris I hoped I might see her again; I was proud to count her among my friends. While Polly and I were looking at dresses Mrs MacDonald brought me a bottle of perfume so exquisite it seemed a breath of heaven—a gift from Mme Schiaparelli!

I was sorry that a frock could not be made for me in a day, but my hands were crammed with loveliness as one robe after another appeared. The model showed me a sunset evening gown she had on with a train. Oh, "how sweetly flowed that liquefaction" of silk and lace! The poet sang, "My love in her attire doth shew her wit," and certainly Mme Schiaparelli's wit scintillates in the gowns that go from her establishment to every land.

Mr Cromwell sent his car to bring us to luncheon, and he entertained us like princesses. As he led me on his arm into the dining room he placed my hand on the gorgeous wall tapestries. Seeing my pleasure, he said, "If you could be here longer Polly would be your eyes to look at the pictures, and I should enjoy them more." M. and Mme Raverat were there. I am always glad to see M. Raverat: he is so interested in the blind, exerting his business and mechanical abilities to lessen or remove the obstacles that circumscribe their lives.

The luncheon was a feast for the gods, and there was a gold service for the occasion! The glasses literally felt like crystal lilies daintily balanced on slender stems. At two-thirty Mr Cromwell took us all to Montevideo, where talking-books are produced. Two lovely children met us at the door and put into my hands great bunches of violets and roses. A film was made, showing a talking-book and a record of what we said. First Mr Cromwell

Helen Keller's Journal

and M. Raverat spoke into the record of the priceless boon those books are to blind persons who have not the sensitive touch required to learn Braille, then I said my word of greeting, and Polly repeated for me the paragraph I had written this morning. Afterwards we listened to the record, and I noted how smoothly it ran until a discordant vibration arrested my attention. On inquiry I found it was my own voice, which did not surprise me—my fingers are never pleased with it when it is recorded. I forgot my disappointment going over the studio and examining the sound-producing discs. I had no idea they could be as light as air, flexible and yet of amazing durability.

Round 5 P.M. Polly and I had tea with Mme Kraemer-Bach. I felt it a privilege to visit a Frenchwoman so distinguished in mind and personality, and I was glad to experience the indefinable charm of a French home. I asked Madame to tell me about her work. It was most interesting to hear of her efforts through the courts to protect unprivileged women and youth. I understood her to say that all professions and careers are open to women in France. I mentioned Mme Curie, for whom I had always had an admiring affection, and I regretted that I could not meet her when she was in America. "It would make me happy," I said, "if I might know her daughter." I heard then that the government had appointed her minister of public welfare, and she accepted, not because she was interested in politics, but to show her solidarity with women. M. Marcel Bloch, a well-known blind lawyer, called. He did not seem blind to me at all, he was so natural and responsive. It was delightful to exchange views with him on the work for the handicapped and the best methods of solving their problems. We agreed that as far as possible they should be given the joy of normal life.

"Lack of sight is not our chief difficulty," he declared, "but lack of understanding and co-operation in our struggle for rehabilitation." I was thrilled because he uttered with new force my message that the blind suffer most from the wrong attitude of the public towards them and that when this attitude is replaced by intelligent sympathy and helpfulness their obstacles will no longer be insurmountable.

Reluctantly Polly and I bade au revoir to such congenial friends. We had been late for everything despite our best intentions, and it was 7 P.M. when we hurried into the George V Hotel to meet some more people. Among them were Mrs Bartlett, the wife of the late Mr Bartlett, the sculptor, and Mary Garden's sister. Mr Borglum was there also. We were begged to stay for supper. Everyone realized what a strenuous day we had lived through and was as kind as could be, but it was a relief to get back to our room and relax awhile before packing up for an early start tomorrow.

Aboard the SS Champlain, February 2nd.

Here we are steaming farther and farther from Havre, and I am still sad over our departure. There is no doubt in my mind that we shall return in 1938, yet it was hard to say good-by to M. Wolf and Miss Slade at the station in Paris. Miss Slade told me Mr Cromwell had been up since 5 A.M., at his desk, as is his daily habit, and at six o'clock he had written me a letter to accompany a box of nut candies as big as a wedding cake. It was a letter

Helen Keller's Journal

of the dearest kind. I wonder why farewells even for a short time are depressing? The emotion, I imagine, is akin to the regret when first love's celestial dream fades, the mother's wistfulness, recalling the joyous moment when she sees her baby taking its first steps or hears his first word. Few pleasures there are indeed without an aftertouch of pain, but that is the preservation which keeps them sweet.

The compartment was full of people, but they talked so quietly that we did not mind. Polly was quite proud when she caught a French word or phrase and could spell it to me. We passed many villages with red roofs which Polly said gave much color to the landscape. Every time the door opened I caught welcome odors from meadows and pastures decking themselves with fresh green garments for spring.

Courteous attentions from the French Line. Even before our arrival at Havre a porter came to tell us that our luggage would be taken aboard the ship as quickly as possible. Everything was made easy for us at the dock. In the midst of the bustle Polly could look about. I wished there was time to drive round Havre, about which I had so often read in history. We were amused at the assiduity with which the customs officials searched through every suitcase for gold. Who would carry gold in a suitcase? I wondered.

The two cabins which the line has placed at our disposal are all that heart can wish. I am now sitting in a comfortable armchair at a splendid desk which accommodates my typewriter, manuscripts and books. The puffs on the beds are dainty, and it is a luxury to find my way about with such ease in this well-appointed room.

Helen Keller's Journal

A French reporter interviewed me before we sailed. After lunch I succumbed to drowsiness and literally crossed the Channel in my sleep. We have just had a light supper in bed, and now the Champlain is anchored in Southampton, 11 P.M. If I let myself look back to all I love in this second homeland, the nostalgia that sweeps over me is worse than any seasickness I can ever suffer....

The passenger list contains the names of some musicians, among them the Australian tenor, Mr Brownlee, who is to sing at the Metropolitan Opera House. There is also Hilaire Belloc, who is going to lecture in America.

SS Champlain, February 3rd.

A dismal day with heavy seas, the ship listing and rolling violently, though fully freighted. Polly and I find it prudent to stay in bed and eat only a chicken sandwich and celery. Writing is extremely difficult, the typewriter slides up and down the table under my hands, and I can scarcely hold onto the chair. However, unless I write when the pitching of the ship lets up a bit, things which enliven this dull time for me will become a blur.

I have just finished Mr Bax's fascinating short book, *Leonardo da Vinci*. Such a revealing book is an event. Of course I have frequently heard Leonardo da Vinci's name, but no literature has come my way that gave the slightest idea of his mysterious, mountainlike personality. I did not dream how amazing his range of achievements was in different spheres—painting, sculpture, music, architecture, botany, astronomy and engi-

Helen Keller's Journal

neering. He must have been a titan, with his double equipment as the foremost artist of his age and a profound scientist. I cannot picture to myself one whose "radiant beauty made sorrowful hearts glad" as loathing life and the procreative law of nature. What a fantastic blend of characteristics—aversion to war as "a bestial madness", truckling to expediency by assisting Florence's enemy, Cesare Borgia, in his campaigns, fastidiousness and a mania for dissecting corpses, vegetarianism!

Another surprise in the book is a passage written by Mr Bax, himself a dramatist intensely alive to art and poetry. Speaking of the conflict between the artistic impulse and the calculating scientific tendency in modern times, he says, "The arts . . . belong to an earlier phase of human society, to a level of the mind which is now becoming archaic. . . . A continual calculation of figures is probably enough to suppress the visualizing faculty. This faculty, it seems clear, is uncivilized. To think in pictures or metaphors is barbaric compared with the abstract thinking of a Kant, a Darwin or any higher mathematician. Such persons as these, therefore, are likely to lose, or never to possess, an interest in the arts. Darwin, as every schoolgirl knows, became incapable of reading fiction because he could not lose himself in a fantasy; and, as every schoolboy knows, there was an eighteenth-century philosopher who, hearing of Lord Melbourne's collection of Greek and Roman statues, said that he could not understand 'his Lordship's interest in these dolls.'"

This repels me—a future civilization likely to be hard, practical, monotonous. I feel fortunate indeed that it has been possible for me to be a barbarian, to enjoy sculpture, the flow of graceful lines on surfaces, poetry, happy make-believe in bleak corners of my limitations. It also seems to me more urgent than ever to foster in the present young generation a spiritual philosophy and imagination that shall keep the morning dew in their souls when an age arrives that knows not the muses or the graces.

SS Champlain, February 4th.

This morning Neptune was still on a rampage. As the ship rose and dived I fancied I could feel his giant hands.

Take the ruffian billows by the top,
Curling their monstrous heads, and hanging them
With deafening clamor in the slippery shrouds.

We did not try to get up, as the pitching of the ship made every step precarious.

Lying on my back, I read another book, Sir John Squire's *Shakespeare as a Dramatist*. It is years since I have come across such a pleasant book on the subject. How strange it is that, according to the author, little has been written about Shakespeare's glorious technique and powers of suggestion as a dramatist, except by Samuel Johnson and Charles Lamb!

This book is free from the voluminous eulogies, "perhaps" and "no doubt" conjectures, interpretations by critics and commentators whose name is legion that used to exasperate me when I studied Shakespeare at Radcliffe College. Sir John Squire discourses interestingly on the stage in ancient Greece and in Elizabethan

Helen Keller's Journal

England where the audiences, thrown upon their own resources, appreciated superb plays with small aid from scenery, lights or any other elaborate modern devices. The melancholy fact is dwelt upon that "our age does not like Shakespeare" because his art is so largely addressed to our imagination, which mechanism seems to have stunted. I have often thought—and this statement confirms my fear—that the present generation is losing the capacity of enjoying life from within. They are sacrificing the delight in handicrafts born with every child to machine products. They demand to be amused instead of amusing themselves. They want machines to sing, play, talk and read to them. They require a play with houses and landscapes complete, so that they do not have to use their minds visualizing or puzzling out the intricacies of a plot. Unless a salutary change checks the process mental erosion will overtake them when they most need inner faculties to keep their youth bright and their age livable.

The storm has now begun to abate, though not sufficiently for me to write with ease.

I tremble to think how lost I should have been without my watch—the inseparable little friend with crystal face and a tireless golden hand, telling me the time. It really seems a sentient creature, responding to my affection. Old and needing tenderest care, it faithfully marks off day that unto day uttereth speech and night that unto night sheweth knowledge. Quietly it assures me that each hour I am drawing nearer to Pflegevater,[1] who presented it to me on my fourteenth birthday. I think it prays with me that the time it ticks may

[1] One of Miss Keller's closest friends, the late Mr John Hitz, director of the Volta Bureau, Washington, D.C.

Helen Keller's Journal

not be long before Teacher welcomes me to our eternal home. . . .

SS Champlain, February 5th.

This morning the ocean seemed all sun, and I wished I could sing as we walked. Truly a golden thread of poetry runs through the daily routine on this ship. Polly and I looked around so that I might get an idea of the ship's handsome architecture—highly polished walls, big mirrors, carved woodwork and massive brass railings. I was delighted with the long, rubber-carpeted decks which lessen risks of falling or slipping, let in whatever sun there is and shut out turbulent winds. Word had been received early by wireless that the water would be rough farther on, and a rope was stretched across the deck to give support when the listing recommenced. It is a pleasure to see the care and consideration shown to passengers. There were many white gulls flying in every direction—young gulls beginning to try their strength against wind and surge.

Reclining comfortably in steamer chairs, Polly and I perused the ship's news bulletin. I was amazed at President Roosevelt's message, launched like a thunderbolt, asking for an increase in the membership of the Supreme Court from nine to a maximum of fifteen if judges seventy years old declined to retire. When I realized the significance of the message I was much interested. I have observed how long it takes to pass amendments to the United States Constitution; and while I admire liberal judges like Brandeis and Cardozo, it seems to me the Supreme Court has blocked important legislation for public utilities extension, minimum wages,

Helen Keller's Journal

shorter hours and industrial co-ordination because it is lined up with corporate wealth.

What the President wrote concerning judiciary procedure applies equally to all departments of life: "Modern complexities call . . . for constant infusion of new blood in the courts, just as it is needed in the executive branches of the government. . . . A lowered mental or physical vigor leads men to avoid an examination of complicated and changing conditions. . . . Older men, assuming that the scene is the same as it was in the past, cease to explore or inquire into the present or the future."

Our lunch—a dry chicken sandwich and a cup of tea and fruit—in the open air had a special flavor. A pleasant surprise was handed to me in the shape of a radio greeting from Mr Borglum, who had passed us on the Europa, bound for New York.

I spent the afternoon trying to overtake the procession of papers and letters unread or unanswered which marches apace mockingly. It is fortunate that I had to stay in bed two days; it has given me rest necessary for a long uphill job.

When we left Havre I solemnly declared to Polly, hand on heart, that I was going to diet, but the dinner tonight—mushroom soup, fish melting in the mouth, meat smothered in juices I had not dreamed of and crêpes Suzette—knocked over my good intentions like ninepins!

The atmosphere is what we like: pleasant people, charming, prettily gowned girls, dignified restraint, excellent pictures and music. This evening we saw *The Plough and the Stars*, picturing the Sinn Fein uprising in Ireland. I felt its overpowering pathos, especially

Helen Keller's Journal

because I had read in *The Blind Citizen*, a Braille periodical for the Irish blind, the incidents depicted. Teacher seemed very close when the picture ended with the words, "Until Ireland is free men will always be fighting and women will always be weeping."

SS Champlain, February 6th.

It was raining heavily when we got up, but the ship was not rolling much. At my desk after a refreshing hour's walk, more mail read and letters answered before I would look at the news.

As we speed homeward the excitement of the duel between the A.F. of L. and the C.I.O. begins to encircle my mind as the flames ringed the rock where Brunhild slept. Yes, an industrial Götterdämmerung is descending upon America, and, unlike Brunhild, I am tensely awake, tremulously aware of the fiery ordeal the American workers must endure to gain their rights as creators of both labor and capital.

The "sit-down" strikers at the General Motors plants are forcing another issue upon us: whether the plants belong to those who produce goods and the capital which is the lifeblood of industry or to those who employ labor. In the sense of human living the plants belong to the producers; in the legal sense only they belong to the capitalists. I did not expect events to show this historic conflict so suddenly in so naked a light.

It is reported that all the demands of the International Seamen's Union have been granted. I sincerely hope so. There is no chapter in the history of labor more revolting than the brutalities inflicted upon sailors until they formed a union. I am impressed by the magnitude of the strike, lasting ninety-eight days. It is more than a strike on the West and East coasts of the United States, it is a sign of the growing solidarity among workers in all lands that alone can make earth a safe home for mankind. . . .

The beautiful, heartbreaking picture, *Camille*, was shown this afternoon. Everybody was moved. I realized how wonderful Greta Garbo must be in her role as Marguerite. Perhaps I acted foolishly in going to see it only three months after Teacher's death. At all events it shook me terribly, and I have not regained my equilibrium since. Marguerite had an unconquerable spirit like Teacher's. With the same sweet obstinacy she rose from her sickbed and put on her brightest looks for the lover who refused to give her up. My tears fell as I remembered how during her last illness Teacher planned a little party at the cottage by the sea where we were staying on Long Island. She was growing weaker, but she wanted to see happy faces about her, and we knew she would get excited if we said no. As she started to put on her shoes with Polly's assistance before the guests arrived, she was seized with violent pain and sank back on her bed. A doctor was summoned at once, and he ordered her in hospital the next day. Despite our protests she sat up and dressed, as it turned out for the last time, holding my hand silently. I sensed approaching death when she spelled, "Dear, there is the ambulance," and Polly supported her downstairs. No; I ought not to have been at the picture which has stabbed me to my soul.

Helen Keller's Journal

SS Champlain, February 7th.

Last night I prayed long, and the Divine Presence poured its healing peace upon me. Not for the world would I let my misery penetrate through the earth-curtain to Teacher. For the first time I understood Wordsworth's poem, "Laodamia," in which the gods gently reproved a woman overwhelmed with rebellious grief for her dead husband. They told her she would not find her way to him through tumult or bitter repining, but rather through godlike calm and mindfulness of his joy in her faith.

The foghorn woke me this morning, but it has sounded only a few times today.

M. Silvestre, captain of the Champlain, invited Polly and me to tea up in his cabin. I liked him very much, though he made me blush with courtly compliments because of my work for the handicapped. One would have thought I was the only deaf-blind person ever taught in the world! I was glad of an opportunity to tell him how many others without sight or hearing have escaped hopeless isolation through a teacher's ministering hand and are living useful, reasonably happy lives.

The captain's dinner took place tonight, although it was Sunday: I suppose because we shall soon be off those redoubtable Newfoundland fog banks. I liked the way everything was arranged—the pleasant dining room, the flowers on the table, the evening gowns of the women and the absence of trivialities like bonbon crackers containing tin whistles, horns and dunce caps.

The concert after dinner was beautiful. Polly was

Helen Keller's Journal

charmed with Brownlee's velvet baritone and with an actress whose very soul vibrated in her voice and shone out of her face. We found out later that she is Russian, which explains the oneness of her personality and art.

Most of the singing was in French. I regretted that I was not near enough to the singers to capture through touch their glorious notes. As the music drifted to me from cello, violin and piano I seemed far away in a room at the hotel in Atlanta, Ga., where Caruso's magnificent voice poured the lament of Samson Agonistes, wave upon wave, into my hand. Again with his enchanting Italian gallantry he said as I read his lips, "I have sung the best in my life for you, Helen Keller."

Memory shifted the scenery, and there I was standing beside Chaliapin at a large hall in Los Angeles. The place was crowded with humble folk, many of them Russian women in colorful shawls. In his brotherly way Chaliapin placed my left hand on his face, and I kept time with the right one as he chanted the infinitely sad "Volga Boat Song" or filled the air with young love's ecstasy or shouted humorous folk songs in which I felt the Russian peasant's big laugh. To my wonderment he said I was well known in Russia. I asked him if he thought the new Soviet Republic could survive the cruel ordeal of famine and invasion. He expressed confident faith in its ultimate triumph. I wonder what his feelings are now. Oh, *tempi passati!*

SS Champlain, February 8th.

Polly and I went up to the top deck for our morning walk. A blustering northeaster nearly blew us over, and we stayed on one side where the sun was warm. There was life in the wind's sting, though, and we held up our faces to its buffetings several times before coming down.

More writing before and after lunch. Had friends to dinner this evening, which was a veritable work of art prepared by the chef. Only the French can make every morsel such a delicate pleasure.

SS Champlain, February 9th.

The usual kind of last day on board. Packing, putting my agitated mind in what order I could for the homecoming and saying good-by to friends.

Lilie de la Nux, sister of M. de la Nux, whom I met in Paris, came into our stateroom to have a few words with us in the sanctuary of friendship. She is one of the few women I have met whose conversation leaves me refreshed—women who educate themselves and one another. Her spiritual insight and exquisite sympathy with my sad thoughts, turning homeward, made me feel as if I had known her a long time. We talked about Provence, where she was born and where I hope to visit her someday. We discussed Victor Hugo, Balzac and the troubadours. It was a delight to compare notes with one so widely read and enthusiastic about books which had fascinated me since my youth.

As the day wore on the grief I had felt on sailing from New York last November threatened to overwhelm me. There was a warmly welcoming radiogram from Dr Saybolt and Judge Richards, but not a message from Teacher, and this finality about our earthly separation seemed more than I could bear. During three months there had been at the core of me an expectation which fact and reason could not break that somehow, somewhere, I should receive a sign from Teacher—and there was none as we drew nearer and nearer to New York.

Has faith, then, proved a mockery? No; but I have been too close to death, too constantly reminded of it in a thousand ways entirely to escape that emotional malady which links all thought of the lost dear one with the ashes that are laid to rest. My soul has not yet reached its full stature. I am not among those godlike mortals "who live above the fog." That is why these clouds of sorrow and loneliness persist in floating about my inner eyes, but since God has laid upon me an experience deep as eternity, high as divinity, I shall become spiritually adult. Then, no doubt, these mists will be low and escapable, and I shall dwell with Teacher in His sunshine. . . .

Forest Hills, Long Island, February 10th.

Under the circumstances I dreaded being interviewed by the newspapers on Tuesday evening as I had always been after a trip abroad. However, the reporters who came on board the Champlain before it docked showed me a consideration for which I shall ever be grateful. Delicately they led me from one subject to another that took me out of myself. They asked me what new work I was interested in; I told them about my planned visit to Japan and stressed the double happiness I should gain from it—a lifelong dream fulfilled of wandering among lovely temples, homes wrought by a nation of artists, cherry blossoms, and being part of a great enterprise which would ultimately rehabilitate the handicapped throughout the Orient.

"Whom do you consider the greatest man in the world?" was the next question.

"That depends on the kind of greatness you admire," I answered. "If you refer to science, of course Professor Einstein is the greatest genius in the world. Or are you thinking of statesmanship? If President Roosevelt maintains his high level of achievement and preserves his spiritual balance with the stupendous power he possesses he will be acclaimed as a truly creative statesman."

I did not mention Stalin because he himself says he is merely an instrument to execute Lenin's purposes. I do not think he has the imagination or breadth of judgment or generous humanity which were among Lenin's most conspicuous characteristics.

There was another question which amused me: "Do you think America has produced any great female artists?"

"How can one pass judgment in such a controversy if one cannot see paintings or distinguish one tune from another?"

I told them sculpture is palpable to the touch, and I was sorry not to have had a chance to see Malvina Hoffman's great work. I could not think of a woman novelist or poet in America today whom I would call "great", but I proudly paid homage to Dr Florence Sabin as a scientist.

I had always been up in arms against the mismanagement at Ellis Island that had so often resulted in needless suffering and injustice. The reporters told me a news item I was glad to hear: ships are not now required to

Helen Keller's Journal

put immigrants off there unless they come from a port where an infectious disease prevails.

At the pier friends almost smothered us with love and "welcome home" embraces. The customs officials, as always, were very kind and helped Polly and me with our luggage quickly.

At home the dogs had been left alone for hours. (There is no one to look after the place when we are away, except Herbert—a true comrade and helper in our household problems.) He met us with the car, and what comfort there was in the warm, strong grasp of one who had so faithfully ministered to Teacher! Several friends accompanied us to Forest Hills, evidently hoping to soften our loneliness.

On our arrival the dogs swept down upon us, a whirlwind of affection. It was fully half an hour before they subsided—and long after they were still saying with tongue, paw and tail how happy they were to have me back. I could not decide which was most adorable—Helga, the golden Dane, with her pathetic lame paw held up for me to caress, dainty Dileas, the Shetland collie in brown and white, brushing my instep to attract attention, his slender, lively mate, Wendy, crowding him away, or dear, homely, fat Maida, the Lakeland terrier.

After the friends left we talked with Herbert until far into the evening, as home folk will. I had wondered how I could endure the house as I had left it, with a baffled hope in every corner, tragedy stamped upon every room. It was a revelation to me how Herbert's sympathy and faithful workmanship had breathed cheer into the place, harmonizing it with Teacher's spirit. When I went through the rooms I found pleasant surprises wherever I looked. Teacher's desk is still there and the chair where she used to sit when she could see enough to read to me. (Her bed is gone, and that is a relief; for it was a bed of pain on which she slept ill during her last days and awoke to tasks for which she no longer had the physical strength.) The books she cherished and kept hoping to read again are there too. When I touched them I was overcome. I had watched the darkness descending upon the eyes she had used during half a century to assist me and enrich my happiness. Only by the hardest work could I shut out that mournful memory and the heart-stabbing loneliness that pursued me every moment.

Forest Hills, February 11th.

My desk and big table are literally stacked high with Braille mail. After unpacking I opened letters, magazines and pamphlets, stopping a few minutes to eat, until I was worn out, and went to bed early.

Today I did not relax until I had put away the magazines, which I shall have no time even to glance at until I return from the East. The *Reader's Digests*, which the American Printing House for the Blind publishes every month in three plump volumes, are especially tantalizing, but the work to be done before we leave for Japan is appalling. Already numberless letters are cluttering up the desk, and I need not be a prophet to foresee the multitudinous interruptions lying in wait for us the next six weeks. The worst is, I have never succeeded in mastering my irritation at being often interrupted. It shuts off my thought flow like an

Helen Keller's Journal

electric current. Yet why should I be put out by such trifles, particularly when everybody is eager to ease my steps over rough paths? Here is the study which Herbert has rearranged so that I shall have more space than ever. With Polly's good-natured helpfulness at every turn, the dogs beside me and sunshine pouring into the room I ought to be equal to a situation not new in my experience.

Forest Hills, February 12th.

This day my thoughts have dwelt much on Abraham Lincoln and how he labored that the United States might be rededicated to liberty and equality. It is true, he saw himself compelled to preserve the Union through war, but as far as might be he stressed the practice of the principles embodied in the Declaration of Independence. A son of the soil, he cut through politicians' verbiage and defeatism with simple, direct speech. He put new vitality into democracy, not by trying to force rhetorical enthusiasm but by encouraging the people's faith in it so that greater initiative and self-government might be the natural result. He reaffirmed their right to alter or overthrow the government whenever it ceased to safeguard their interests. He pointed out that there should be a fuller representation of the workers who create both the products of labor and capital.

It is well to consider these facts now, while the Senate and the press at large are raising a clamor about "changing" the Constitution, which has already been changed in many essential respects since 1790.

I have just read an adage that peoples are ungrateful. Unfortunately we do not often render thanks as we should for work nobly done. We are prone to denunciation without making our criticism constructive. We have a chronic habit of complaining that the President, Congress and state legislatures muddle things.

But deep down in the hearts of the American people, I believe, there is a grateful sense of indebtedness to Lincoln. Long they have waited for another leader who speaks their language, feels poverty's buffetings, and their disappointment has grown more bitter as one party platform after another has failed to meet their demands. This day it is my wish that under President Roosevelt's leadership the American people may advance further towards fulfilling Lincoln's dream of a democracy free from privilege and economic injustice....

The telephone has rung so frequently, Polly and I could not get a quiet moment to go over the mail. My unpacking continues between tasks assigned by the Foundation. One was to write immediately to Speaker Bankhead, Senator Black and Senator Walsh, if I remember correctly, requesting that they do what they can to get passed Bill 168, increasing the present federal appropriation from $75,000 to $175,000 for talking-book records for the blind. This continuous whirl of tasks and names taxes my distracted mind to the utmost.

Forest Hills, February 13th.

It is no exaggeration to say I have raced from 6 A.M. to 6 P.M. to clear my desk of tasks which must be done *first*. I was beginning to feel in myself "an ancient and owlish demeanor" when Amelia,[1] whom we had asked

[1] Mrs Thomas Bond, secretary to Mr Migel.

Helen Keller's Journal

to dinner, entered the study. I awoke to her cheerful greeting and to the fact that tremendous changes are taking place around us. She was looking out of the windows at two artificial lakes which have been made recently. The vast marsh which Teacher and I loved for its delicate beauty in the spring, its long bright summer grasses, the wild birds that flew over it on their autumn migrations, is being transformed into a beautiful parkway. This is part of the magnificent preparations for the World's Fair which will be almost at our door in 1939. Certainly our little house will no longer be the quiet spot, only fourteen minutes by train from the Pennsylvania Station, which has rendered my work possible for twenty years!

Forest Hills, February 14th.

Mr Gutzon Borglum surprised me this morning with a very pleasant Valentine greeting. I regret that we did not have the chance to see him again while he was in New York.

Mr Migel called this afternoon. I love the way he greets me. It is like light from the sun—warm light bringing life to growing things, shining benignly upon the shadowed and the forgotten. We talked much about how to make the trip to Japan effective. Mr Migel seeks with charm, stimulating interest and energy to win friends for the blind everywhere. That is why I call him Prospero: he is always conjuring up beautiful visions of a kindlier world for the handicapped, and the Foundation is his island where he rescues many a life, shipwrecked on the rocks of darkness.

Helen Keller's Journal

Forest Hills, February 15th.

The cold wave is broken, but the ground is still hard with frost, and the dogs refuse to stay out long.

Herbert brought Wendy home from the hospital with five puppies born yesterday. She let me take one or two in my hand—the daintiest bits of downy silk imaginable! Polly thinks two look like Dileas. Teacher's happy exclamations, her tenderness caressing these tiny creatures and pride in her darling's offspring—how vividly I can imagine every detail!

The past two days Polly and I have given every hour she could spare from household matters to business papers, reports on work for the blind, correspondence connected with the trip to Japan, and at night I was too weary to write more than a line or two in the journal.

Forest Hills, February 16th.

This morning my heart sank as I noted a bulletin of renewed dust storms in the Middle West, and that so soon after the flood. Sometimes I wonder if the federal measures to prevent that once wonderfully fertile territory from becoming a desert are too late, but I am resolved to hope for the best. . . .

I had the pleasure of seeing Mr Raymond[1] again today at Mr Migel's office. As we talked it seemed as if we were back in Boston, serving together on the Massachusetts Commission for the Blind, 1906. There were

[1] Mr Robert Raymond, Boston lawyer and family friend.

Helen Keller's Journal

only a few minutes for reminiscence, however. Mr Raymond had come to help me fulfill Teacher's wish that the provision I had made for her in case I died first be transferred to Polly. The change saddened me as I counted over the years he had been Teacher's and my faithful trustee. He holds a special place in my memories as one of the few links I have left with Boston.

This afternoon I was absorbed in work which required concentration when I was called down to see two reporters from the Associated Press and the New York *Times*. Reporters have given valuable publicity to my work for the blind, and I am always glad to show my indebtedness to them. All the same, any interruptions shake my mind when it is fixed on a subject, and it is actual pain to pick up the broken threads of thought again.

Forest Hills, February 17th.

Polly and I went to town by the new subway just opened from New York to Forest Hills. It is local, but I believe there will be an express later. Where the car stopped Polly spelled names of streets new to me— Sixty-seventh Avenue, Sixty-third Drive, Roosevelt Avenue (Jackson Heights) and Queens Plaza. I was glad of a subway ride and shall take one as often as possible coming home. I like any mode of transit—subway, elevated or the bus—that brings me into closer contact with people. Polly describes their faces or their talk. Through the sense of smell impressions tell me much— powder, perfume, tobacco, shoe polish. I also sense freshness and good taste in the odors of soap, clean garments, silks and gloves. From exhalations I often know the work people are engaged in because the odors of wood, iron, paint or the office cling to their clothes. In an automobile I miss these intimate revelations of how my fellow creatures live.

Forest Hills, February 18th.

I was distressed this morning that the "safety" net at the San Francisco Bridge gave way, plunging ten men into the water, 280 feet below. Polly and I are to sail from San Francisco April 1st, and as we pass the bridge I shall bow my head, remembering the lives which have gone into its construction.

Touched by this emotion, I dropped everything and turned belatedly to an article in the *Reader's Digest*—"John L. Lewis, Labor's Looming Force"—first published in *Fortune*. This is the first time since Eugene Debs's earlier years that I have had any lively hope of a labor movement in this country. Whether John Lewis is a genuine radical or not I am uncertain, but he appears to have courage, wisdom and the wide influence required to organize the less skilled workers who are the majority of the American population. If he succeeds in mobilizing even a part of the laboring class to bargain collectively for wages, hours and better living conditions they will thus secure a voice in the government and make it more truly a democracy. His massive personality, amazing powers of persuasion and defiance of the lightning—corporate wealth mightier than any political empire earth ever witnessed—command my admiration. . . .

Andrea called this afternoon with Mr Peter Lubbock

Helen Keller's Journal

and two Japanese reporters. I was agreeably surprised on hearing that Mr Lubbock is the son of the distinguished naturalist. He showed delight when I told him that as a child one of my favorite books was his father's *The Beauties of Nature*. He asked me if I perceived differences in places I visited. This was a chance for a little dissertation on what I find out from smells about a city or town. I tried to describe London's odor peculiarities—large smell areas of fresh grass and hawthorn blossoms in springtime, broken up among the thoroughfares; in winter a heavy, smoke-clogged mist. I spoke also of the towns in California, Oregon and Washington State which have different fragrances according to the kinds of fruit growing around them.

The Japanese complimented me by saying that the story of Hanawa, the great blind scholar, and my own were an encouragement not only to the handicapped but to normal people in their country. They expressed pleasure when I praised the courageous activities of Japanese women as teachers, philanthropists and social service workers. Among them I mentioned Baroness Ishimoto, the Margaret Sanger of Japan, who is at the head of the birth-control clinic in Tokyo. The reporters wondered if I would speak on peace as well as the education of the blind and the deaf. I feared the militarists would repent allowing me to enter Japan if I did.

"But if you pray for world peace as a part of your good-will message," they assured me, "it will be an influence for higher things."

In today's mail I received a cordial note from Speaker Bankhead, promising that he would do his best to get Bill 168 passed. There were lovely letters from my English friends, and not a word have I written them

Helen Keller's Journal

since I left Britain! If this congestion of work continues this journal will turn into another "Diary of Revolution."

Forest Hills, February 19th.

The singing-book for the blind has come! There was an editorial in the New York *Times* today about a singing-book called *Wild Birds of America*. It told how Albert Brand, of Cornell University, studied bird notes, placing a sound-reproducing apparatus near the nests and catching the songs all the way from the chipping sparrow to the cardinal. What a joy this book will be to blind people! It will mean a new interest for them, identifying the birds they hear and studying their habitats and migrations.

We were with Amelia twice in the city today. She and Polly worked on our bank accounts before and after lunch. I was gratified when Amelia, whose fine business sense I admire, declared to me that Polly is an excellent bookkeeper....

Lunched with Mr Julian[1] at the Waldorf-Astoria. He is a friend whose enthusiasm and resourcefulness in saving human eyes make me glad and confident in my work. With him are associated tasks which appeal to me most—pleading with people over the radio to safeguard their sight, showing in pictures how they can improve their vision and writing letters about prevention of blindness. This time he talked about a new series of radio playlets he is preparing. His idea is to broadcast outstanding episodes in the lives of several groups of distinguished men, like George Washington

[1] Mr M. J. Julian, president of the Better Vision Institute.

and Benjamin Franklin, and scientists and physicians who were persecuted for asserting that the prevalence of blindness could be much lessened.

While we were at table a lady came over and made herself known to us. With emotion I heard her name—Warden Lawes's wife. I mentioned the articles I had seen by Mr Lawes in the *Reader's Digest* and told her how deeply I honor him for his humanity to prisoners. She said there were two blind men at Sing Sing. She pressed my hand tenderly when I exclaimed, "That is the only real darkness, is it not?"

Forest Hills, February 20th.

This is Polly's birthday, and I am grieving that Teacher is not here to celebrate it with me. I could not think of a way to make it the joyous occasion it should be. There were tears in our eyes when I wished her happiness which neither of us could feel. But at least my wishes reflected the tenderness with which I remembered the twenty-three years she had devoted herself to us both.

We read that China has made peace with the Reds. I hope that means a strong united front in solving the gigantic problems which have convulsed the country....

I was wrought up over the worst siege Madrid has undergone. Such fratricide revolts me all the more because I used to hear my father tell what a shambles the South became during the American Civil War....

This afternoon two ladies called—a teacher from the Clark School for the Deaf at Northampton and a Japanese student who is preparing herself there to teach the deaf in her country. The student spoke English charmingly and was full of interesting talk about places she hoped I would visit in Japan.

Our trip will soon be all planned, I believe. I expect hard but interesting work. I have been requested to speak for the deaf as well as the blind—a double task I have not attempted before on a single tour. I understand that we are to appear six times in each place—at a mass meeting, a children's meeting, before women's clubs, social service workers, specialists and at schools for the handicapped. I do not yet know whether we are to speak once or twice a day. . . .

Amelia invited Polly and me to a birthday dinner at her apartment and put forth a world of kindly art to brighten us up. Afterwards we went to the theater to see three of Noel Coward's playlets. Two I liked very much were "Still Life" and "A Family Album", but I was disgusted to be caught falling asleep off and on. I was not the least bit bored either; I had got up at 5 A.M. to allow myself time for interruptions and was more tired than I realized.

Forest Hills, February 21st.

This morning I was sad because of heart-hunger. I missed the old Manse in Scotland and the beautiful service at St Bride's which Polly and I had attended every Sunday. Then came gladness that I had long ago formed the habit of holding a little service by myself Sundays—a chapter in the Bible, a Psalm and short prayers. Who is like unto God—the Teacher who is above all temples and dogmas?

Helen Keller's Journal

With pleasure I noted in *John Milton Magazine*, a Braille interdenominational religious monthly for the blind, that three hotels in New York provide a chapel where one may worship or meditate alone. Only religion which evenly blends the personal gospel and the social gospel can endure or keep the church alive.

There was another item in the magazine that set me thinking. At the suggestion of an atheistic society the Gideon Bibles were removed from a six-hundred-room hotel. The very next night two hundred inquiries were made for the missing Bibles. This seems to indicate that, despite all statements to the contrary, a deep religious sentiment is silently developing in America.

I remember how I was irritated not long ago when a man insisted on discussing atheism, although no one in the company was interested. I felt like saying to him, "This is a world bewildering enough without your telling us that God is a tyrant and our comfort a delusion. If you can only sneer at the island of faith in our ocean of uncertainties you are inhuman to do it."

This evening a man prayed over the radio. Polly noticed how he rattled off his words like Mother Goose's rhymes. How different from her brother's sincere, carefully enunciated prayers. I have been sorry to hear frequently that many devout American worshipers have no sense of rhythm or beauty in chant or prayer.

Forest Hills, February 22nd.

The *North American Review* contains an account of George Washington's inauguration that surprises me as truth stranger than fiction. On March 4, 1789,

Helen Keller's Journal

Washington was to have been officially proclaimed first president of the United States. Only the day before was it discovered that a sufficient quorum could not be raised either in the House or the Senate. Without the quorum the electoral votes could not be counted. Letters were dispatched to the absentees in frantic haste, but not until April 6th could a quorum be raised. A week was spent discussing the title to be used in addressing the chief executive. Many felt that the mere title of president was too plebeian—did not fire companies and cricket clubs have presidents? To this day the question is still unsettled.

On April 30th, just before Washington appeared, the Senate was in confusion because no one knew whether to stand or sit while the president delivered his address. This question was sidetracked when they found that they had forgotten to send the proper committee to escort the president-elect from his lodgings to the Capitol. The committee was rushed off. Then it was recalled that there was no Bible upon which to administer the oath of office, and a messenger was sent posthaste to a Masonic lodge near by for a copy!

I do not know which touches me most—the valiant general's timidity as he spoke with a shaky voice, the spontaneity with which the entire assembly arose and stood all the time he was reading his address, or the courage with which he and the inexperienced nation shouldered the new democracy. . . .

Dr Fosdick's remarks about labor in the New York *Times* interested me. He says the verdict of history will be that labor in the main was right. He thinks, too, that those who are at the top are not essentially "bad"— they simply do not feel the hardships of industry as the workers do. I wonder! I know some lovable personalities that walk serenely in the vineyards of abundance with no comprehension of economics. On the other hand, it cannot be denied that there are capitalists who have *seen* and *felt* the wretched life conditions under which millions toil—and yet, once having won a comfortable existence, cling to things as they are with hidebound selfishness. . . .

What a commentary I read on the stupidity of styles in modern shoe wear! Nine out of every ten persons in the United States suffer from foot defects. . . .

This morning while searching my files for some papers I had mislaid I came upon a portrait in relief of Sir Arthur Pearson which he sent me twenty-seven years ago. I could not recollect when I had touched it last; but the moment it met my hand he seemed to be right at my side. Tenderly my heart repeated his story—how after losing his sight in middle age and relinquishing his chief work, conducting newspapers and periodicals, he refused to look upon the disastrous side of blindness. He threw himself into one enterprise, then another, developing the activities of the National Institute for the Blind, collecting the Prince of Wales Relief Fund at the beginning of the World War and establishing St Dunstan's Hostel for Blinded Soldiers and Sailors. As he told me he created the hostel so that sightless men discharged from hospital "might come into a little world where things they could not do would be forgotten and the principal concern would be with things they *could* do." I am moved as I think of his offer to have whatever I wished to read embossed free. Among the books he had transcribed for me were Turgenev's *Spring Freshets* and *Smoke,* Conrad's *Youth* and *The*

Helen Keller's Journal

Heart of Darkness, Under Western Eyes, Swinburne's *Atalanta* and *Songs Before Sunrise*. It is indeed a rich store of happy memories that the kind face I touch in the portrait evokes.

Forest Hills, February 23rd.

The Supreme Court reform battle continues unabated. . . .

I received a letter from Senator Black saying he would try to have Bill 168 reported out of committee soon as I requested. Also a dear letter from Lilie de la Nux thanking me for a copy of my book, *Midstream*, and charmingly describing the big house where she is spending some weeks in Canada. . . .

This has been one of the rare days on which Polly is left undisturbed long enough to read me the large batch of mail always waiting for us. Then followed a long sitting for me, answering letters, autographing books and pictures which Polly wrapped and addressed. After seventeen hours we are just beginning to relax.

A gust of irritability is blowing through me just now because there has been a recurrence of a tendency in some people to try to run my affairs. This seems all the stranger to me because since I was seventeen I have arranged my own life. At the age of twenty-two I began working very hard for whatever money I have earned the past thirty-four years. Of my own accord I have undertaken public responsibilities in America and other lands. After Teacher's health broke down I worked very much alone with Polly's hand to furnish information and her voice to reinforce my halting speech. Yet there are still those who appear to think it is incumbent upon them to alter my life according to their own ideas! There was some excuse when I was young and bewildered in the search of something worth doing. But Mother and Teacher knew me better than anybody else ever did, and they never dictated the course of action I should follow. There have always been other friends with power to advance the work for the blind, and they respect my desire as a human being to be free. It is beautiful to consider how their co-operation has increased my happiness and rendered possible whatever I have accomplished. However, unless I keep on my guard against uncalled-for though well-meant interference they cannot help me any more than they can help any other person who weakly surrenders his will to another.

Forest Hills, February 24th.

Polly and I had appointments early this morning, she at Dr Hinsdale's, 8.30 A.M., to have her ear treated, and I at the dressmaker's, nine-thirty. I stayed there an hour and a half. I know I shall need many frocks on the Japanese trip, and planning such a wardrobe in the midst of pressing duties is a problem, no matter how fond a woman may be of pretty clothes.

Called at 11 A.M. for the first time on a literary agent, Mrs Carol Hill, whose advice will, I am sure, be very helpful to me in new ventures as an author.

Home to lunch. Barney[1] came to tea at three, and we had a long chat—we had not had a chance before to tell her about our visit to Scotland and Paris.

[1]Mrs Saybolt, wife of Miss Keller's family physician.

Helen Keller's Journal

Nella Braddy[1] was here for dinner. She gave her news and heard ours. (I had written her only once this winter.) We talked about Teacher and how it still seems as if she was here but yesterday, how I plan everything with her in mind and watch for her morning and night. Nella showed a letter from Mr Schramm to Doubleday, Doran and Company about my refusal to have the comments on Lenin in *Midstream* omitted. Mr Schramm intimated that they would exercise their authority over me and see to it that I fulfill my obligations to the German publishing firm. Nella said everyone in the House of Doubleday feels as I do about the right of freedom of utterance and they are going to write Mr Schramm to that effect.

Not a line written today. It is ludicrous and disconcerting how circumstances thwart me just at the times I most want to settle down for a steady pegging away at my desk.

Forest Hills, February 25th.

Today's news concerning armaments was not reassuring. Last year millions in America and Britain were living on the dole, and many countries were confronted with a serious shortage of decent dwellings for the workers. Yet the nations found altogether eleven billion dollars to continue the insanity of war preparations. Now the British government is planning to spend seven billion five hundred million dollars strengthening the

[1] Mrs Keith Henney, as Nella Braddy, author of *Anne Sullivan Macy, the Story Behind Helen Keller*.

army, navy and air forces, so as to "cope with a potential enemy clearly indicated, but not named."

There was an item confirming Jesus' declaration that wherever two or three are gathered in the name of the Lord, His strength shall go forth with them. Two church leaders, Michael Cardinal Faulhaber, Archbishop of Munich, and the minister of the Confessional Synod of the German Evangelical Church have led devoted followers in bold campaigns to prevent the Nazis from controlling the churches and using them as channels, like the universities, for government propaganda. It remains to be seen whether Hitler will carry out his decree of a free church plebiscite and full self-determination.

With a thrill I learned that the sweet potato can be used for starch in many industries as well as for food. This is another chemical miracle made possible by the genius of Dr George Washington Carver. It would be a beautiful experience if I might meet Dr Carver, whom I venerate as a brilliant scientist and as a saint. Humbly I, who have enjoyed every advantage that love and education can bestow, meditate upon his story—no record of his birth, no knowledge of his parents, a childhood spent in slavery, an education earned by ceaseless drudgery, a passionate desire to serve his own people which was fulfilled when Booker T. Washington invited him to teach at Tuskegee. Who can harden his heart against a man so Christlike in his unworldliness, giving the results of his experiments free for the benefit of humanity, refusing a salary of one hundred thousand dollars? What incalculable wealth there is in the three hundred products he has extracted from the peanut and the one hundred from the sweet potato! And all he asks is to have it devoted to the well-being of whites and Negroes alike throughout the South. Among the historic sayings of our time posterity will no doubt quote oftenest Dr Carver's words to his students, "When you do the common things of life in an uncommon way you will command the attention of the world."

My good friend, Alexander Woollcott, invited Polly and me to his apartment, and we called this afternoon. We had a quiet but pleasant visit. He was tenderly understanding when we spoke of Teacher and the difference her going had made in our home. He said he was going to broadcast a tribute to her the evening of March 2nd and asked me what recollections I had of the day she came. I recalled standing at the porch door, feeling Mother's steps when she returned from the station and loving arms, which I did not recognize, thrown about me. How wildly I tried to escape, not knowing it was a friend with a key for my release from the worst jailers—isolation and anger! The contrast was startling as I remembered the day Teacher bore me, screaming, upstairs for a lesson and the heavenly morning when I discovered that words were a means of getting whatever I wanted, and the joy of *knowing* irradiated my darkness.

The next topic was the trip to Japan. As Mr Woollcott has traveled there he laughingly advised me to practice sitting on the floor before we started. We discussed Japanese etiquette, and I trembled to think how many "breaks" I might commit. He related how once he was invited to a Japanese dinner and how a lovely geisha girl kept passing wine around. Each time she came to him Mr Woollcott nodded and smiled, meaning that his glass should be refilled, but to his astonishment

Helen Keller's Journal

it remained empty. Afterwards he found out that the girl thought he was declining the wine and that he should have held out his glass for her to fill it.

As we talked a darling coal-black cat, soft as eiderdown, nestled up to me, and Mr Woollcott's beautiful Alsatian, Duchess, also black, kept laying her head on my knee. As she is a "Seeing Eye" dog she knew how to make friends with me quickly. I decided then and there that I would give Mr Woollcott one of the Shetland puppies, black with a white tip on his tail—I thought they would all go together handsomely in the color scheme. Besides, Mr Woollcott is a true lover of animals, and I was sure Teacher would wish him to have such an exquisite pet in return for all his dear kindnesses to her.

Forest Hills, February 26th.

Early this morning at the dressmaker's again—a long time. From there Polly and I went to buy materials for more dresses. Andrea went with us. It is a pleasure to shop with her, for she has perfect taste and a good fairy's delightful way of helping out in difficulties.

We three lunched at the Mascotte, an attractively quiet French restaurant on Sixtieth Street which Andrea knows well. Polly and I recounted our adventures in Paris, Andrea talked about the airship Hindenburg on which she flew during its second voyage. We told each other that we would cross the Atlantic on the first transoceanic passenger plane. Andrea was the same sweet, animated queen of hearts as ever—all the graces in one. I do not wonder people everywhere are attracted by her beauty and vivid intelligence. . . .

Helen Keller's Journal

The air had been full of snow for some time. Back home, I felt a New Englander's joy in the light, soft, virgin snow mounds on the privet hedges and white festoons on the vines at the front door. The flakes are big and will be gone by tomorrow or Sunday; but a beautiful snowstorm like this is unforgettable, especially to one who wearies of hard pavements and brick buildings in the city during winter.

Forest Hills, February 27th.

Work the livelong day. But there were glad thoughts to lighten my tasks. This morning I received the good news that a commission for the blind has after long years of effort been appointed in Oregon, and there will probably be another in Washington State this spring. Thirty states have established commissions for the blind since I served the first one in Massachusetts, 1906, and this alone would make me feel repaid for the struggle of almost a lifetime to interest people in the handicapped. But I had a wonderful surprise today, learning that a Mr Duff, who, it is thought, heard me speak for the foundation in Washington, D.C., 1926, had left us a hundred thousand dollars! I thought such big contributions to the work for the blind were forever of the past, since financial depression had either crippled or put a quietus on numerous philanthropic activities in America. Now I dare hope again that I may raise the second million to set the Foundation firmly on its feet as a national agency rendering effective service to those deprived of sight in every part of this country. Mr Migel is planning a campaign to begin next October which he thinks will be successful. Instead of holding meetings as heretofore we intend to call on different groups of influential givers and solicit donations. It would seem that the Foundation had by now established itself among the societies upon whom even the most capricious dispensers of bounty would look with favor.

With this hopeful prospect smiling upon me I remain exceedingly grateful for the first million which was given dollar by dollar at public meetings in 143 cities during two years.

The Arches, near North Philadelphia, February 28th.

The weather was overcast when Polly and I left for Philadelphia at 2 P.M., but the thought of Mrs Walz, with whom we are always happy at the Arches, made sunshine for us. Going down on the train Polly read from the New York *Times* a statesmanlike speech by Governor La Follette supporting the President's plan for changes in the Supreme Court. I realize more than ever what a regrettable spectacle we have had of a few judges blocking beneficent legislation for a hundred and thirty million people. The danger of having the Constitution twisted and misconstrued to support vested interests and prejudices must be guarded against if American democracy is to maintain a progressive character....

My heart leaped up to salute the courageous geisha girls of Osaka, striking not only for more pay but also for their human rights to education, healthful living and personal freedom. In such women speaks the voice of all that is noblest in the hearts of the Japanese....

I know Britain does not desire to fight. Its craving for empire has been satisfied, and I hope that in some mysterious way its terrifying armament program may stem the lust of hungry imperialistic nations. But if that happens Britain will prove itself exceptional in the history of empires. Its victory will be one of mind, not force.

There was a verse that stirred me as if it had been a rallying call from Teacher:

> *Stout heart to steep hill!*
> *Earth melts behind you.*
> *Firm faith and strong will!*
> *No mist shall blind you.*
> *Up, up the crag, bravely endeavor,*
> *Stout heart to steep hill,*
> *Starward forever!*

Mrs Walz welcomed us at the station in flutters of delight and brought us in her car out to the suburb where the Arches stands—large, love-filled, cheery with her own brightness. For a few minutes we three sat in the sun parlor chatting over a cup of tea. Mrs Walz happened to tell us that Mrs Edward Bok was speaking at the Civic Club not far from here this afternoon, and I was eager to go there. It was years since I had seen Mrs Bok, and her friendship is woven into the warp and woof of my story. I never forget her husband's generous enthusiasm when he urged me to write my autobiography for the *Ladies' Home Journal*. I bless the vision that caused him to open the periodical to my articles on the causes of blindness and its prevention, despite the fact that in those days other editors held the subject taboo. It thrills me to recall how he helped me with his eloquence and five thousand dollars to launch splendidly the campaign for the blind of America

Helen Keller's Journal

in November 1924. The warmth with which he praised Teacher as a great woman is another cherished memory. Since he died Mrs Bok has continued to take an interest in me, and her sympathy has renewed my courage when obstacles seemed insurmountable.

We went to the club. As Mrs Bok was to speak, I did not wish to disturb her, but on hearing my name she greeted me affectionately. As she went on the stage she touched my cheek softly, saying, "I wish you might put wings on my words—I fear you may find the subject dull."

No, indeed! It was a topic especially appealing to me —community life.

Mrs Bok is the chairman of the Community Association, which her husband founded, and she explains its work to young people who do not know about it. Many constructive activities are carried on—establishing schools, playgrounds and shops where they are needed, safeguarding public health, planting trees and flowers wherever possible, fostering the neighborliness upon which true civilization rests. If similar associations might be formed in every town and city, what a wealth there would be of alert, healthy men and women, well-ordered cities and picturesque country life in America.

The Arches, March 1st.

After breakfast we sat with Mrs Walz and her son Edward in the sun parlor, soaking ourselves in the warmth of a spring day. We talked about aviation with Edward, who is deeply interested in air travel. He says, and I can believe it, that according to accident statistics motoring is more dangerous than flying. So keenly aware am I of this that it always makes me nervous to have anyone leave my home in a car. Many friends have been seriously injured in automobile smashes in spite of strict precautions. Personally, I prefer the subway or the elevated. "I wonder how many people will be able to stand airsickness?" I said to Edward. With pleasure I heard that ten thousand feet up in the air it is calm, and few if any will suffer at that height. Edward predicted that before long airships will be constructed to fly much higher and faster. What an exciting prospect—leaving New York in the morning and arriving in London in time for dinner!

It is refreshing to converse with a friend like Mrs Walz who loves pictures, flowers, young people, finds beauty in simple things, creates joy for others and herself wherever she goes. . . .

We arrived in Washington at 4.30 P.M., where we are spending the night with Lenore and Phil.[1] At the station I was overjoyed because their pretty daughter Constance walked down the platform to meet us. Only last December my heart had been wrung by the news that she was stricken with infantile paralysis—Constance, seventeen years old, one of the brightest, most active girls I ever knew. I did not expect that she would be able to walk again without crutches, and there she was moving towards us as if nothing had ever laid her low! Her case illustrates what may be accomplished by prompt treatment of the dread disease when its symptoms first appear.

We found Lenore in bed with a broken ankle which

[1] Dr and Mrs Philip Smith, friends of Miss Keller's since her college days. Dr Smith is chief Alaskan geologist of the United States Geological Survey.

was likely to keep her confined for three weeks. She was all eagerness for our news since she saw us last, November 2nd. Remorsefully I realized how far I had fallen behind in letters to my closest relatives and friends. As I sat on her bed other scenes rose before my mind—her coming to our home as soon as she knew Teacher was dying, her tender ministrations to Polly and me in our anguish, her helpfulness every hour—telephoning, meeting people and advising with us about funeral arrangements. In memory I felt Lenore's comforting handclasp and Phil's, too, as we sat together at the impressively touching service the afternoon Teacher's ashes were placed in the Chapel of St Joseph of Arimathea in the National Cathedral at Washington. Thus death has rendered even sweeter the friendship which bound Teacher and me to these two dear people in college days.

Lenore's cheerful talk brought me back to the present, and we were soon deep in the Japanese trip. We recalled that Dr Davis, a prominent oculist, had urged me when I was here before to go to China with a message for reducing the frightful prevalence of blindness in the East. I had just received a cablegram from Mr Fryer, director of the School for the Blind, Shanghai, begging me to come to China and plead the cause of its sightless multitudes. We got in touch with Dr Davis by telephone, and he called this evening. He is still enthusiastic over the idea of my visiting China, and what I hear from him further will dictate my next step.

Constance and her sister Katharine make me feel young again. I enjoy "powwowing" with Phil over the delightful times Teacher and I had with him, Lenore and John in Cambridge and Wrentham.

Helen Keller's Journal

Forest Hills, March 2nd.

We bade Phil and Lenore good-by early this morning, as I had an appointment with Bob[1] to meet several senators and, if possible, persuade them to report Bill 168 out of committee before I leave this country. (Fears had been expressed that it might get pigeonholed after it passed the House.) It is important to get the bill passed now, so that the Foundation may purchase additional equipment and double the output of talking-books. We were at the Senate Office Building two hours, traveling miles up and down in the elevators and across long corridors in the hope of capturing this or that potential champion for the blind. First we met Senator David I. Walsh, of Massachusetts. He was in a great hurry, as is his wont, but his greeting was friendly, and I succeeded in making my request before the interview was cut short. Next we descended upon Senator Hugo Black. He bore my invasion with gracious Southern courtesy, asked why I wanted Bill 168 passed and, after some discussion, said he would do what he could for it. I had gone to see him last spring in an effort to obtain a federal grant for pensions to the blind, and I was glad he was willing to listen again amid a heavy pressure of other more important duties. His son was there and kindly volunteered to guide us about the building. With his help we located Senator Royal S. Copeland. I told the ex-physician how deeply interested I was in

[1] Robert Irwin, executive director of the American Foundation for the Blind.

his public health campaign, for I felt the physical welfare of the people should be the government's first and last concern. He assented heartily and expressed a sympathetic attitude towards the handicapped. He seemed reserved about the bill, but somehow I think he will support it. Also we saw Senator La Follette. To my delight he shook hands with me so cordially that it seemed as if we had long known each other. I asked about his mother and his sister, Miss La Follette, whom I had met at the Civic Club in New York years ago, and was pleased to hear good news of them. I said I was confident that all would be well with the American people, since strong men like his brother and himself are giving vitality to the concepts of justice, public welfare and economic freedom. Then I suggested that he serve the majority of the blind who demand talking-books by voting for Bill 168. He was noncommittal, but he said he would be glad to help them in any way he could. Somehow it seemed that my endeavors to interest the Senate in the bill had not been wholly futile.

I was amused when we went down to the basement and got on the tiny subway car which the senators use in going to and from the Capitol. We stopped at the House Office Building, where Mr Kent Keller, of Illinois, met us. He introduced me to several members of the Committee on the Library who had recommended that Bill 168 be passed, among them Congressman Lord, of New York, Mr Holt, of West Virginia, and Mr Gale. I understood that some members were strong for the talking-book but equally interested in Braille. I stressed the fact that the great majority of those who lose their sight are adults and find Braille difficult or impossible to learn. The talking-book will never take the place of

Helen Keller's Journal

Braille in a blind child's education, but it is an indispensable source of diversion and knowledge to an ever larger number of people blinded in mature years.

I had a few minutes with Mr Keller after the others left the room. It was a pleasure to talk with one so genial and expansive. He said he wished there was time to show me the city. He described the magnificent view which inspires him at his work from one window—the dome of the Capitol, the Lincoln Memorial and George Washington Monument, the Potomac and in the distance Arlington Cemetery. Also he described to me the diagrams of the building to shelter the Mellon art collection, which will be a superb structure.

It was nearly half-past twelve when Polly and I rushed off to catch the one o'clock airplane that was the only way I could get home in time to see a Japanese reporter who was coming at 3.30 P.M. On the ground a high wind was blowing, but as we ascended it became calmer. We had met the pilot on the plane several times. He spoke to us, and I was amazed to hear how much faster we were going than the last time we flew from Washington. It took only an hour and twenty minutes to reach Newark! The day was beautiful, and the flight was perfect. I felt at home as the plane climbed the winds and shot forward among the sunbeams and the clouds. I was sorry when we arrived at our destination, for I had enjoyed a delicious release from the physical restraints that beset me in the house and on the street.

Sitting in an airplane, I always perceive many sensations. I catch the throb of the motor like the insistent beat of a drum in an orchestra of vibrations. I sense the machine trembling like a thing alive. I feel its straining and tugging upward as strong winds tug at a tree, and

Helen Keller's Journal

I know when we return to earth by the downward gliding motion of the machine.

Herbert met us at the airport, and Polly said he looked very ill. He was in great pain and had all he could do getting us home. We sent for Dr Saybolt at once; he found Herbert down with serious gall-bladder trouble and ordered him in hospital tomorrow. Polly and I talked to the reporter as best we could between interruptions. He asked if I would send a message to the women of Japan, and I wrote it for him on my typewriter.

At 7.30 P.M. Alexander Woollcott broadcast a moving tribute to Teacher—"a memorial to one of the great women of our time—or any time." His words, full of perceptive tenderness, caressed my fingers as Polly spelled them. She said he spoke beautifully, with a throb of emotion in his voice. Tears welled up in my eyes as he told how fifty years ago tomorrow Anne Sullivan "started a work which has been recognized the world around as one of the heartening triumphs of the human spirit." I never felt prouder than when he said she "was made of the original stuff of creation." The sense of responsibility made me tremble as he spoke of the torch "handed on from Dr Howe to Laura Bridgman, from Laura to Anne Sullivan, from Anne to Helen Keller, from Helen to . . ." We clasped hands as he ended with "This to Helen Keller and Polly Thomson as they start for the Far East. Our prayers—and Anne Sullivan's, too, maybe the prayers of all of us go with you to Japan and back—now and always."

After the broadcast I sat quietly by the fire with the dogs around me, my thoughts straying far into the happy thirds of March when Teacher had lived at my side. I resolved that each third of March I live alone shall justify her faith in my will to be happy in sunshine and strong to endure in the shadows.

Forest Hills, March 3rd.

Herbert was still suffering terribly this morning. He did not want to leave us in the midst of everything, but I knew he must go, and Polly took him to the hospital.

Heartsick and discouraged, I went down to see Wendy and her darling puppies. It was a comfort to stroke their lovely forms and notice how they grow. By their uncertain motions I know they have not got their eyes open yet.

No sooner had Polly returned than we hurried away to take out her naturalization papers. Judge Richards had done all he could to expedite matters, but we were kept an hour and a half. Polly was asked innumerable questions. Then I was called in as a witness. Barney, who had come with us, took me to the desk. I was required to hold up my hand and swear that I am a citizen supporting the government of the United States. Then the judge placed my fingers on his lips and asked my name and where I live. I answered, and, turning to Barney, he told her to repeat his words while I read them from her lips: "Do you recognize Miss Thomson as a citizen of the United States?" Dr Saybolt also served as a witness.

Polly did not get her papers after all, because there are some details about which the immigration authorities are not quite satisfied, and she must appear be-

Helen Keller's Journal

fore them again in the autumn. Those alien laws are most exasperating and confusing.

It was nearly three o'clock when we five lunched at the Pomonok Country Club. It was Judge Richards' birthday, and Polly and I arranged a luncheon in honor of the occasion. I would have given much to be in a festive mood: he has such a big, warm heart and never lets go a chance to do us a kindness.

Stopped at the hospital a few minutes to see Herbert; then I wrote until and after dinner. This is the strangest, saddest third of March I ever spent, and Teacher has not seemed so far away as tonight.

Forest Hills, March 4th.

The weather turned bitter cold during the night; the furnace fire died down; and this morning Polly found one of the puppies sick. She gave it a little whisky and put it in another room. I kept Wendy and the other puppies in my study for warmth.

Another fitting at the dressmaker's. While there we received a telephone message from the house that the ailing puppy was dying. We got back as soon as we could, hoping to save it, but in vain. Nothing is more pathetic than a tiny, dainty creature dead before it has known the joy of living in the light.

Wrote to Mr Woollcott, thanking him for his perfect tribute and requesting a copy so that Polly may have it put into Braille for me and place it among the treasures in the Helen Keller Memorial Room of the American Foundation for the Blind.

Herbert is no better. He is to be X-rayed tomorrow.

Helen Keller's Journal

Polly is up at daylight to start things going, let the dogs out, prepare breakfast. A girl, Lena, helps clean the house, but she is young and cannot cook or do the countless things Herbert does so excellently. We have jumped many hurdles in housekeeping, but never one like this! However, I am thankful to have a pair of hands available for other work besides writing.

Forest Hills, March 5th.

Continuous writing. I am seeing nobody for a day or two until I catch up with a month's accumulated tasks sufficiently to know "where I am at."

Wendy is sick with milk fever. Polly took her to the vet but she has returned and Polly is feeding her with milk every few hours.

Forest Hills, March 6th.

Still very cold. Polly was up in the night and again at six o'clock to look after Wendy. I told her she must not kill herself trying to be companion, secretary, housewife, international worker and nurse all in one. Finally she fixed Wendy and the puppies up nice and warm and sent them back to the vet's, where I know they will be taken care of properly.

A long letter from Mr Iwahashi, giving our itinerary and program. It sounds as if we were expected to make six speeches in each city. That is a physical impossibility. I shall consult with Mr Migel and see what can be done. Such a crowded schedule would prevent us from

Helen Keller's Journal

accepting invitations or seeing the country or observing the courtesies that guests should not neglect. At Mr Iwahashi's request I wrote a greeting to the Japanese people which they are to receive before we arrive. . . .

No doubt Mayor La Guardia's words about the "brown-shirt fanatic in a chamber of horrors" have laid the train for an explosion of Nazi hatred and caused uneasiness among the prudent, but whatever the consequences may be, they will not daunt Fiorello La Guardia.

How impressively he rises before my mind as I saw him in November 1934 at Evangeline Booth's farewell meeting in Madison Square Garden! I had paid an admiring tribute to my friend, the commander—the great woman leader with followers in eighty-six countries—and Polly and I were waiting for her to address the immense audience. Beside us sat the mayor, who had just been elected. Again I feel his hand vibrant with sturdy manhood. In reply to my congratulations he thanked me and spoke grimly of the deep-rooted obstacles that must be wrenched aside before New York could be made a home fit for the whole population to live in. Ever since, I have felt his Herculean energy tugging at those myriad obstacles—graft, social blindness and greed—and my wonder grows as they move inch by inch before his undiscouraged onset. A few years ago when he was a member of the national House of Representatives he and Senator Norris got Congress to pass a bill outlawing the "yellow dog contract" that forbade workers to organize or join a union. Surely if he is re-elected he will go far towards supplying food for the undernourished in the city and ameliorating the lot of the unemployed. . . .

Helen Keller's Journal

This afternoon Polly and I went with Amelia to see *Richard II*. I had not read the play since I was a girl, and I regretted that I had not had a chance to go over it again. I was deeply stirred by Maurice Evans' tragic power in the role of King Richard II, especially in the surrender of the crown, Ian Keith's superb dignity as Bolingbroke, the weeping queen in the garden and the speech of John of Gaunt. I was especially interested in Augustin Duncan, whose wife, Margherita Sargent, I have known since we were classmates at Radcliffe College. Mr Duncan plays the part of John of Gaunt with a peculiar appeal because he himself is blind. It fills me with glad pride that one who trails the dark way should have such an impressive role in a drama which many people consider the finest production in New York for many a year.

We had Leslie,[1] Jan Wasilewski[2] and his wife to a belated dinner. Lena waited on the table nicely, and everyone seemed happy. The Great Adventure—Japan—excited them not a little. Mayor La Guardia's unfortunate remark was commented upon. Jan had much to say about economic difficulties in his country.

Now the guests are gone, and Maida is begging me to come to bed. She stands up and lays her smoke-blue head on my knee, now she slides down on her forepaws, turning her head in a manner that reminds me of a Chinese idol. I wonder if a Lakeland terrier does that when he digs a hole in the earth.

[1] Leslie Fulenwider, conductor of the Famous Features Syndicate.
[2] Jan Wasilewski, Polish vice-consul in New York.

Helen Keller's Journal

Forest Hills, March 7th.

Mr and Mrs Migel and Mr Wright[1] were here this afternoon. We discussed the Japanese program, and all agreed that it is too strenuous. Mr Migel said he would send a letter to Japan by air mail suggesting that our visit there be extended or the dates cut in half. He wishes me especially to be here next October, fresh for the campaign to complete the endowment fund.

I was glad to see Mr Wright. He is another loyal friend who has been interested in all that concerned Teacher and me since I was fourteen years old. He was delighted that I am to say a word for the deaf as well as the blind. "The deaf of Japan need friends even more than the blind do," he said.

Herbert looked brighter when Polly saw him this evening, but there is a probability that he will be operated on this week.

Forest Hills, March 8th.

This morning's New York *Times* states that the blind workers under the Pittsburgh branch of the Pennsylvania Association for the Blind have entered the second week of their sit-down strike. Naturally I am entirely on their side. . . .

Nella was here all day helping Polly and me with materials we shall need for our lectures in Japan.

Herbert was very ill again last night. The X-ray

[1] Mr John Wright, founder and director of the Wright Oral School for the Deaf in New York which Miss Keller attended as a child.

photographs show gallstones that must be removed. The only comforting thought at this time is that the earthborn clouds which darken our days do not touch Teacher's heavenly blessedness. It is well for me to work, work and again work. Trouble may not leave me altogether, but work forces it to take its normal place in my life, having no more importance than many other experiences.

Forest Hills, March 9th.

After thirty years the steel industrialists, the bitterest foes of organized labor, are capitulating to the C.I.O. A momentous chapter is being written in United States history.

Forest Hills, March 10th.

At Dr Berens', 9 A.M. My eyelids have been inflamed for some weeks, and he is treating them. Then to the dressmaker's. A hurried lunch at Schrafft's. After an hour at the dentist's we spent the rest of the afternoon shopping at Bendel's. Leslie met us there and came out to dinner. His charming Southern ways and pleasant talk were just what I needed. The news of Herbert's serious operation did not tend to soothe my nerves.

Forest Hills, March 11th.

I was writing this morning when lo! my fingers slipped off the typewriter keys, and I caught myself bending over. I had fallen asleep, owing to the sudden change of weather from sharp cold to sunshine like June. I jumped up, tidied my chiffonier drawers to shake off drowsiness and returned to the desk as fresh as ever.

A very sweet woman, Kathryn Cravens, of Columbia Broadcasting Company interviewed me this afternoon. She talked interestingly about her work as a radio speaker. I knew we understood each other when I learned that we both love beauty, travel and dogs. What a bewitching picture her five white Spitzes must be at her feet! We both think life a wonderful game and are determined to play it to the finish; we believe that courage is a cure for every sorrow. With tender tact Miss Cravens asked how the world I live in seems without Teacher's physical nearness. She read wisely my silence of love which let me say only that from the moment I wake in the morning until I lie down at night there is an ache at my heart which never stops.

Polly and I saw Herbert for five minutes tonight. I was quite broken up. Polly wept as she noticed how startlingly he resembled Teacher in her last days. I had feared he would be low. I had often heard about major operations and the agony endured, but the reality appalled me. He cannot take any nourishment except through a vein. I passed my hand cautiously over the apparatus used to feed him drop by drop. It takes six hours for his system to absorb the liquid food. His one chance of recovery is that he has always had a strong, sound body and wholesome habits. Knowing how Teacher loved him, I said he must do his best to get well for her sake as well as Polly's and mine.

Helen Keller's Journal

Forest Hills, March 12th.

My heart gives the echo to every word of Heywood Broun's editorial in, I think, the *World-Telegram*, on the shocking attitude of those who oppose the Child Labor Amendment. Except religious hypocrisy, there is nothing else which causes indignation to blaze up in me like profits extracted from the souls and bodies of children. It is the blackest crime for which plutocracy is to answer in posterity's judgment of this civilization.

An hour at the dentist's and the rest of the morning in the shops. Home to lunch. . . .

Yet another scene to be enacted in our Japanese drama. A request from Honolulu to speak before the legislature for the blind of Hawaii. I shall comply, as the boat stops there for a day.

Mr Schramm has written a lengthy letter in reply to mine which means another idea-battle for me when I have a free hour.

As Polly was leaving for Mr Street's[1] office at 2 P.M. she blurted out, "Oh, that dreadful income tax! The report must be ready for Monday, the fifteenth, and it robs me of precious time I want to give you and other people." I am in the same boat—I have not even put two thoughts together for my Japanese speeches.

A poor little black cat came to our back door tonight. It cried and cried, and Polly let it in and tried to give it some milk, but the dogs nearly went insane barking, and it was so nervous she had to let it go out in the cold again.

[1] Charles H. Street, New York lawyer.

Helen Keller's Journal

Forest Hills, March 13th.

It snowed this morning, to the evident joy of Dileas and Maida. They love to roll in the white down dropped from Winter's wings.

Rumors are flying around that keep my interest in the trip to Japan screwed up. A friend writes that she hears we are going to Turkey! That is more than we know about ourselves.

Bob has sent me two encouraging notes he received from Senators La Follette and Copeland saying that they will support Bill 168 if it comes up before the Senate Committee. The doctor and Barney wanted us especially to spend this week end at their farm in Pennsylvania, and we should have loved to: it would have been such a welcome bit of play before our lectures begin. We could not go: there is too heavy a load on our minds at present.

Herbert continues to hang between life and death, and that only twelve days before we start for San Francisco.

Forest Hills, March 14th.

While Polly and I were at breakfast the old loneliness came upon me overpoweringly, and I could not help saying, "I can never, never get used to the house without Teacher."

"Nor can I," she answered. "Not once in all the twenty-four hours does it seem like our home without her."

Helen Keller's Journal

"Somehow it does not seem a part of her life," I went on, "and that strengthens my sense of separateness between body and soul. Teacher's real self is alive with us, yet it was never in this house. The home of her personality was in Wrentham, and something I cannot control turns my thoughts to her there. Only her poor tortured body sojourned in this place. No! Not even in my loneliest moments do I wish her back here. All the same, this strangeness bewilders me. . . ."

Before going to see Herbert with Polly this afternoon I put on the suit I bought at Bradley's, thinking it might please him. Barney kindly took us over in her car and went in with us. I was thankful to notice a decided improvement in Herbert's condition. The feeding tube had been removed, and he could spell nicely. His hand was not limp as it was on Thursday evening. He said, "It will not be long now before I come home." He will have to be very careful of himself for two months, however.

As we were coming back we passed the two lakes, part of the exposition. Polly's hand flashed up excitedly: "Oh, Helen, they have already brought such a swarm of gulls! It is a bit like Looe in Cornwall—you remember how they used to lull Teacher to sleep."

I accomplished a great deal before supper in getting together my eight or nine speeches for Japan, and that will help me tremendously the next crowded two weeks.

It was cozy eating sandwiches by the fire in the sitting room—our usual Sunday supper—with the dogs basking in the warmth of the fire and snow falling outside.

Wendy is nearly well, and her puppies are getting bigger each day.

Helen Keller's Journal

Forest Hills, March 15th.

At the dentist's, nine forty-five. It was half raining, half snowing, and the wind was high. As I closed my window before leaving the house I had felt the sleet pecking at the panes. The vibration of icy wind on the glass felt like the tapping of a big bird's bill. It was nasty underfoot. I was glad of my fur coat, although it is too heavy, and I refuse to wear it any more than I can help. It has served me well during many long winter drives to and from meetings for the blind in all weathers, but that time is past. The other day I was putting on the Glasgow coat which, besides being warm, is less cumbersome, and I lost my temper because Polly said it looked shabby and I could not wear it to town. (I call it the Glasgow coat because I bought it in Glasgow several years ago. It has a handsome fur collar, and I have got much pleasure out of it.) Afterwards I gave myself a "Hail Columbia's happy land" for letting trifles like that rumple up my good nature.

After supper we went by subway to New York to meet Elizabeth Bain's friend, Major Hunter, aboard the SS Caledonia, which was to dock at six-thirty. Both the ship and we arrived on time. The major seemed really glad to see someone to speak to; he said he was lonely. I was sorry to observe that he was far from well. We went to the Pennsylvania Hotel and tried to make him feel a bit at home. Leslie joined us at dinner, and the major gave news I was glad to hear of the Bains. He spoke of the war, which ruined his health, and the insomnia from which the soldiers suffered. He could see no way out of another world conflict, and evidently that depressed him greatly. It had not stopped raining a second all day, and torrents were pouring out of the sky when we got home at eleven-thirty.

Forest Hills, March 16th.

At the New York *Times* studio from 9 A.M. until noon, having pictures taken. I need many photographs for the Japanese trip. Marion's[1] dear smile, Bill's[2] cheery teasing and a reporter who wanted details of my work in Japan helped me face the camera dutifully.

How often Teacher and I used to go to the *Times* building to be photographed or interviewed! How beautifully everyone there understood our unity in work and the rays of wisdom that flashed from her spirit into mine! Her thought-stimulating talk and quick laughter were often released in that studio.

While Polly and I were there, in came Dr Finley, greeting me with the dear big hand the blind love. "How nice it would be to have a photograph of Dr Finley and Helen together!" said Marion. I was indeed proud to have his picture taken with me. Ever since I met him as a young woman his friendship has been a precious support to me in my endeavors for the sightless. I still wonder that he is ever ready to send word-rays of light into their darkness when his range of interests is so amazing and he is so constantly sought as a pillar of constructive good works struggling for recognition. The magnanimous sentiments and sym-

[1] Marion Morgan.
[2] William Freese.

pathy flowing from the inexhaustible treasure of his heart are, as it were, wealth tossed on the highway. They are more than a contribution to philanthropy, they enrich us with faith. For he discerns and reveals the good hidden in men and in things—good which only exceptional spirits can see and which few have the gift to present interestingly to the unobserving eyes of the crowd. That is why Dr Finley's influence wielded for peace and international amity, on the platform and through the New York *Times*, makes its mark on his time and gives a special luster to the humanitarian activities in New York.

There is no counting the occasions when the *Times* held high for us the banner of the blind in an eloquent editorial, an account of our meetings or an appeal so skillfully worded that the subject was kept urgent in the public mind.

Polly and I took Marion to lunch at Sardi's, where we had a quiet, cozy visit. As we had not seen Marion this winter, we had much to tell her about our trip abroad. Speaking of Teacher, she said, "I feel as you do, Helen, that your dear one is not gone from you. Teacher is only farther ahead, lighting for you a road to new goals, and that is why you do not see her." Mr Sardi and his wife greeted us with Italian cordiality.

Half an hour at the dentist's, then to Bendel's, where I had a three hours' ordeal trying on evening dresses, hats and shoes. But it was an ordeal tempered with the helpfulness of the girls in the shop and my wonderful luck finding just the simple, cool, soft summer gowns I wanted. Everybody liked me especially in a cloud of Caribbean blue voile.

We came home as tired as dogs after the chase, but

we knew Herbert was waiting for us, and after dinner we were off to the hospital. He is not so well as he was Monday. I fear he will have some trying ups and downs before he gets definitely better.

Forest Hills, March 17th.

This morning brought a flare-up of telephones, mail, letters still unwritten, promises unfulfilled to autograph books and pictures. I received a lovely letter from Mme Kraemer-Bach, thanking me for Teacher's book[1] and my picture sent to her. There is also a letter from Dr Lewis B. Chamberlain, president of the John Milton Foundation that publishes the *John Milton Magazine* for the blind, also *Discovery* for sightless children. He asks me to help raise funds for *Discovery*, which is a bright, suggestive little messenger of spiritual joy to the young. Regretfully I must decline, as it takes all my time and strength to solicit money for the American Foundation.

Mrs Maeno, a delightful Japanese woman, called this afternoon. She is the principal of a combination school for the blind and the deaf in Tokyo. She is visiting schools for the blind in America so as to learn how to teach handicrafts to the sightless in Japan. Her husband, who conducted the Tokyo school, died last year; and she bravely took up his work. She cannot speak English, but two other Japanese came who interpreted, and what she said charmed me, it was so full of sweet intelligence. She had arrayed herself in her wedding gown, thinking I might like to see a Japanese bride.

[1] *Anne Sullivan Macy, the Story Behind Helen Keller*, by Nella Braddy.

Helen Keller's Journal

The dress was a luxury to the touch—layer upon layer of silk soft as flower petals, shimmering with varied colors. She wore a broad silk obi holding the little sword that, according to Japanese custom, she had put into her husband's hand during the marriage ceremony. I believe this sword symbolizes protection of home and purity.

Mrs Maeno had some gifts for me. One I could feel—a gorgeously caparisoned model she had made of the white horse on which the Emperor of Japan rides. Another gift Polly described—a painting on silk which Mrs Maeno had copied from a famous Japanese picture, "Cherry-blossom Feast." It represents young girls clad in rich fabrics on a lawn, one playing the koto, another singing, the others dancing under cherry trees billowing with rosy blossom. She also traced for me in delicate picture writing two sentences uttered by the emperor:

"The burden is heavy, but I will carry on for the sake of the nation.

"Though I cannot run a race with other people I will go the way of righteousness."

I asked Mrs Maeno how many deaf and blind there were in her country. She replied, if I remember correctly, "About one hundred thousand deaf and a hundred and sixty thousand blind, of whom only four thousand are being taught."

With much feeling she begged that we pray for each other in an effort to reach all the handicapped.

This evening Polly and I spent half an hour with Herbert. She said he looked much brighter, and I knew his hands were firmer. He is very impatient to come home, and I fear he may try it sooner than he should—before we leave for San Francisco.

Helen Keller's Journal

Forest Hills, March 18th.

The sun this morning was like May, and I have kept the heat turned off in the study until now. Maida and Dileas rolled on the grass to their hearts' content. The ground had thawed out, and the result was that they came into the house looking like little mud mounds. Polly and Lena did their best to remove the "muddy vesture", but their long fur sticks out in tufts that look like roots, and I do not recognize them.

This afternoon Ethel Freeman, her nephew Frederick, his pretty wife and their darling little girl, Gabrielle, had tea with us. I was especially happy to welcome them, as Teacher and I used to visit Ethel's family near Boston when I was a child. Dr Edward Everett Hale was living then, and I love to recall how he would drop in while we were playing games or telling stories. After we grew up I saw Ethel seldom; but our friendship has remained sweet through the years. Today we were gaily reminiscent of our youth. We recalled a jolly visit we had together once in the spring at Smith College while I was at Radcliffe, also an evening in 1914 when I was speaking at Northampton and met M. Brieux. Ethel still wonders how he and I managed to understand each other: he could not speak English, and I could only muddle through French after a fashion. Yet he divined my meaning as I tried to say I honored him as a true hero who broke the prudish silences of society on questions of sex and hygiene. I also declared that he and Shaw would surely overthrow many giants of ignorance and cowardly pretense, and his warm

Helen Keller's Journal

approval gladdened me when I told him that as a young woman I had insisted on discussing publicly the cause of blindness in the newborn and its remedy.

Ethel told me how happy she is at Journey's End, where she continues to give poor people vacations out among the fields and woods every summer. She also paints and writes, and I was not surprised to hear that she had recently taken up modeling—she is always cultivating a new interest. I was delighted with an adorable head of a child she had just modeled. She was very tender to Helga, and the golden Dane put up her paw for her to caress—a special favor.

"Do come to Journey's End, you and Polly, after your return from Japan," Ethel said; "then you will know another part of me, and I will model Helga." I shall look forward to that cozy visit with lively pleasure.

Dined with Nella this evening in Garden City. The conversation shifted from one topic to another—people we know, Remus the Unsubduable (one of Maida's puppies I gave Nella last November) and television. I asked Keith[1] how far he had penetrated into the mysteries of ether and was astonished to hear that many scientists do not believe there is such a thing as "ether"! They do not know what medium light travels through. I wonder how many theories of the universe I shall find "gone with the wind" when I have leisure again to read books on science.

Mr Maule, of Doubleday, Doran and Company, and his wife came in later, and we had a nice talk. Mr Maule's kind expressions of the interest the House of Doubleday takes in me were pleasant to hear. He discussed plans for a new edition of *Midstream*, then

[1] Keith Henney, editor of *Electronics*.

mentioned the voluminous letters we both had received from Mr Schramm. He was sure that if I replied at length Mr Schramm would keep on arguing by post for years. His suggestion was for me to write briefly that I had turned the business details over to my American publishers and then drop the subject. Mr Maule said most generously that he would stand by me even though he did not agree with all my opinions on Russia and some other questions. He thought Mr Schramm would keep his word and not publish *Midstream* any more, but he could not be positive. "The Germans, you know, may call contracts, as they do treaties, scraps of paper—and we may as well be prepared for some disagreeable surprise or another."

Nella spelled all that was said to relieve Polly. She whetted my appetite for *Gone with the Wind*, which I shall read on the voyage. We inquired if each of us had made the acquaintance of a certain author, and we both said no regretfully. Then we made a bargain: Nella would read Knut Hamsun if I would read Sigrid Undset. That means a good time for us comparing notes someday.

Forest Hills, March 19th.

Dr Berens was pleased with my eyes, which are improving rapidly. From his office we rushed to the dentist's and afterwards lunched at the St Regis Hotel with Edith Cooper. She had interesting things to tell us about her recent trip to Mexico—the incredible ignorance of the peons; the hundred and sixty million pesos they send annually to Rome, Aztec gods worshiped as well as Christian saints, and how beautiful Mexican babies are. . . .

Helen Keller's Journal

At Bendel's an hour, then to Bonnie MacLeary's studio. She made a cast of Teacher's hand, thinking it might comfort me. It was a touching tribute to Teacher wrought by a true artist encompassed by unending silence. I summoned what composure I could to touch the graceful outline of the hand and the thumb and index finger forming the letter L, suggesting Love. I traced each line in the palm, startlingly distinct and true—a likeness snatched, as it were, from death's relentless waves. In spite of myself I succumbed to the old heartbreak; my tears fell; and I could not speak. It troubles me that I could not more fittingly thank the artist who had earnestly striven to express a lovely thought for my consolation.

I was cheered tonight to find Herbert much better—looking quite like himself, Polly said.

Forest Hills, March 20th.

I worked on speeches for Japan all day. That includes practicing them, so that Teacher, wherever she is, may not feel her labors wholly lost. I am like a cripple without a staff, so grievously do I miss her skillful counsel in matters of enunciation and vocal quality, but Polly is using her good ear to the utmost to preserve my speech.

I was moved to tears over another big pile of letters (Polly had them transcribed), with donations in response to my appeal for the American Foundation last November. There is unmistakable sincerity in the declaration of many who have little that they would gladly give more if they could. There are tender words from those who have lost a wife or husband or friend.

Helen Keller's Journal

One woman writes, "I know, dear Helen Keller, your heart is crying out as mine is for the loved one, and our only comfort is to do what good we can in the world." Another woman (not a medium) believes she is able to communicate with the other world and wishes she might put that blessing into her gift. One giver is deaf, another suffers from insomnia, a third from arthritis; and all say that, once having looked into darkness of one kind or another, they have a fellow feeling with the shadow-immured blind. Let the worldly wise say what they will to disparage mankind, they cannot gainsay the endless beautiful story of goodness in the human heart unfolding before me—a story aglow with romance, adventure and prophecies of the day when the race shall attain and keep undimmed the nobility of which I catch frequent thrilling glimpses! . . .

This evening when we returned from visiting Herbert in hospital, about 5 P.M., Polly stopped short at our door.

"Helen, oh, Helen, there is a bird singing such a lovely note." It kept on singing in one of the evergreens, and somehow we were as excited as if we had found Teacher in the house.

Forest Hills, March 21st.

There was a beautiful editorial in the New York *Times* on the school disaster in Texas—a big heartbeat of sympathy for the stricken parents not only from Americans but from people everywhere who cherish the world's most precious treasure—children. I have an unfaltering faith that little ones who die enter a beautiful, unclouded childhood, acquire glorious knowledge

Helen Keller's Journal

beyond our imaginings and grow up to achieve mightier works than earth ever knew. But my heart grieves over the parents for whom there is no comfort here below....

Usually I rest Sunday morning, but this time the speeches claimed every moment, as I knew we should be away from home in the afternoon.

God's voice was peculiarly moving as it spoke to me through Isaiah, Chapter 40—"Comfort ye, comfort ye my people"—which I read this morning. Every Sunday my heart cries out for the large number who, amid laborious days and nights heavy with anxiety, have no inner refreshment; but I experienced this emotion more strongly than usual today after reading about the many young people in America who turn to crime and the workers who in the struggle for existence have lost faith. I am glad Dr Stanley Jones has organized a mission to bring the church as a body and labor closer together. No matter what advantages the workers may win, it is imperative for them to enter more fully into the treasures of the spirit if they are to keep their own souls strong and the nation's ideals undimmed. Material poverty can and must be abolished; but there will always be many poor in spirit who need peace to sweeten their daily routine, aspirations to enrich a narrow environment, a beacon to illumine the darkness between this life and eternity.

Mr Migel was here this afternoon. Speaking of our trip, he said he hoped the President might write me a letter conveying a message of good will from America to Japan. I was excited thinking what a beautiful gesture that would be; but I realized that permission must first be obtained from the State Department, and the result is still uncertain.

Helen Keller's Journal

He also discussed plans for a campaign to start next October to complete the endowment fund which will support the American Foundation in its ministrations to the blind throughout the country. I told him I was more than ready and that my mind would not be at rest until the second million dollars was raised. He said he thought it could be done—God bless him!

Between 4 and 5 P.M. Polly and I went to a tea given by Mr and Mrs Lewis at their apartment in Gramercy Park. (It was Mr Lewis through whom the Thomas Paine Memorial Society had asked me to speak in Paris at the unveiling of the Paine statue.) Among the guests I was happy to see Lilie de la Nux again. I had not expected that pleasure until 1938, when I hoped we might come together in southern France. Rosika Schwimmer, whom I had seen and heard at the peace meeting where Professor Einstein spoke in 1928 or 1930, was there. I was introduced to Charlotte Lund, a Norwegian with a rich, soul-stirring voice. She sang "At Parting", and the pathetic refrain, "I gave you a rose, but oh, you took my heart!" blended softly with my daily feeling that the dearest, most inspiring element is gone from my earth life. With surprise I discovered a friend from whom I had not heard for many years— Professor Joseph Jastrow, who used to teach psychology at the University of Wisconsin. How pleasantly his name brought back the summer Teacher and I spent at a cottage on Lake Wollomonapoag in Wrentham, while I was in college, and the visit he paid us. I smiled, thinking of the endless questions he asked concerning my mind processes, sensations and dreams. He asked them so charmingly and with such variety. He had learned the manual alphabet so as to converse with me

Helen Keller's Journal

more freely. It is to those interesting discussions dashed with humor that I owe much of what I afterwards wrote in *The World I Live In*.

Polly and I met Mr Leigh, a distinguished artist who has spent much time in the Arizona desert. He told us what a wonderful place it is for painters, poets, writers. I spoke of the day, 1925, when some friends and I visited Harold Bell Wright's house built of great stones picked up in the desert, several hours' journey from Tucson. Mr Wright was away, but we were shown the armchair in which he writes on a leather desk, the elaborate stone fireplace and various Indian curios. Learning that Mr Leigh had spent some years among the Navajo Indians, I asked him to tell me a little of their history. People kept coming to speak to us, which rendered sustained talk difficult; but it was fascinating to hear about the Navajos, Hopis and other so-called "Indian" tribes who two or three thousand years before had crossed Bering Straits in canoes from Asia, an old civilized country, to an unknown continent. Curiously enough, as a student I had never believed the old theory that America was settled by Orientals driven by storms across the Pacific Ocean. How could they have traveled such enormous distances in the inadequate, small craft built in those ancient times? Mr Leigh also spoke of the Maya Empire extending from Greenland through South America to Cape Horn. It started me to think of such an immense dominion and the ever dwindling few thousands of Indians now left in the United States. However, Mr Leigh seemed to think the Indians would not disappear in South America or Mexico, especially as they were acquiring enlightened ideas of government. "Who knows," I reflected, "they may be the 'small remnant' the Bible speaks of who shall lead the whites in the only path to peace and true progress throughout the Western Hemisphere."

Rosika Schwimmer and I spoke of the apparent triumph of militarism everywhere. I hoped President Roosevelt's plan for a closer union between the Americas might facilitate the task of establishing universal peace. She said we needed another Thomas Paine with irresistible eloquence to clear the way for a world federation of nations, which would render it impossible for any state to call out its fighting forces without the consent of the rest. Alas! when shall we ever have such a desirable council of man? That saving day seems remote indeed at present....

Round 6 P.M. Polly and I met Bess Hay, and she came out to Forest Hills for the evening. It was good to have an intimate talk with her, she had always been so sweet to Teacher. For the first time I could talk without trembling all over about Teacher's last days on earth; but I have not the courage yet to review the harrowing details in a journal, although I think that would free my mind from the nightmare that lowers over it when my attention is not concentrated upon a hard task. Bess told me the latest news of her family—the Hays in Dingwall with whom we used to visit so often—and as usual a wave of nostalgia came over me as we wandered through Ross-Shire in reminiscence. It was peculiarly sad as Teacher had spelled into my hand towards the end, "Let us go back to the old farmhouse at South Arcan; perhaps I can find the peace that filled you while you walked up and down those golden lanes."

Helen Keller's Journal

Forest Hills, March 22nd.

Up at 5 A.M., knowing I should be away all day. Barney came for Polly and me in her car at 8 A.M. We went to Dr Hinsdale's first, then Polly remembered another appointment which it was too late to cancel and which prevented her from taking me to the dentist's. We telephoned Andrea, who went with me. She was kindness itself, conveying to me the dentist's directions. That was one of the countless times I bless my stars because I can read other people's lips, although I prefer the hand alphabet.

When Andrea and I joined Polly we did some shopping. In one place, as I laid my hand on the counter, my fingers lighted upon artificial flowers which astonished me with their lifelike delicacy—lilies of the valley, windflowers, narcissi and jonquils. I remembered reading in Pepys's diary that a picture he saw of a plant in a flowerpot looked so real, he had to put his finger on it before he would believe it was only a painting, and I smiled to think I escaped self-deception merely because the flowers had no odor.

Lunched with Nina Rhoades, whom I had not seen since that heartbreaking moment when she came into the sickroom where Teacher lay unconscious and tenderly caressed her face, which she had never beheld with her physical eyes, then took me in her arms, too overcome to speak. Today, as Nina greeted me, it seemed she had never been so bright with the spirit of youth. It is always a delight to visit her in that apartment full of the Braille books on nearly every subject with which she has spent most of her seventy years in joyous companionship. We laugh together over old times when she and I whiled away hours in long arguments as we walked arm in arm in the enclosed piazza at her summer home on the New Jersey coast, and I love her for the tolerant sweetness with which she listened to me.

Although I still have the argumentativeness of the Adamses, I like it less and less. It reminds me too much of a sword pulled out of its sheath in season and out, and not everybody meets it, as Nina did, with humorous good sense. As firm as a rock in her conservatism, she never dismisses scornfully what I say when we discuss radicalism. This afternoon she said next winter she would send me a life of Lenin, because the author has tried earnestly to see every aspect of that baffling, many-sided personality. An hour later she met us at the dressmaker's and drove home with us so that she could see more of us. I was sorry she could not stop for a cup of tea.

With fear and trembling I worked on my speeches (there will probably be ten or twelve in all) until and after dinner. My heart beats like a drum as I wonder how well I can say them. Trying to keep one's speech up to a particular standard is extremely difficult when a multiplicity of tasks prevents one from practicing an hour and a half each day as should be done, and at night weariness defeats the best intentions.

Helen Keller's Journal

Forest Hills, March 23rd.

Up again at 5 A.M. Maida, who sleeps with me nights, put up her funny short paws on my knee as if to say, "Why are you working at such an unheard-of hour? It's too dark for me to see you except with my nose!" Barney drove us to town early, as we wished to finish our errands today if possible.

Polly and I rushed to Battery Park to see about her passports, then to the customs, where she and the officials went through the usual questions and answers. We attended to our tickets and arrived in good time at Le Voisin, where we had invited Andrea, Lilie and Mrs Lewis and her daughter Claire to lunch. The place was crowded, and it was not easy to carry on conversation; but Andrea spread ease and pleasantness about her, and we enjoyed the luncheon. Reggie Allen came in and greeted us with the bright young smile Teacher loved. How she would have talked and laughed with him, and what interest she would have taken in his splendid career as manager of the Philadelphia Symphony Orchestra! Another welcome surprise was seeing Alexander Woollcott at another table. He said he would try to call tomorrow afternoon....

I was glad and at the same time fearful of Herbert's overdoing when I found him at home. He said the doctor had been "good enough to let him come back so that he might get our final directions when we left," but the doctor insisted that Herbert must be brought over in the ambulance. We have engaged a nurse, Mrs Loughran, who was with Teacher last October.

Helen Keller's Journal

I was still deep in another speech when that inexorable engagement book warned Polly and me that we must go to Dr Saybolt's to be examined at five-thirty. He was pleased with our state of health but descended upon us both with intense earnestness, admonishing us against too continuous work and overexcitement.

Tonight I shall work until midnight collecting the papers and notes I require for the trip. *Absolument il le faut!*

Forest Hills, March 24th.

Once more I have broken the doctor's commandment, working 5 A.M. until now, 10 P.M. Five more speeches finished, waiting to be memorized and practiced. Polly and I, between constant interruptions and telephone rings, plowed our way through mail that could not wait. Packing three steamer trunks and a dozen cases, rendered necessary by our voluminous papers and varied clothes for an unprecedented social and lecture program, is a rather staggering proposition.

Herbert is still weak, but he declares with emphatic spelling that being at home will do him more good than any medicine. This morning I caught him half reclining in bed, writing out the labels for our luggage—and that is the kind of man Herbert is. I scolded him as roundly as I could without being brutal to a sick person, and he laughed.

Dileas runs after me every time I come downstairs, and sticks so close I almost stumble over him at every step. He is a timid dog, and he has never done this before. He knows, I am positive, that we are leaving tomorrow. Helga, too, gets in my way, limping, pushing

Helen Keller's Journal

me to attract notice, and there is a lump in my throat as I count the hundred and fifty days during which I shall be separated from the most loving dogs in the world. Poor Wendy. Two more of her puppies have died, and there is no telling whether the others will live, or when she can return from the vet's. I hate to go away without giving her a good-by hug....

If possible I shall get Mme Sugimoto's *A Daughter of the Samurai* to read on the way to San Francisco. I have already chosen *Gone with the Wind* for the voyage, which will give me the alternating light and serious reading I like.

En route from New York to Chicago. March 26th.

In retrospect yesterday makes me catch my breath. At dawn I packed my two cases. Then Polly began feverishly going over unfinished tasks so as to wind up our affairs for a six months' absence. We had breakfast at my desk, so as not to be disturbed, and we never left the study until lunch.

Barney came over to see what she could do for us. She joined forces with Mrs Loughran and Lena to pack the trunks and suitcases. We had not a moment to give them instructions. Consequently we did not know where they packed any of our belongings, and now it is taking us forever to reorientate ourselves, going through all the luggage in a crowded drawing room of the Twentieth Century Limited. But the thought of their eagerness to help us puts a grateful warmth into our hearts.

Helen Keller's Journal

At 4 P.M. Polly and I were still working. The three women made us stop to get dressed. Barney's and my hands raced as together we locked my typewriter, put the Braille writer into its case, tidied the tables. I shall not be surprised if I keep missing things which I forgot in the scramble.

Herbert cried as we said good-by: that was not his nature but sheer bodily weakness. Downstairs I called the dogs to give them a parting pat. Helga and Maida answered, but poor little Dileas would not come. Barney picked him up in her arms, and how sad he looked as I caressed him! I wondered if he had grown suddenly wise, seeing the luggage carried out of the house, and realized that his two mistresses would not be back for a long, long time.

With kisses and hugs the women fairly pushed us out of the house. It was raining in torrents, and they were afraid we might be delayed and miss the train. The cases were piled into Barney's car until there was hardly a foot of space where we could sit. Anxiously Barney steered through traffic which our nervousness made us imagine grew worse every instant. We dared not look at a watch lest we should collapse.

At the station a crowd gathered about us, and I felt little hands trembling as they pinned a lovely gardenia bouquet on my fur. I asked Polly who it could be, and she said it was one of the ladies in the Japanese delegation who had come to see us off. They stood silently about while I shook hands with as many as time permitted. As we walked down the platform more friends surrounded us—Mr Migel, Amelia, Leslie, Lilie, Marion, Mrs Lewis. Literally they loaded us with gifts, good wishes and cautions to keep well. On the train steps

Helen Keller's Journal

Polly and I were photographed for the press, and almost before we knew it a unique journey had begun.

After dinner we opened the gifts which sprawled over the drawing room in the train. There were all kinds of sweetness to tell us of our friends' loving bon voyage wishes—letters, telegrams, roses, lilies of the valley, fruits, candies, exquisite sachets and perfume. What, oh, what have I done that such a wealth of kindness should be poured into my hands?

Strange to say, I did not feel homesick as I expected, but rather glad to leave behind the unsatisfied longing that had pursued me every hour in a familiar yet tragically different home. It was bracing to know that I was about to throw myself into an adventure unlike anything I had ever had—to live for a while in a land with traditions, customs and a philosophy new to my experience. Only when the Japanese delegation greeted us at the Grand Central Station did I sense the fact that my childhood dream of visiting the Far East had come true. This excited me so much, I found it hard to get to sleep.

I like an upper better than a lower berth. It gives me more freedom, and its springy motion has a soporific effect. But last night the engine, probably overburdened with a heavy train, shook me like jelly even in my dreams and jerked convulsively every time it came to a standstill.

This morning we are speeding through a white landscape. I think the chill wind I felt blowing through the car last night was the tail end of the gale reported in the papers which hit Buffalo Harbor. Just now the sun is comfortably warm, and spring seems nearer.

The thought has just flashed across my mind that

it is the consciousness of wings which is lifting me at this time above nostalgia and casting such a glamor upon the trip to Japan. They tell me a bird poised in mid-air is a picture of repose and trust, and that invisible hands seem to bear it up. That is the beautiful, sustaining experience I am passing through as I take new wings unto a morning of new opportunities and points of view.

With surprise and regret I read that John Drinkwater is dead at the age of fifty-four. He died when his powers were at their height, and there is no measuring what he might have accomplished if he had been spared. But his play, *Abraham Lincoln*, remains with us, a perennial beacon of courage and idealism. It seems to me that, while he was not a great poet, he depicted forcibly, with a wisdom from within, the panorama of American life in the 1860s, its crudity and its vast problems, its democracy ever on the point of succumbing, yet gathering new strength. With poetic impressionism he brings together many details—a gesture, a phrase, a letter, a vision—to form a picture of Lincoln the lonely which will be remembered by everyone who reads it: the American in the sense of a man who serves his fellow creatures, a statesman diverting strife and hatred into new channels of good will.

En route from Chicago to Kansas City.

When we got off the train in Chicago this morning we again faced the newspaper cameras. A reporter held me up with "Are you for or against President Roosevelt? Do you support his Supreme Court plan?"

Helen Keller's Journal

I replied that any plan was desirable which would more surely safeguard the liberties of the people, as set down in the Declaration of Independence, and I hoped the President's changes in the Supreme Court might prove beneficent.

Mrs Trude, who knew our friend, Colonel Walter Scott, of New York, was waiting at the station to take us to the other train. Mr Migel's son Richard, who had flown to Chicago last night to wish us a successful trip, was there also. How easy they made everything for us in the transit! We had never before crossed so quickly from one station to another. It was just like Mr Migel to reach out a helping hand to us, so to speak, in our journeyings. Again flowers and sweets were showered upon us as we settled down for a day's run to Kansas City.

I only wished we could have stayed longer in Chicago and surveyed the changes which I believe have taken place since my lecture days in 1922. Chicago has always interested me on account of its miles of fine parks, its high public spirit and the colorful Lake Michigan along which Polly and I used to walk whenever we had a free hour. There was also the delightful Blackstone Hotel with its choice meals and comfortable, attractive bedrooms. For Teacher especially, it was a blessed return to civilization after the shabby hotels and poor food we endured while lecturing in the Middle West.

As it was, Polly could see only the tracks, big factory buildings and freight yards as the train pulled out of the city. Now we are passing one drab town after another, and I am sadly disappointed that there has been no improvement in this respect since we last traveled through this section. I can but hope the Resettlement

Administration agencies may extend to the Middle West in the near future....

In the *Braille Weekly* I see that during the frightful battle round Madrid anti-Fascist soldiers led the attack upon their fellow countrymen. Those who wage war in a foreign land have in their hands a sword that slays two ways. This should serve as still another warning to governments not to permit volunteers in any fight where a nation is divided against itself. With emotion I note a report that more than half the Abraham Lincoln Battalion, comprised of Americans fighting for the Loyalists, have been wiped out.

Kansas City, March 27th.

Yesterday afternoon Polly and I resumed our interrupted winding-up jobs, never stopping until eight-thirty. But we did not mind the fatigue. A light dinner, much bustling about to get our dispersed articles together in the cases, and with buzzing heads and arms full of parcels we found ourselves on the platform in Kansas City, where we stopped over to spend Easter with Bryson and Alice Jones.[1] Suddenly I felt Teacher close to us; and no wonder, for those two beautiful friends had welcomed and entertained us three every time we had stopped there on our trips across the continent. Time, distance and fewness of letters had not lessened their stanch affection, and there are no words for the hospitality with which they are brightening every moment for us two lonely women in their home.

Just as we were starting up to bed at 11 P.M. a re-

[1] Old friends of Miss Keller, Mrs Macy and Miss Thomson.

porter called, and our pictures were taken. Alice gave a charming interview to save us, and in another hour I was in slumberland, "exempt from public haunt."

Today three nations are filling the newspapers with loud wrath as a result of Italy's failure to stop the flow of volunteers into Spain. How futile it all is! Britain knows perfectly that in the first place it should have taken prompt measures to aid Ethiopia before Italy started the invasion. Britain also knows that if it had shown firmness in keeping Italian volunteers and its own as well out of Spain, the situation would have been less dangerous than it is now. Both Hitler and Mussolini are fully aware of the role as aggressors which they are playing, yet they manifest surprise that their relations with Britain should all at once become strained to the breaking point. Instead of blaming one another they should set their wits to work formulating peace measures that shall avert the ruin of both the conquerors and the vanquished which everyone with a grain of sense dreads.

There could be no easier place for us to rest than this house. For the two short days we are staying here Alice has placed at our disposal two bedrooms and a charming study to write in whenever we wish. Alas! the telephone bombarded us the whole morning, and very little writing was done. Alice answered every message herself, so that Polly could read me some important letters and articles. With tact and humor she held off importunate people who wanted us to appear at a tea or meeting or dinner. One person made matters disagreeable for us all. I recognized her as the woman who years ago had written a nasty letter to the effect that I had neglected my kin, and then asked me for an autobiographical article to read to her English class. I would not see her on any terms. I knew, and I said so, that she had not shown the slightest interest in me since I was first taught. Bristling with impertinence, she told Alice that she had not kept in touch with me because Miss Sullivan had prevented us from meeting or exchanging letters. She could not have told a more outrageous lie. Teacher never knew her and therefore could not have held a grudge against her.

After that encounter Alice was still her smiling, serene self and would not let Polly answer the many messages which took her precious time.

This afternoon Alice invited a few people to tea, among them Mrs Drage, a childhood friend of Alexander Woollcott, Mr Haskell, editorial writer for the Kansas City *Star*, and his wife. Mr Haskell asked me if I remembered Colonel Nelson, owner of the *Star*.

"How can I ever forget a man with whom one of my most gratefully happy memories is associated?" I exclaimed. "Was it not his fearless crusading spirit that broke the cowardly, harmful silence concerning the two most terrible diseases which destroy sight in the newborn?"

With animation Mr Haskell told the company how Teacher and I visited Colonel Nelson in his office and acquainted him with the facts about blindness in newborn babies, and the prompt, effective, simple measures which should be taken for its prevention, how the kingly fighter against graft and injustice wept over the little ones needlessly doomed to lifelong darkness. He said, "I will publish anything you say if you will write an article on this subject."

I wrote the article, and often I have been thanked for the eyes I helped save. But it was the gallant colonel

Helen Keller's Journal

whose straight-from-the-shoulder sincerity wrought this blessing to thousands in Kansas City, and through them to thousands in other parts of the United States.

After the callers were gone Bryson told me at length what generous patrons of art Colonel Nelson and his family were and described the splendid gallery for which they bequeathed large funds to house works of art. It has been built since their day and is now one of Kansas City's crowning glories.

It is inspiring to dwell on the regal spirit which I admired twenty-two years ago and which is still living in the institutions of a wide-awake, beautiful city.

How different my last Easter and this one are from all others! Besides its own blessed message for mankind each Easter used to bring in a new way the thrilling sense of my own resurrection when Teacher awoke me with a word, a touch, from the only death I can imagine—dark silence without language or purpose or faith. Easter, 1936, walked by me like a sad ghost. Teacher was wretchedly ill, and for the first time I feared she would never be better. Now there is no greeting from her on earth, and the vibration of the anguish still quivering in my heart muffles the joy-bells of other years. But there remains something breath-taking about Teacher's personality—the miracle that lives here and now, awes, charms and spurs me onward. This experience gives a new meaning to the Gospel of the risen Christ who shared with sorrow-laden mortals the joy of eternity interpreted by love. May His presence drop dews of refreshment more and more, until the bondage and the strife are lifted from all souls, and the beauty of His peace shines in their fear-liberated lives!

While breathing this prayer I do not forget the dis-

Helen Keller's Journal

heartening retrograde apparent at present in civilization everywhere. Times have changed. Tyranny in its worst forms, denying human rights, has enslaved three peoples who were supposed to be progressive, and they are suffering themselves to be led into the accumulation of armaments which threaten mass murder in all lands. Without a critical survey of the situation or a show of self-respect they support governments that openly trample upon liberty, self-expression and culture bound up with a humane humanity.

However, these symptoms of social darkness do not discourage me. They only emphasize the commandment for us who have our part in the Resurrection to be steadfast. If the higher ideals we pursue are threatened with repression or extinction they can be obscured only locally and for a time. They will grow through the ineradicable might of the Divinity which transformed a few timid, unknown, simple disciples into a constructive power for good that made history both in the ideals and the temporal affairs of the race. I believe it is because these very ideals are pushing their way to the front harder than ever that the world is in such commotion. They are rousing fiercer opposition in the forces they are to cast out—greed and hate, fear and prejudice and intolerance. Today it is as in the beginning—Darkness is upon the face of the deep. And the Spirit of God is moving upon the face of the waters. In time the light shall shine more and more into a true Easter, and in that light we shall behold a heaven-upon-earth civilization. . . .

In the April *Reader's Digest* I have just read Mr Flagg's article on beauty in women. How true it is, as he says, that thousands upon thousands of modern women have a beauty which is vulgar and unsatisfying! Their ambition is physical perfection, and in its pursuit they are starving their minds and stunting their souls. The only truly beautiful women have well-stored minds, poise, strength for serious discussion and a gift of blending laughter with fragrance of the heart. It is this beauty, "incandescent with the spirit", which Alice Jones possesses to a rare degree.

Kansas City, March 28th.

We had a delightful talk with Bryson and Alice about one of the many talented young people they befriend in difficulties, Homer Koyama. (How similar that name is to Omar Khayyam!) Polly noticed his exquisite paintings of the Arizona desert and marveled at the delicacy of his colorings and effects. Bryson told how he and Alice had given Homer an opportunity to leave his humble home in the desert and study at the Kansas City Art Institute. But Homer gained little or nothing from the white man's philosophy of art and went back to his primitive environment because only there could he enjoy true communion with the Great Spirit. The Joneses regard his attitude with a gentle philosophy. They feel as I do that individuals cannot contribute to art or civilization unless they remain loyal to the genius of their race and the language in which the universe speaks to them.

At noon the Joneses took Polly and me to breakfast with Dr Frank Ridge and his wife at their charming apartment. Dr Ridge's specialty is geography of medicine. He talked very interestingly about his experiences with patients in different localities and climates. He said often the only way to cure their ailments is to find out the region they inhabit—the soil, the water they drink, the conditions under which they live and work. For instance, if the water lacks iodine, goiter becomes common and cannot be eliminated unless a proper amount of iodine is put into the water. How futile one's own endeavors seem when one considers the vast areas which physicians and scientists are redeeming from diseases which once seemed inevitable!

The Ridges have two Sealyhams who claimed their share in entertaining us. They were not exactly arrayed in their Sunday best—they had been out in a pouring rain for a walk, and their long hair, as it dried, felt like bits of candied orange peel sticking out all over them, but I loved their joyous friendliness.

The rain was still with us when we returned. Now I must pack up and write until it is time to start on the third lap of our journey.

En route from Kansas City to San Francisco,
March 29th.

Yesterday before I left Barcia and Lucia Doris[1] brought their lovely children over to hunt for Easter eggs and play with balloons shaped like great ducks. I spent a few minutes watching them, and they were delighted when I caught the balloons they tossed up in the air. One dear little fellow, Stanley, four years old, saw me reading his mother's lips and without the slightest shyness asked questions about the trip. To my surprise I understood him easily, despite his baby accent.

[1] Barcia and Lucia Doris Jones, daughters of Bryson and Alice.

Helen Keller's Journal

"What boat are you going on to Japan?" When I said the Asama Maru, he inquired what that word meant, and I told him the ship was named for a famous Japanese volcano. "Is it day here, Miss Keller, and night in Japan?" he demanded, and the bright puzzlement on his upturned face was adorable.

It was hard to bid Alice and Bryson good-by at the train. Polly and I felt depressed, much as we did when we left the old Manse last January. At times life seems nothing but a series of meetings and partings.

As the train bore us across Kansas it was light enough for Polly to see the grain mills and huge silos so characteristic of the Middle West. The sun has kept me company nearly all day, warming my fingers deliciously as they moved over the cold typewriter keys. I have not stopped working, except to eat lunch and dinner, until now, 8:30 P.M. . . .

Since we stopped in Denver this morning Polly has seen one blizzard after another, broken by bursts of sunshine and whole mountain ranges enveloped in snowy whiteness. Now we understand why our friends would not let us fly to California as we greatly wished to. They realized the serious risk of ice formations on the ailerons of the plane. To our disappointment we find we shall not arrive at Salt Lake City until 1 A.M. Polly would love to see once more the magnificent mountain wall rising about the city.

En route from Kansas City to San Francisco,
March 29th.

We are crossing the Nevada desert. It takes a lavish sun and all the resolution I can muster not to be op-

[265]

pressed by desolate seas of coarse grass, endless expanses where nothing seems ever to have grown.

More mountains mantled with snow and tremendous icicles. Just now Polly told the porter she could see the tracks of animals in the snow. "No, no!" he declared with a flash of white teeth, "I have been traveling round these parts for thirty years, and I have never seen any lions or tigers." I was glad of the good laugh he gave us. . . .

"Trees, Helen!" I could feel the shout in Polly's fingers. "The first trees! Small, but something good to see after the great, bare distances between Denver and western Nevada."

"Spring! Spring!" she said. "My eyes are simply feasting on soft, green grass. . . ."

"There begin the sierras and the pines," Polly commented an hour later. For the first time my nostrils caught the welcome odors from a soil that was alive. Another excited gesture from Polly: "I am looking into an ocean of pines. Their branches are interlaced so that you could almost walk from one to another all the way. . . ."

"How I wish you could reach out your arms far enough, Helen, to touch those feathery billows of blossoms on the hillsides—plums, peach and cherry," she kept saying. "The whole country seems one gigantic pink, white and rose bouquet, and oh, those blessed streams, so restful to the sight after the desert!"

From Sacramento onward the name of almost every place where the train stopped brought back to me a meeting for the blind or an appearance on the stage. How happy Mother and Teacher were when they caught the shimmering, dreamlike loveliness of the blossoming fruit trees along this route! Every pleasure I then had was the sweeter because it was shared with them. How tantalizing it is now to feel them ever nearer and not to be able to pour into their ears my overflowing new experiences and catch their reassuring words in the strangest, most bewildering journey I have undertaken. As I contemplate the immeasurable changes in my life since the death curtain fell between them and me, this country, not Japan, seems the foreign land. . . .

We have just stopped in Berkeley, where Ned Holmes met us when we came this way first and brought me a bunch of breath-of-heaven which sent an enraptured thrill through my senses.

St. Francis Hotel, San Francisco, March 31st.

Last night I stopped writing abruptly as Polly said, "Come quickly to the other side. There is the new San Francisco bridge—another world wonder! Helen, I need a new language for its magnificence. It looks like one gigantic span of amber lights."

Still atremble with excitement, we stepped off the train and were instantly surrounded by reporters and cameras. Another Japanese delegation met us, and friends of the blind begged me to visit this or that place or speak a message to the sightless. As usual I wished I might be a sextet so as to comply with last-minute requests in a day of only twenty-four hours.

I was deeply touched by the helpfulness of two young newspapermen who, seeing that Polly and I were alone, piloted us to the ferry and accompanied us all the way from Oakland to San Francisco. One of them had been employed for a while on the construction of the cables connecting the two new bridges, and his comments gave me an exciting sense of the titan labors that brought those bridges into existence. Once more I was wrapped in the wonder that had always quickened my pulse crossing San Francisco Bay—the very soul of the city. I regretted that before long those ferryboats would no more ply leisurely on water iridescent by day, glorious at night, shimmering with mountain shadows and reflections from mighty buildings.

Entering our hotel room, we found the furniture and every corner full of roses, gardenias, fruit-blossom sprays and forsythia from a friend's garden. Another shower of bon voyage telegrams and letters from home made us feel the sweet impact of friendly thoughts on all sides and prayers for our well-being and safe return.

Today is unforgettable—a leaf out of *The Arabian Nights*. This morning Polly put into my hand a letter addressed to me by President Roosevelt. As her fingers unfolded his beautiful message of good will given through me to the handicapped of Japan our voyage assumed a romantic meaning. His noble words deepened my sense of responsibility towards those without sight who are still waiting for a friend throughout the Orient:

Warm Springs, Ga.
March 20, 1937

DEAR MISS KELLER,

I have learned that in response to an invitation from a Reception Committee representing various Japanese associations and sponsored by the Japanese government, you are to visit Japan this spring to give a series of lectures there. I feel confident that your presence will prove a lasting inspiration to those Japanese laboring under physical handicap, and that your association, brief as it may be, with Japanese individuals and groups interested in humanitarian endeavor will contribute to promoting that spirit of friendship and good will between our people and the people of Japan upon which good international relations must rest. As you are so well qualified to convey to the Japanese people the cordial greetings of the American people I take this opportunity to express my hope for the success of your mission...."

I thanked the President for his splendid message. Then it was as if something I could not resist took hold of my hand to write these words:

"It would be wonderful if a host of men and women might bear good-will messages from America to a world still groping its way through fear and anger. Then all the militarists and dictators united could not drive it into another war and the frightful increase of handicapped human beings which war inevitably creates. Sadly I reflect that such reconciling words might fall upon unheeding ears, but surely universal peace cannot remain only a dimly encouraging dream always."

A long cablegram from Honolulu, where the Asama Maru is to stop for a day. I am to speak before the legislature, urging them to provide a Bureau of Welfare for the blind of Hawaii and an adequate appropriation, and arrangements are being made for me to give an informal talk to the Honolulu Lions at a luncheon. Mrs Grace Hamman, who is in charge of the work for the blind there, had previously written that after the meeting she would show Polly and me around Honolulu!

Helen Keller's Journal

What a breath-taking thought! Only a week more, and we shall be seeing Waikiki Beach, the volcano and the most enthusiastically praised climate in the world!

My letter to the President was actually sandwiched between newspaper interviews and picture taking which lasted from 10 A.M. until one o'clock. Polly was so besieged by the telephone, she could neither spell the questions I was asked nor tell me which way to look for a picture. Luckily one of the reporters offered to answer calls for her, and his cheerful, capable service smoothed out another rough place in the day's crowded San Francisco program. . . .

This afternoon Polly and I spoke to the Japanese branch of the Young Women's Christian Association in this city. First Polly asked me a few questions, so that they might become accustomed to my imperfect speech, then I told them how happy I was to be on my way to their country of which I had dreamed as a child. I went on to speak of happiness and the heartbreaking experiences which sometimes shake our belief in a purpose of good in the world. "We look around us in fear and doubt; it is as if a light were suddenly blown out, and we were left in the dark. At first we are stunned, but the urge to escape is strong within us. After a while we feel the wall of life on which we lean, and lo! there is a door within our reach. . . . I want you to know the door which has been flung open for me in a deep sorrow is the passage to Nippon."

Polly described to me the lovely young Japanese girls in costume. One of them performed two famous Japanese dances, one ancient and the other modern. Afterwards she let me feel her dress and the fairylike fan she had woven. There was divine poetry in her twinkling

Helen Keller's Journal

feet and hands, so suggestive of bird wings and flower petals fluttering down the wind. Another girl played on the koto a composition by a blind musician. I sat on the matting close to her so that I might watch her playing. Wonderingly I noted how skillfully she swept the strings with the ivory at her finger ends. What a cascade of dainty notes fell on my hand as raindrops on autumn leaves! Every now and then a startling cry of distress burst from the quivering instrument. Shriller and sadder it rose, then sank back into soft wistfulness. Near her was a Japanese screen with a single dainty plant in front of it, and Polly said that was all the setting needed to heighten the effects of beauty and harmony.

Pictures were taken of me with the dancer and the koto player, then Polly and I were photographed. So many people shook hands with us after the meeting and had so much to say, we were quite limp when we left the hall; but that was not strange, since we had not been in public life a long while.

Elsie Sperry,[1] who was at the meeting, took us in her car to her home in Berkeley where we had a family dinner. We crossed over the bridge, eight miles in length, including the approach at either end, which now connects San Francisco with Oakland. Mr Sperry has a book of pictures taken of the bridge during construction —and how I envied Polly as she looked them over! Unless there happens to be a model of a building or a bridge I cannot form a correct mental picture of it. However, it is not the spectacular grandeur of those enterprises that especially moves me, but the idealism, the human labor, skill and suffering out of which they spring.

[1] Mrs Austin Sperry, an old friend.

Helen Keller's Journal

Aboard the Asama Maru, April 1st.

Why, oh why did I start this diary, knowing how crowded my life had been for many years? When it is almost impossible to write letters it seems the height of absurdity to attempt self-recording of any sort. As it is, I can only snatch moments to jot down fragmentary paragraphs or ideas which I have no time to develop, as a hungry man seizes mouthfuls of food. But having gone so far as I have, I cannot now let go the raw material I have retrieved from oblivion; it will brighten my dull moments in retrospect.

A hectic morning. A good-by interview with reporters who asked for my impressions of the San Francisco bridge precisely at the moment when I felt most idealess. . . .

Kate Foley[1] called. She knows the hand alphabet, and as we have long been comrades in the struggle towards a happier world for the blind, we spent a cozy hour together. Now there is another close bond between us. Her sister, whose discerning sympathy and rich helpfulness carried her through innumerable difficulties, passed away last year, and Kate is quite as much alone as I am on the dark trail. More than ever I admire the cheerful courage with which she raises the newly blinded out of despair and pushes forward the campaign for the prevention of blindness. With modest simplicity she startled me by saying she would travel all by herself to the convention for the blind in Toronto, Canada—she, Kate Foley, who is both crippled and without sight!

[1] State home teacher of the adult blind in California.

Helen Keller's Journal

Finished my packing in breathless haste, and Polly and I found ourselves in Elsie's car skidding through a pouring rain and congested streets. The Asama Maru was due to sail at noon, and I felt the last warning whistle as we arrived. A large throng—Americans and Japanese, including the deaf and the blind—greeted us, and I almost disappeared beneath a mound of hothouse and garden flowers. Elsie and "Pussy Willow" parked the car, but evidently the crowd swept them aside, for they were nowhere to be seen when Polly and I came on deck to wave good-by. With imperative fingers Polly spelled, "Helen! a picture," and though the rain came down in torrents we swung into a pose for the camera. Already I know the Japanese will want to photograph us constantly on our way to the Orient and back.

When we sailed through the Golden Gate a god plucked me by the ear, as the Romans would say, and winged memory bore me back twenty-two years to Mount Tamalpais where Teacher, Polly and I sat one heavenly day with San Francisco Bay gleaming, green-gold-blue, and the giant sequoia forest below us. Ned Holmes held us spellbound with romantic tales of the ships that entered the harbor, laden with jade, ivory, mahogany, myrrh and frankincense from the Far East. As we listened Polly and I resolved (I did not then know our wish was simultaneous) that sometime we would go the way of those ships from the Golden Gate to the Orient. Wonder-smitten, I felt the Asama Maru bearing us like a mighty genie at the command of Aladdin's lamp through that world gateway. In a mist of rain we moved slowly under the great Golden Gate Bridge which is almost completed, and past the cliffs that rise sheer out of the sea. Then I had a sensation as if we dropped out of a life into another—into unknown vastitudes of experience.

Yet I did not feel lost; rather I exulted in the thought of new horizons opening before my mind. Perhaps that was the beginning of my release from the torturing sense that a world had been burned out with Teacher's passing. Certainly she seemed nearer than she had since she last kissed me. My purpose was revitalized, as if she had spoken from her celestial home, encouraging me to go forth into the darknesses and the silences yet untouched by hope. With her earthly presence is gone the dear familiar home atmosphere, and it may be that the task now required of me is to grow a new self out of the emotions and impressions I shall no doubt bring back to America. My heart is still like a house where friends come and go, but no one else can ever be Teacher or Mother or Father to me, and that means that one intimate chamber remains closed until I, too, depart. Since I have no husband or child I do not know if other rooms will be opened for satisfying human relationships, but "before me, as behind me, is God, and all is well."

Our stateroom resembled a conservatory. One unusual basket of flowers was sent by the Japanese women of San Francisco. In this most touching gesture sixteen groups—including Buddhists, Shintoists and Christians—were represented. There was a delectable basket of fruit from Mr Pfeiffer[1] with a warmhearted letter of good wishes and a check for Polly and me which he hoped we would use to pick out a souvenir we especially liked in Japan.

I find it more blessed to give than to receive—and here I am receiving far more than I shall ever be able

[1] Mr G. A. Pfeiffer, trustee of the American Foundation for the Blind.

Helen Keller's Journal

to give. But this multitude of kind thoughts and prayers is gratifying, since it springs from the very generosity that has enabled me all these years to raise funds for the blind of America....

Captain Kaneko called soon after the ship left the harbor. From his handshake I know we shall like his friendly personality. The second Japanese we met on the voyage was Mr Ishi, a wealthy tea merchant of Yokohama.

We were almost crowded out of our room by the flowers and had them taken to the dining room so that they might be enjoyed by the other passengers. Overcome by a drowsiness natural on the first day out at sea and after long excitement, I sank down on the bed and never moved until Polly waked me for dinner.

Aboard the Asama Maru, April 2nd.

Slept late this morning. Still rainy, windy and quite cold. Anxious friends had so loaded us with directions about Japanese food, we hardly ate any lunch; we just picked a tidbit or two from the soup, the fish, the chicken, which was not half cooked, the apple and celery salad and the cheese. I was hungry, of course, but in a day or two I trust we shall accustom ourselves to the new dishes as befits travelers in far parts of the earth.

It is pleasant to touch the palms, dwarf Japanese pines, spruces and other plants all over the ship and to see with what painstaking care they are sheltered from the sea winds. I wanted to read Lafcadio Hearn's *Out of Unfamiliar Japan:* it tells much about Japanese

Helen Keller's Journal

gardens, which are like nothing else in the world. But a painful duty drove this exquisite joy and rest out of my mind. Before leaving home I learned that a friend I dearly love was much hurt by something I had said. It is one of those miserable misunderstandings that menace the strongest ties of affection, and it really seems as if I might have been spared such an extra burden at this critical time. I spent the afternoon writing to explain the situation to her at considerable length, but I realize that such a task seldom does much good, and the bitterness lies upon my soul like a stone.

Aboard the Asama Maru, April 3rd.

The rain has dwindled to a drizzle, but walking on deck is not yet pleasant. A busy morning with autographs, my speeches for Honolulu and mail we had been forced to leave unread the last breathless ten days.

We had an enjoyable little visit with the captain over a cup of tea up in his cabin. I asked if he had read any of Conrad's works. He replied, "Yes. I have read *Youth*. I liked it very much."

I said Conrad's tribute to the sea and to sailors was the noblest I had ever read.

"Seamen everywhere are united by a spirit of brotherhood and tolerance," he replied. "If they had their say in world affairs there would be no next war."

I agreed with him, for I think their influence is growing stronger from port to port, and their voices may yet be heard above the hysteria of fear and nationalism.

The welcoming committee at Honolulu sent me a cordial "Aloha" by wireless this afternoon. Three times

Helen Keller's Journal

an inquiry has been cabled from there whether I would permit a broadcast of my speech for the people on seven other islands beside Hawaii, and three times I have signified my consent. Could they have failed to receive two of my replies? It seems strange. Whatever the trouble may be, the nearness of Hawaii is now a thrilling reality. Polly is whetting my impatience to reach that Blest Isle by recalling the blue, blue mountains round Honolulu which she saw years ago on a world cruise. She says they resemble those on the island of Jamaica, where Teacher took her last trip by sea with us a year ago last October.

How my heart contracts with anguish every time I think of Jamaica. That trip was one of Teacher's efforts to get over the distressful illness that was shattering her vitality. She could not enjoy the sail beneath a wondrous October sky as she hoped to, and for days after our arrival she could not rally sufficiently for a motor drive. Stricken to the soul, I realized then, though I would not admit it even to myself, that no rest, no splendor, not even Puerto Rico in which her vibrant, poetic soul had reveled, would ever renew her health. The roads over which we sped seemed interminable to her as she bravely tried to distinguish with her glimmer of sight the vast banana groves, smooth bamboo hedges and the dizzying jumble of mountain grandeur. Not until we reached St Ann's Bay at the other side of the island did she discover anything that recalled Puerto Rico—the ravishing color of the mountains, the beach, the Caribbean Sea and the coconut palms with their feet in the water, rustling endless gossip to the waves. But she was so exhausted, I wondered if it had been worth while for her to come so far in pursuit of that smiling "phantom of delight." She missed the picturesque little churches and shrines that she had seen at every turn in Puerto Rico.

We went back to Forest Hills as quickly as possible, and, trembling, we three groped through the darkness of another year. Again Teacher fought for better health after the unsuccessful operation on her eye in the spring. With tears I smell in retrospect the firs and pines on the marvelous walk Herbert made for me up at the big log camp in the Canadian mountains where we took Teacher for the summer; I pace back and forth by the quiet little cabin on the edge of Lac Archembault where Teacher tried to sleep, listening to the murmur of the waves, the dip of oars and the songs of birds, hoping against hope that they might soothe her. The anxious days passed, and she did not improve. Heartsick, I helped her get dressed the thirtieth of June when she went back to New York to consult doctors. "Wait for me and be of good courage, dear," she said as she was lifted into the automobile. She never saw that wonderful camp again—the one place in which she would have found peace if she had only been free from pain.

I cannot stop this onrush of sad memories. Teacher's last attempt to throw off her illness at the little cottage by the sea on Long Island ... the month in hospital during which she hung between life and death ... her piteous eagerness to get home. I ache all over as I remember how she grew thinner and thinner. I was glad she could not see my swimming eyes as I massaged her and noticed skin and bones where I had once felt the firm softness of her chest and shoulders.

I live over the last few minutes of her earth life: the death rattle after an eight-hour struggle for breath

Helen Keller's Journal

... her darling hand growing cold in mine ... the smell of opiates heavy in the room ... sorrowing friends who drew me away so that her body might be prepared for the funeral ... the Gethsemane I passed through an hour later when I touched, not Teacher's blessed face, but fixed features from which expression had fled. I feel again the recoil, the cry that escaped me, "It is not Teacher, it is not Teacher!" ... The next thing I knew I was sitting in the chair up in the attic-study desperately trying to efface that still, cold image—as final for me as the sound of the last shovelful thrown upon the coffin is for those who hear. There, in the sunshine, by the window where she had sat reading to me while she could see, a merciful Power restored to my imploring fingers the warmth, animation and soft contour that only the soul can impart to the face.

When she breathed no more, somehow the faith she had wished she could hold with me rose up stronger than ever and, leaning over, I said, "You know, dearest, don't you, that life is beginning over again, glorious with light and peace." Then it came over me that she was thinking of the joy of being reunited with her little brother, and I talked about him, feeling his nearness vividly. I wonder if her mind answered mine from afar? There was such a surge of memories sweeping over me, and I remembered the first joyous days of release when we spelled winged words to each other, and life was a continuous great discovery ... our white farmhouse in Wrentham with the wind soughing in the evergreens ... our walks in the pastures bounded by old stone walls and through woodland silences with the soft light she loved filtering through the leaves. As I murmured to her I still felt the indefinable response of the spirit in her face. The change I sensed afterwards was more than I could bear. Everything was blurred. It seemed as if I should henceforth tread paths that led nowhere, climb steps that would lead to nothing because they could not bring me to her.

But while I communed with her among the books she had cherished I had a new consciousness that "the body is only the shadow of the soul." I knew she would never be far away. The paths we had walked over side by side would still blossom with her personality; life would always speak to me of her through the things we had done together.

It has not been possible until now to ease this cumulative grief even a little with the narcotic of words. Perhaps this clutch of haunting remembrance may be loosened soon. I do not believe in special "providences" because that implies special neglects; but I am positive that, if we let Him, God strengthens us for heavier trials, and that through this trip He is guiding Polly and me to a new purpose of good.

Aboard the Asama Maru, April 4th.

This morning the sun burst through the clouds, and there was brightness in my heart too. I was glad to think I was a day nearer to Honolulu. My fancy ran forward impatiently to the azure waves singing on the coral sands, the dazzling spray flung from the surf, the mountains with hearts of fire and palms climbing up their slopes, golden fruits "suspended in their own green heaven" and—I was going to say, the witchery of the ukulele beneath the moon, but I shall be there only

Helen Keller's Journal

until 5 P.M., and there is no telling if the despotism of circumstances will ever let me pass this way again.

At noon, jaded with work that never gets finished, Polly and I reclined on deck, soaking ourselves in sunshine. I started *Gone with the Wind* in Braille. It is in twelve volumes, and I do not know when I shall finish it, as I allow myself the luxury of reading only on deck or under bedcovers. I shall have to rob myself of sleep if I am to return the book this spring, which I am anxious to do because other blind people are waiting for it eagerly.

How charmingly the book opens with a placid life on a Georgia plantation! I have known women like Mrs O'Hara—ministering angels with comfort in their hands and voices for the unfortunate, yet amazingly blind to vital truths. Ignoring subjects that are not pleasant or sanctioned by the proprieties, they unconsciously create a shelter under which insidious evils eat their way like rust into the framework of society. For instance, there is the obstinate silence of many women concerning venereal disease which is only just now being broken and which has rendered almost impossible the discussion of methods to check its appalling increase.

Mammy's warmhearted loyalties, comical tyrannies and drawling dialect are adorable. Scarlett I like not at all; I fear she will turn out an utterly selfish creature like Regan in *King Lear* or Empress Catherine....

A woman has been hanging around our door with an obvious intention to take up our time with her trivial chatter. At such moments I want to crawl into a rabbit's hole. Those insistent, persistent and empty-headed persons are the hardest to get rid of because one in my position must remember there are malicious individuals who misconstrue even the most necessary acts of self-defense as pride or snobbery.

We are keeping to ourselves severely until we arrive at Yokohama, realizing that our absorption in others' affairs will be complete for the next three or four months; and at present I have so many personal obligations to meet, I sympathize with the old woman who lived in a shoe. I am not even sure, figuratively, to whom I should give bread or soup, or whom I should spank and send to bed. Unanswered letters keep turning up reproachfully under my hands, and my thoughts fly about distracted, dropping speeches and memoranda. I wonder the crash is not heard, it is so real and alarming to me. Why should this be? I wonder. Perhaps the demands under which we both stagger are just part of the unrest and soul-hunger throughout the world. . . .

By this month's *Ziegler* I see with mingled regret and pride in the blind men's courage that the sit-down strike at the workshop for the Pennsylvania Association for the Blind in Pittsburgh is still on. There are 173 workers, and 107 have taken possession of the factory itself.

Sometimes the sightless are most unreasonable in their demands. They forget that it is impossible for those who see to grasp the big, black realities of blindness or wholly to reinstate them in a world of the eye and the ear. Where others are free to rebel and have a fighting chance to improve their living conditions the blind must think long and move quietly before they risk losing their small gains. A rebel myself, I have begged them to go halfway whenever decency or manhood permits—yes, even two thirds of the way, to meet their sighted fellows.

The Pittsburgh blind workers have appealed to the

Helen Keller's Journal

management for an increase of wages and for weekly pay rather than by piece work. The association says it would be impossible to do this, as the shop is already run at considerable loss. The association has said that the average wage of the 173 workers is $13.68. With a weekly pension of $6.92, the total amount is a little over $20 a week. With prices rising and living conditions becoming more insecure it is obvious to me that $20 a week is far from adequate for a seeing breadwinner, let alone a blind one. I am glad that Matthew Dunn, the blind representative from Pennsylvania, is in sympathy with the blind strikers. . . .

I see that New Jersey will collect nine million dollars in levies on the estate of the late Arthur Brisbane. Justice on the spot for once!

With amused approval I read these rhymes printed by the *British Medical Journal* in a lecture on nutrition:

> *Eat all kindly nature doth bestow;*
> *It will amalgamate below.*
> *If the mind says so, it shall be so,*
> *But if you once begin to doubt,*
> *The gastric juice will find it out.*

That is the attitude with which I shall eat Japanese food. Thus far I like most of the dishes I have tasted. The chief trouble is to get their names straight. . . .

There is a touch of grim comedy recorded in what seems to be Germany's unbroken tragedy of repression. In Berlin a man was dismissed from a government position because he allowed his wife to henpeck him. I am speculating as to whether there is not some truth in the contention that if he cannot stand up before his wife he lacks the ironclad spirit required for heavy responsibilities in public life. . . .

It is a delight to me to notice how everything of any literary value enjoyed by the seeing is embossed for the blind as quickly as it is asked for. There are *The Toilers of the Sea*, which I remember Teacher started reading to me when I was about twelve but never finished because her poor eyes gave out after the first few chapters; *Les Miserables*, which I suppose I shall need a whole summer holiday to go through; and Olive Schreiner's *The Story of an African Farm*. How well I remember Teacher and Polly sobbing aloud over the last book on our cruise home from California through the Panama Canal!

Aboard the Asama Maru, April 5th.

Another big smile of a day in the blue Pacific, the air caressing, the ship's motion smooth and swift.

I was pleasantly surprised when a telegraphic ray of good will was flashed to me across the immense distance we still have to traverse—"Welcome to the land of cherry blossoms." Japan seemed very near indeed, and my sense of oneness with another part of the human race was gratifyingly confirmed.

America seemed close, too, when Polly and I met on deck this morning a niece of my beautiful friend, Mrs William Moore. Mrs Bullard and her two charming daughters, Jean and Carol, are on a world cruise. I told them how Mrs Moore had entertained us several times in her New York home, how dear she was, leading me from room to room, placing my hand on some of her

Helen Keller's Journal

choicest art treasures—jade Chinese vases and bowls dating back many hundreds of years, ivory statues, a lovely bas-relief of Kwannon and fearsome dragons. "And oh, the fragrant Chinese tea distilled from dewdrops on the leaves of the lotus over which we chatted!" I added. Mrs Bullard spoke of her home in Santa Barbara. I hope we shall see more of her; it is cheering to have such a sympathetic spirit near on a fateful voyage like this.

The atmosphere we are living in these days is not foreign—nothing human is foreign to me—but it has a quality all its own. Like a new language, it commands my attention, tests my capacity to learn, lures me on to fresh discoveries. There are handsome, quiet Japanese aristocrats, there are brisk, shrewd businessmen. Others appear much interested in athletics, and their deck sports are fascinating to watch. Others, like the captain, are thoughtful, troubled by the disorder and suffering in the world. But through these different types runs the same untranslatable race conjugation. I also perceive in them a conflict between an ancient civilization and modern times. Young and old alike seem pulled this way and that by opposing forces which they must try to comprehend quickly if they are to preserve their national life. Some are nervously self-conscious, as if trying to fit in with Western ideals and methods that are changing the face of the earth. Unflinching loyalty to their emperor and intense patriotism are still a fundamental part of their mental equipment. At the same time they are more international minded than Americans. When most aggressive, they show a courtesy that conquers more surely than force. Even if a fanatical militarism should drive them further in empire building,

Helen Keller's Journal

I am sure they will never lose their catholicity or their benevolent neighborliness.

The captain believes it is the women who have for ages kept Nippon vigorous spiritually and socially. "The woman in the home has been the country's faithful guardian," he says. He has sincere compassion for the women who work from dawn until dark, seldom if ever gathering life's flowers; he wishes everything possible to be done for their education and the enrichment of their lives, but he feels that their place is still in the home. Having observed the discontent, the instability and aimlessness of many "free" women in my country, I wonder if he may not be right to a large extent. Gently he regrets the passing away of the old Japanese culture with its soul-illumined beauty and artistic power, and he thinks that only by keeping their place in the home can the women save a part of this priceless heritage for their children. Certainly there have been few nations like Nippon which continue young, forward looking from age to age; and it is to be hoped that only the best modern ideas will be accepted by the Japanese in adapting themselves to changing circumstances.

Aboard the Asama Maru, April 7th.

A day at Honolulu.

The Arabian Nights now seem pale beside yesterday with its shimmering, romantic memories. It was many things in one—a lei woven of splendor-filled moments that sped like heartbeats, a bewildering rush from one meeting to another, a mantle of dreams spread under

Helen Keller's Journal

my feet, a fleeting contact with a region isolated from the rest of the world that in retrospect will stir a poignant longing to come back and explore it at my leisure. I am so weary this morning, it seems as if I had worked night and day for a week; but the poetic hospitality with which we were entertained and the assurances on every hand that my visit would prove a help to the Hawaiian blind compensate me richly.

We arrived at Honolulu 6 A.M. I was hardly up when a Braille copy of the program for the day was brought to me. I noted that two extra meetings had been put in between that of the legislature and the Lions' luncheon. That meant remarks to be made on the spur of the moment.

Polly and I were on deck at 7 A.M. A committee headed by Commander Todd, aide to the governor of Hawaii, and including representatives of the blind, the deaf and the Lions, welcomed us. The leis—veritable living jewels to my enraptured touch—were heaped upon me until my dress was completely hidden. From Polly's enumeration of colors they must have had a rainbow glory—white, red, pink, orange, gold. Their blended fragrances intoxicated me—gardenia, pekokee (very much like the scented wisteria), plumeria, mock orange—so that I forgot the weight and the heat of the flowers on my neck. The music of "Aloha Oe" was in every word spoken, every kindness shown, on my first visit to Honolulu.

As we drove through the wide, pleasant streets I knew by smell it was a garden city. Mrs Grace Hamman, director of Sight Conservation and Work with the Blind, took us to her home for breakfast. From there Polly could see the heavenly jade sea, the surf dashing white

Helen Keller's Journal

against the reefs and Diamond Head in the distance. (I prefer its Hawaiian name, Laihahee.)

Senators Elsie Wilcox, Mrs Cudingham and W. J. Heen escorted Polly and me to the governor's office in the building which was formerly the royal palace. Governor Poindexter greeted us cordially. I was touched to learn that he had come out of hospital for the occasion. He told me the office used to be Queen Liliuokalani's bedroom, and that the representatives met downstairs in the sometime throne room. I said I had read her pathetic story as a young girl, and told how I shed tears hearing that the Hawaiians had shut themselves up and wept after her abdication. Again the view from the windows held Polly entranced, and I could imagine how Her Majesty's eyes must have rested upon their soft, luxuriant greenness with a poet's intense love.

From the office several representatives escorted Polly and me to the House, where we were to speak. The response was encouraging, and I am sure the blind of Hawaii will obtain the Bureau of Welfare they need. I felt handsomely complimented when the legislature passed a long resolution extending to me a welcome on behalf of the people of Hawaii.

It was very interesting to address a legislative body representing widely different groups on the island—Chinese, Japanese, Hawaiians, Portuguese and Anglo-Saxon. I believe they are working out slowly but surely a solution of interracial problems. Hawaii is fortunate in a geographical situation that sets it somewhat apart from the fettering prejudices and rabid nationalism which retard endeavors to achieve permanent peace. It is easier for the natives to adopt a detached attitude in politics and commerce, to emphasize the points of unity instead of the differences among them. Their minds are more open to biological truths concerning the oneness of mankind and to history based on enlightened economics, taught without a false patriotism. While I deplore the imperialism that has subjugated Hawaii under a foreign yoke I think a unity of mutual aid and support is developing which may prove mighty enough to resist the estranging, maddening propaganda of racial supremacy. I shall follow with special interest any news concerning the Hawaiian Americans of different national backgrounds who are steering through human confusion and blindness from past antagonisms to a sanity of heart that will modulate their desires to the key of good will and intelligent co-operation. I have just gained a new hope for peace from reading an article on the harmonious relations between the racial groups in Hawaii by Mr Hume Ford and a splendid letter written to me by Mrs Satterthwaite, a member of the Pan-Pacific Union. (She was among the members of the Honolulu Business and Professional Women's Club I met yesterday.) She describes at length the efforts of the union to bring about amicable discussion and settlement of problems confronting the fourteen countries which border on the Pacific, where more than half the world's population lives.

As Polly and I were coming out of the palace we were surrounded by a large crowd of schoolboys and girls, and I was asked to say a few words to them from the balcony. Afterwards we were taken to the Territorial School for the Blind and the Deaf, and fresh leis were rained upon me by delegates from the Honolulu Junior League, the Japanese Junior League, the Hospital Social Service, the Chamber of Commerce and the

Helen Keller's Journal

students. Then I learned what those works of art meant —the wreath weavers rising at dawn, picking masses of blossoms and spending hours threading them together petal by petal. What a lavish, colorful welcome to bestow upon a visitor! And I counted between twenty and thirty leis round my neck. I especially loved a lavender passionflower lei presented by the blind children and a cerise strawflower lei made by the deaf. I am sorry that the blind and the deaf are taught in the same school. The combination method does not produce the best results. For it imposes a heavier burden upon those who teach two entirely different groups of handicapped, and it is not possible to give each group the special attention it requires. But I was delighted to find the Territorial School in spacious grounds where the students can exercise freely and develop happily, with beauty calling to the eye or the ear in mountain, sea, bird songs and brilliant vegetation.

The luncheon with the Honolulu Lions and the Business and Professional Women's Club took place at Fuller Hall. Before I spoke the orchestra, led by one of my sightless fellows, sent out deep, sweet vibrations that I could feel a long way off. Then I stood beside him and kept time while he played the ukulele. The selection was the heart-melting song "Aloha Oe" sung by Queen Liliuokalani. As the plaintive notes floated about me it seemed as if there had never been a sadder farewell to friends, happiness and queenly power.

Our charming hostess was the governor's daughter, Helen Poindexter. His Excellency placed his automobile at our disposal for a ride round Honolulu. It had grown quite hot, and I was glad when we stopped at the pineapple factory, where we enjoyed the coolest, most de-

Helen Keller's Journal

licious pineapple juice I had ever tasted. To my regret I found we did not have time to pay our respects to the active volcano, Kilauea, but we drove far enough into the mountains to be overpowered by their magnificence. Polly said they seemed to float in an ocean of unearthly blue, and the rounded green slopes were beyond description. I felt the car zigzag up corkscrew roads between hibiscus hedges, groves of palm and bamboo, pineapple fields and homes built on the summit or near it for the fascinating view in every direction. Mr Palmer, who teaches the deaf, was of the party. Between his wealth of legend, history and Hawaiian names liquid with vowels, Polly's color-filled fingers and the smells that flooded my nostrils I received a Niagara of impressions which I have not yet formulated.

We got out to visit Queen Emma's summer palace with its wide cool rooms. I was permitted to touch the enormous beds on which the natives sleep, the cradle of the queen's heir, her sewing table and her mat-weaving loom. In the hall was the royal standard made from the long, slender feathers of the frigate bird. Everywhere stood great vases containing gorgeous bird-of-paradise plants, "cups of gold"—blossoms as big as my two clasped hands—and no end of lilies. A glass case was opened so that I might see the queen's amazing cape made from the plumage of a black bird with green feathers under its wings. It took several generations to collect the feathers in the molting season and stitch them together. Then we walked into the "grass hut" or pavilion where the king sought refuge from the cares of state. It had many windows as well as dry grass between strong, smooth bamboo logs. What romance it suggested—revelers under the tender

Helen Keller's Journal

dreaming evening sky, graceful slender hula dancers, the ukulele sending its wistful notes out over the sea until the stoutest hearts succumbed to the love spell!

We drove on to the great Pali, or cliff, where Laihahee towered majestically close by; and the masses of white surf beating against the rock caught a rainbow glory in the sun. On the exposed side a furious blast buffeted the car. Its vibration, which caused the windows to rattle, was startlingly like the roar of Niagara Falls which I have visited several times. I was told that wind had turned over a number of automobiles.

As we returned down the mountain a sudden pungent whiff made my heart jump with delight—the fragrance of eucalyptus trees which mingles with all my memories of Los Angeles. The giant banyan tree where Stevenson used to sit writing or gazing seaward was pointed out to us, and we walked round it—a circumference of about a hundred feet. No one knows how old it is. The size of the branches in every direction and the tremendous roots I scrambled over gave me the impression of a grove, but really it is one colossal tree.

Back in Honolulu we walked over the enchanting grounds of the Hawaiian Imperial Hotel. What an ideal place to have dinner in the open air among tropical shrubs, trees and potted plants. . . . Before leaving the island Polly and I had a cup of tea at the house of Governor Poindexter, which rested us somewhat after our deluge of beauty. Miss Poindexter drove us to the dock. Reluctantly we said good-by to the warmhearted friends who had made the day a sunburst of hospitality and pleasure for us, but their Alohas cheered us with the knowledge that we would be welcome if we came back for a longer stay.

Helen Keller's Journal

Aloha means farewell to thee,
Aloha means good-by:
It means until we meet again
Beneath a tropical sky.
Aloha means good morning
And always to be true,
But the best thing that Aloha means
Is that I love you.

The Asama Maru was gorgeous with streamers as it moved out of Honolulu. Although Polly and I could scarcely stand from fatigue we went on deck for a glimpse of the beautiful harbor and Laihahee. People were waving to the ship, singing, shouting, the very automobiles seemed to honk "Aloha!" until we were a long way from the shore.

When we entered our hot stateroom and saw leis piled high on our beds we groaned—in fact, I could have screamed. I was so surfeited with sweet smells and crazy to stretch out, I simply threw the wreaths on the floor. I understood as I had never before the painful effect of a dazzling spectacle too prolonged upon the eyes of those who see.

While we were having dinner in bed two boxes were brought in filled with an odorous miscellany of flowers which I was about to send away when a Braille label caught my finger tips.

These are some of the lovely flowers that grow in Hawaii.
TERRITORIAL SCHOOL FOR THE DEAF AND THE BLIND.

I found they had with Aloha thoughtfulness fastened a Braille card to each blossom, giving its name and colors, and for an hour I forced my drowsing mind to identify them. There were also some queer natural curios —a branch from the sausage tree, the shower pod—a long stiff receptacle filled with seeds that, shaken, vibrated like a baby's rattle—and the baobab bombax (the rat tree). All night I dreamed that I was being smothered with sweetness, and this morning I ache every time I recall the leis pressing upon my shoulders.

With twitching fingers Polly has done her best to spell the endless pen-written Honolulu messages, and with hands quite as tired I have gone over the Braille Alohas. Now I am oppressed by the prospect of thank-you letters I am to write to Governor Poindexter, the school and many others. . . .

How did we drag ourselves on deck? I wonder. After a chicken sandwich we stretched out in the steamer chair and closed our eyes. While we were resting a distinguished, dignified gentleman called on us for a few minutes—Mr Mitani, who, I believe, is an important official connected with the Japanese embassy at Paris. Without meaning any discourtesy I fear I was languid, acknowledging the honor of meeting him. Mr Mitani said his sister met me years ago during her student days at Radcliffe College while I was there. He went on to say there were between three and four hundred Japanese aboard the ship going back to their native land for the cherry-blossom season. When I told him how interested I was in Hanawa he asked me if he might cable the welcoming committee at Yokohama inquiring if arrangements could be made for me to visit Hanawa's birthplace. How wonderful that would be! I doubt, however, whether we shall have time. I am under the impression that the program will be a staggering one. . . .

Helen Keller's Journal

After yesterday's excessive handshaking I notice cramps in my palms. It relieves me to confide to this insentient, imperturbable typewriter my misanthropic mood. I have resolved that I shall not risk paralysis by shaking every hand extended to me or grow dumb by talking from breakfast until midnight each day in Japan. I have frequently been asked if it tires me to talk, and I have replied, "Did you ever hear of a woman who got tired talking?" I am that woman for once today!

We were invited to a Japanese dinner tonight, but I would not go. Polly was weary, and we thought it a good plan to eat carefully. We are still sampling Japanese dishes, as cautiously as if we were playing with fire, and my brain feels like mush.

Aboard the Asama Maru, April 8th.

At half-past five Polly and I pulled ourselves out of bed. We had told each other solemnly that we needed exercise, and the speeches must be practiced while few people were around. We paced the upper deck an hour. It was cool and pleasant. The sea was a soft gray, and I felt a light spray as the ship plowed along. Some gulls circled overhead, and my spirit rose with a hymn to the fresh, still morning. There is no blessedness for one task-driven like "being aware of a morning hour upon sublunary things." We met a Japanese in his kimono, chanting, and I thought he must be a priest. I began practicing, and then had a heart-sinking emotion because three of the speeches I had prepared did not please me. During the harum-scarum rush of the seven weeks

Helen Keller's Journal

we had been in Forest Hills I had not had a sufficiently calm mind to examine them critically.

After breakfast I wrote and rewrote the speeches until I felt mentally black and blue. They must be as short as possible if I am not to overtax my listeners' patience with my halting delivery, and I am anxious to put over as many worth-while ideas as I can in my pleas for the Japanese blind.

Again we had lunch sitting on deck so as to be by ourselves. I became absorbed in the part of *Gone with the Wind* describing Scarlett's frantic ministrations to Melanie in her childbirth agony, her flight from Atlanta and how she killed the thief. No light reading—far from it! But I am glad to see Scarlett being transformed from a spoiled belle into a courageous, responsible worker. Rhett Butler is out of the picture at present, much to my relief. He is one of the sensible people without heart whom I shun as heartily as any fool—he is supremely selfish, sarcastic and bitter. I hate his truths conveyed with a sneer no less than falsehood. . . .

More work on the speeches. Then there were pictures and autographs. There seems to be no escape. I sign them and sign another bunch and another until I feel like the man in the tale who was bound hand and foot when ants attacked him, and died a slow death.

Tonight we had a pleasant time dining with Captain Kaneko up in his cabin. In the middle of the table was a small stove on which he cooked a delicious Japanese dish, sukiyaki. First he put oil into the saucepan, then all kinds of vegetables, rice and bamboo and juicy meat on top. He kept putting nice morsels hot from the stove on my plate and was most careful cutting them up for me. He said we would often have sukiyaki dinners

Helen Keller's Journal

in Japan. Polly and I were glad to hear that; we knew we should be sure to like it. At first I was a bit perturbed finding chopsticks beside the plate—I had visions of dropping everything and making myself ridiculous—but I managed better than I expected, and the captain was so courteous I felt quite at my ease during the meal. With simple dignity he dwelt most on the quiet kind of work he enjoys doing in his leisure moments—writing up sporting events for the papers and tending plants.

This evening we were at the cinema. The picture that interested me especially was *The Island of Mahi*. It showed how the sugar cane is cut on the great sugar plantations, crushed in the mills and sent down the railroad to the sea. I do not care for the cheap love-making pictures shown on this ship.

Aboard the Asama Maru, April 9th.

Up soon after 5 A.M., so that Polly and I could rehearse more of the speeches on deck. The decks and windows were being washed, and we had to move about gingerly. But these are days when we cannot afford to have any inconveniences put us out, and it was interesting to watch the sailors at work in the sweet, soft, gray calm of a Pacific dawn.

Oh, those speeches! Every time I go over them I feel as if I were sitting on a volcano. I know there is going to be an eruption of unexpected circumstances connected with the lectures, and I have no idea how much time I shall be given to speak or how I shall arrange the material to suit the purpose of the meeting. Owing to the difficulty of communicating with the workers for

Helen Keller's Journal

the blind of Japan over eight thousand miles, it is still impossible to plan our work or to anticipate any plans they may have made. Nor can I be sure what the attitude of the audiences in some parts of Japan is towards the handicapped. Alas! with all the advantages of the telephone, telegraph, cable and airplane, distance can still be a terrible obstacle to quick, effective action.

The captain came in before lunch and gave me an autobiographical sketch which I know I shall enjoy if Polly and I ever get a chance to read it. His cheerful serenity despite ill health and heavy duties and his pleasant talk helped me forget my nerve-trying uncertainties, and I started work again refreshed.

Gone with the Wind is still delightful, though repetitious at times. It stirs in me a nostalgia for the drowsy, sweet spring and early summer days in Tuscumbia, the red earth, the huge old magnolia trees and live oaks. Again I smell Mother's royal wealth of roses, the masses of tangled honeysuckle and paulownia blossoms heavy in the afternoon heat. Again the air about me vibrates with excitement as the men fulminate against some political group or refight the Civil War. Or perhaps it is the big spring to which my retrospective thoughts drift. There the Negroes come, young and old, with buckets to fetch water. Picturesque in bright-colored bandanas, barefooted, always singing or dancing or performing a cakewalk, they warm my heart, and I long for the joyous pickaninnies who so good-naturedly played with the insatiate tomboy I was. But time's disillusioning searchlight has years ago fallen upon those days, which seemed to me a glorious playtime forever. Sadly I recall the degrading poverty, the ignorance and superstition into which those little ones were born and

Helen Keller's Journal

the bitterness of the Negro problem through which many of them are still living.

Aboard the Asama Maru, April 10th.

The ship was rocking more than it had since leaving San Francisco when we went on deck at 6 A.M. Occasionally the spray flew over us in light wreaths. Heavy clouds foretold rain before long, but Polly said their dull gray was restful to her eyes, and I was glad of the coolness after the oppressive, sticky heat of the last two days.

For the life of me I have not been able yet to memorize all the speeches. I am almost in despair. I can practice only an hour and a half without getting hoarse, and that does not give time for more than four or five speeches. After saying them over I find the others have slipped out of my mind as if on roller skates, and I swear silently and relearn them. Are they worth all this trouble, I wonder, and will my message impress the Japanese sufficiently to bear practical results?

This afternoon I received a welcoming cable from Mr Iwahashi. I understand there is to be a tremendous crowd to greet us at the dock.

This evening we saw a remarkable Japanese comedy, *The Barber*, in which a troublesome neighbor starts a vociferous quarrel between a man and his wife who have hitherto lived in peace. The acting was so clever and the facial expressions so full of speech, Polly could give me the play without understanding the words. I was really proud of our cabin steward when I found that it was he who impersonated the barber. It seems to me all classes of the Japanese show fine dramatic instinct as well as artistic sensibility.

Eight thousand miles! It does not seem possible that we should be voyaging that far, and I still feel at home on these waters. But then I have always by temperament been a citizen of the world. My inner freedom from the limits of space and time is a precious possession. At this distance Forest Hills, with all I love in it, is vividly present to me, and I know that individuals and places in Nippon will be quite as near and real after I leave that country this summer.

Aboard the Asama Maru, April 11th.

During the night the ship rolled a good deal. But when Polly and I began our walk the wind had fallen, I fancied, like a mighty bird folding its wings. Sea and sky were enveloped in a gray mist, like soft chiffon, and it was an hour or so before the sun brushed the film aside and warmed the chill air.

While I worked one greeting after another was cabled to me from Nippon. Prince Tokugawa sent this poetic message: "The committee, the nation and the cherry blossoms await you." Requests were wired for greetings from me to the Tokyo Asahi, which I managed to send between speeches. An article about how I spent the time on the ship was wanted which I would not write because I knew that if I complied I should be swamped with requests for similar articles.

The pleasant-faced man whom we meet chanting in the mornings seems troubled because no meetings have so far been arranged in his city, Yokohama, where there

Helen Keller's Journal

is a school for the blind. He talked to us about it at length today, and I had difficulty in keeping a straight face; for I have had no say whatever in the program, and I do not even know where we shall begin or who will conduct us through the cities. Our only information up to now is what we learned before sailing—that we are under the auspices of the Osaka Asahi, the Japanese Department of Education, the minister of foreign affairs and the minister of home affairs....

Polly has had a busy day. She has been making out a declaration of our luggage, having our money changed from dollars to yen, issuing ultimatums to people who invaded our privacy too much, giving battle to a host of autograph hunters and reading the cables to me. Why does the impression persist, I wonder, that this is a pleasure trip for us and that therefore I can be at everybody's beck and call morning, afternoon and night?

The captain is as kind and understanding as he can be, and really concerned when he tells us how heavy our program is likely to be. He had spoken much of Hanawa and would like us to be free to visit the little old wooden house where that wonderful scholar without sight was born. How I should love to do that before we return to America!

Mrs Bullard has radiated cheer and friendship to us ever since we left Honolulu. She will be in Tokyo a day or two, and we hope she can spend a quiet evening with us at the Imperial Hotel. We were discussing *Gone with the Wind* today, and she delighted me by saying she had a mammy who was as faithful as the one at Tara, and who was constantly misquoting fine things she had picked up in Shakespeare. For instance, she would say "trembling like an aspirin." Her daughters' bright presence rests me after hours of severe mental effort. Without conceit I think two high-strung women like Polly and me, thrown upon our own inner resources, have good courage to undertake the strangest expedition of our lives with as little fussiness as we do.

Aboard the Asama Maru, April 12th.

Last night my heart almost stopped when I read in *Gone with the Wind* how Scarlett, finding her mother dead, felt that she had come to the end of the road—to a dead wall from which there was no escape. But resolutely I said over and over, "In the Divine Bosom is our dwelling place where all limits vanish."

No sooner had Polly and I come down from our walk than another batch of welcoming cablegrams was handed to us. The National Christian Association, the Women's Federation of Clubs in Tokyo, my Japanese publishers and many individuals whose names caused me to quake because of their difficult spelling. My satisfaction in having voyaged these thousands of miles dissolved and I trembled lest my ignorance of this or that celebrity might seem an affront. Mark Twain was right when he said that as soon as we are at rest in this world off we go on something else to worry about.

Sometimes I wish these too, too solid limitations would melt; I feel positively bruised with their impacts! Day and night, in torrents of letters, under an avalanche of compliments I am reminded that I cannot see or hear when I know perfectly well that in the eternal sense I do. The spirit, like the sea, is greater than any island or continent of sense-experience within its waters. It has an infinite horizon of ideas that bring new facts and a way of living in accordance with them. My deep-rooted feeling that I am not deaf or blind is like the feeling that I am *in* the body but not *of* it. Of course I know that outwardly I am a "deaf and blind" Helen Keller. That is a transitory ego, and the few dark, silent years I shall be here do not matter. I use my limitations as tools, not as my real self. If others are helped through them that is the seventh heaven of happiness for me. The rub comes with the everlasting absorption in problems of deafness and blindness that keeps me from oftener looking out upon the universe through book windows or listening to the many-voiced course of things. . . .

How exciting it is to be several selves at once! There is the beauty of Nippon calling insistently to one part of me, the dubious task of interesting the Japanese enough to start a nationwide movement for their blind, while a third part—a pretty equal one—is brooding anxiously over the desperate world situation.

Apprehension has filled my thoughts since I read two weeks ago that Hitler had ordered the army to be ready in case of a sudden coup d'état. He would not attempt it alone, surely, but there is no conjecturing as to what direful events may result from his interviews with Mussolini. Those two ruthless leaders may yet lay the train for another war. Even if Germany collapses in its insane pursuit of power—and Thomas Mann believes it will—Italy still appears vigorous and capable of inflicting terrific defeats upon Europe before the other nations succeed in crushing its Hydra-headed militarism. This is not a bright outlook for one with my passionate desire that no more men be blinded or maimed in war, and here I am on my way to another country where the party in power is not a friend to peace. Fervently I hope Norman Davis, one of the few Americans who understand European affairs, may suggest a constructive method to direct the efforts of the nations towards peace and co-operation.

Aboard the Asama Maru, April 13th.

It seems as if my track across the Pacific had been strewn with welcomes from Nippon; messages by radio and cable have continued since early this morning. Such cordiality is overpowering. Every faculty in me prays that I may accomplish half the good they expect.

Polly and I kept at the desk from before breakfast until seven-thirty. Then we thought we had time enough to put on our prettiest gowns for the captain's dinner, but we came to grief. We had not worn them before, and it was slow work fixing the diminutive hooks and eyes, fastening the lilliputian lingerie straps and putting in clips. Our nerves were like fiddlestrings when we finally arrived, but the gay atmosphere restored our good humor. The room was adorned with lighted lanterns, potted shrubs, artificial cherry-blossom garlands and festoons. There were models of a temple, a sampan and a Japanese house with cherry trees, all of which I was permitted to touch. The ice cream was cut in the shape of a cherry blossom. It was fun watching the dancers and tossing the bright-colored balloons in every direction. The captain's geniality made everything still pleasanter.

Helen Keller's Journal

Our dreams are becoming strange like everything else. Polly has repeatedly dreamed of a bird that keeps following the ship and trying to get into our room, but is driven away. I dream of a little child that plays and plays hide-and-seek with me, though we never succeed in finding each other because a mist always rises between us....

How endearing is this bit I have just read about Jizo, the little ones' god! He says, "I will hide thee in my sleeves and keep thee from all evil and play shadow-play with thee."

For the first time I am beginning to form a clear picture of the dreadful Reconstruction Period in the South from *Gone with the Wind*. The criminally stupid descent of the North upon prostrate states with a deluge of carpetbaggers and scalawags turns into a mockery the bloody Civil War fought to emancipate the slaves.

Aboard the Asama Maru, April 14th.

A mist was floating round the ship like incense out of a burner when Polly and I took our last walk on deck at 6 A.M. We were silent, but each knew what the other was thinking—"This is Teacher's birthday." That thought has continued uppermost the whole day, however busily I might attend to pressing tasks with the surface of my mind.

When I awoke this morning I started to find Teacher and tell her somehow my joy that the world had been blessed in her birth. Then I remembered and was transfixed with pain. There was no language for my yearning to see her—to keep not merely reaching out through aching heartbeats but to be with her and a part of her other home where joy is in its fullness. I felt like the monk of De Machlinia's tale who was walking with his beloved patron, St Nicholas, in a vision. They came to "a full glorious wall of crystall whose height no man might see, and length no man might consider and a shining gate with a cross in the middle." The cross was lifted to give free entrance to those who were admitted but let down to prevent others from coming in. St Nicholas entered, holding the monk's hand, with a prayer that they might be received together, but was forced to let him go as the cross descended between them. Heartbroken, the monk stood before the shut gate, thinking he was the one who had died, just as I think in such forlorn moments.

But those moments are only shadows on life's dial; and by tracing them back to the Divine Sun, I again find the brightness of Teacher's spirit living with me, no matter what barrier may hide one from the other....

Ever since I started reading about the religious beliefs of Nippon I have had a very warm sympathy with the Buddhist in his attitude towards immortality. It is a religion of affection which regards the departed not as dead but as a part of the home life of those who love them. Unseen, they guard the house and watch over everyone in it; every night they hover in the glow of the shrine lamp, and the stirring of its flame is said to be their motion. Dwelling mostly within their memorial tablets, they observe and hear everything that happens to the family; they delight in the voices and the warmth about them. Sometimes, it is said, they can animate a tablet, change it into a human body and thus return to aid and comfort the living.

While the ancestor worship and the animistic element

Helen Keller's Journal

in this creed do not appeal to me, the Buddhist's confidence that the invisible world sustains and nourishes the visible is refreshing in the midst of present-day vagueness and agnosticism.

Thankfully I gather courage from the innumerable details in Swedenborg's writings concerning the other world. For they help me to share by imagination Teacher's limitlessly varied, colorful, many-worlded experience. "Plucking the flower of life," the Chinese say of death, and how magnificently that flower spreads out before me in Swedenborg's word pictures! I can think of nothing to suggest its richness even slightly except the emblem of perfection—the sweet-scented lotus opening in the morning sunshine with curving petals and leaves whose shiny surfaces reflect every mood of the sky and constantly change colors as the day passes over them. As I contemplate it the curtain between Teacher and me becomes no longer the devouring silence of death or the desert, but rather a silence interpreted by the music of nature and "scanned by the prosody of humanity."

What is so tragic to me on this anniversary is that I lived too long with Teacher's scintillating, unique, stimulating personality to be content among ordinary folk. Always I shall look about, despite myself, for the sparkle with which she charmed the dullest person into a new appreciation of beauty or justice or human rights. My fingers will cry out for her descriptive touches which were nuggets of gold, her exquisite tenderness, her bright summaries of conversation or books not in raised print. Then, too, the trust I had in her from childhood was a support not easily to be replaced. Anyone who knows how sentiments shrivel "in the gradual furnace

Helen Keller's Journal

of the world" will understand the enthusiasm such memories awaken and the loneliness after such a parting.

However, I am certain that Teacher is exceedingly with me on this voyage. Both Polly and I notice that strength flows into us for tasks to which we never dreamed we should be equal. Surely it is towards this supreme undertaking that Teacher strove with such an urge in her heart. It was for this that she worked so painstakingly, making the most of the circumscribed life with which I was equipped.

In a book on China I read that a man had a small rock garden with a pool, a pavilion and bamboos. His wife was a poet, and he wished her to have a quiet spot for meditation. He separated this retreat from the rest of the garden with a hedge of dwarf pines. It was contained within a few yards, but he so carved the flat land that he produced a perspective seemingly of many miles. The winding path went by a waterfall, climbed through mountain foliage, passed a flower-sweet dell, entered a forest, came out by a lake where tall lilies bloomed, followed a slow river through a sunny green field and terminated at the door of a rustic cottage. Even so did Teacher gather into the small compass within my reach knowledge, beauty, chances of usefulness—and lo! the path we followed during fifty years has wound magnificently across the world to Nippon! Having come thus far, she will reinforce my labors with an inner power given only to those who have loved deeply and believed unwaveringly. . . . And as I stood on deck this morning in the mist of dawn, looking westward to the land where a great adventure awaits me, I thought I could feel her by my side.

Index

Aberdeen, Lady, 45, 46–47, 67, 83, 97
  Lord, 46, 98
Æ., 139–140
Æsop, 73
Ainsworth, Robert, 150
Alexander I, of Yugoslavia, 16–18
Allen, Reginald, 251
Amelia, *see* Bond, Mrs Thomas
Andrea, *see* Berens, Mrs Conrad
Argentina, La, 23
Attlee, Clement R., 154

Baillie, Joanna, 108
Bain, Andrew, 82, 92
  Elizabeth, 82, 83, 92, 235
Baird, Mr, 46
Baldwin, Stanley, 10, 147
Bankhead, William B., 196, 201
Barley, Major Leslie, 24, 25
  Mrs Leslie, 24, 25
Barney, *see* Saybolt, Mrs William
Bartlett, Mrs Paul, 178
Bashkirtseff, Marie, 21, 36–37
Bax, Clifford, 139, 151, 180–181
Bell, Alexander Graham, 12, 70, 141
Belloc, Hilaire, 180
Berens, Conrad, 230, 242
  Mrs Conrad (Andrea), 149, 213, 249, 251
Brand, Albert, 202
Black, Hugo, 88, 196, 208, 220
Bloch, M. Marcel, 177
Bok, Mrs Edward, 216–217
Bond, Mrs Thomas (Amelia), 196–197, 202, 204, 228, 254
Booth, Evangeline, 227
Borglum, Gutzon, 160–162, 170, 171, 178, 185, 197; and Thomas Paine statue, 8, 106, 157, 158; and Rodin statues, 161, 164–167
Braddy, Nella (Mrs Keith Henney), 210, 229, 238, 241, 242
Brandeis, Louis D., 184
Bridgman, Laura, 223
Bridie, James (Dr O. H. Mavor), 33, 40–41, 66, 91–92

Brieux, Eugene, 240–241
Broun, Heywood, 232
Browning, Robert, 58
Brownlee, John, 180, 189
Bullard, Mrs Sellar, 284, 301
Burns, Robert, 69

Canterbury, Archbishop of, 64, 109
Cardozo, Benjamin N., 184
Carmen Sylva, 175
Carnegie, Andrew, 124, 125
  Mrs Andrew, 125–126
Caruso, Enrico, 189
Carver, George Washington, 211–212
Chaliapin, Feodor, 189
Chamberlain, Lewis B., 238
Chang Hsueh-liang, 92–93
Chaplin, Charlie, 72
Charnwood, Lord, 71
Chiang Kai-shek, 92–94
Cierva, Juan de la, 55, 56
Clemenceau, 167
Cockin, Mr, 22
Connelly, Marc, 20
Conrad, Joseph, 207, 276
Coolidge, Calvin, 97
  Mrs Calvin, 97
Cooper, Edith, 242
Copeland, Royal S., 220, 233
Coward, Noel, 204
Cravens, Kathryn, 231
Cromwell, William Nelson, 159–160, 171, 174, 176–177, 178–179
Cudingham, Mrs, 288
Curie, Marie, 177

Dalou, Jules, 168
Davidson, Jo, 161
Davies, W. H., 19
Davis, Norman, 304
  William T., 219
De Chavannes, Puvis, 167
De la Mare, Walter, 22
Deland, Margaret, 13
Dickens, Charles, 60

Index

Dickinson, Emily, 51
Disraeli, Benjamin, 28-29, 46, 83-84, 95
Drage, Mrs, 260
Drinkwater, John, 256
Duff, Mr, 214
Duncan, Augustin, 228
    Henry, 109
Duranty, Walter, 91-92

Eagar, Jimmy, 12, 13, 14
    W. McG., 12, 13, 14, 21, 148
    Mrs W. McG., 12, 13, 147
Eden, Anthony, 11, 123
Edward VIII, 48-49, 56-58, 59-61
Einstein, Albert, 76-77, 105, 136, 192, 246
Eliot, T. S., 138
Elizabeth, Princess, 22
Emerson, Ralph Waldo, 1
Emma, Queen, 291
Evans, Maurice, 228

Fabre, Henri, 63
Fairbanks, Douglas, 72
Fairhaven, Lady, 14-15, 151
Faulhaber, Michael Cardinal, 211
Finley, John, 236-237
Flagg, James Montgomery, 262-263
Foley, Kate, 272
Fosdick, Harry Emerson, 206
Ford, Hume, 289
Fraser, Sir Ian, 7, 22, 70, 147, 151
    Lady Ian, 151
Freeman, Ethel, 240-241
Freese, William, 236
Friedel, Capt., 4-5
Fryer, George B., 219
Fulenwider, Leslie, 228, 230, 235, 254

Gale, Mr, 221
Gandhi, Mahatma, 89, 137
Garbo, Greta, 187
George V, 46, 49-50
George VI, 66
Gladstone, William E., 28-29, 46, 83, 95, 98
Goebbels, Joseph, 121, 123
Goering, Hermann, 121, 123
Goethe, 122-123
Graham, Lady Jean, 39
Grahame, Kenneth, 21, 69, 73

Grenfell, Wilfred T., 83
Guedalla, Philip, 8
Gunther, John, 121

Haas, Herbert, 193, 195, 198, 226, 278; illness, 223, 224, 225, 229, 230, 231, 233, 234, 238, 239, 243, 244, 251, 252, 254
Hale, Edward Everett, 240
Hamman, Grace, 269, 287
Hanawa, 201, 294, 301
Harrison, Pat, 88
Haskell, Mr, 260
Hauptmann, Gerhart, 122-123
Hay, Bess, 248
Heald, Miss, 12, 13
Hearn, Lafcadio, 275
Heen, W. J., 288
Henney, Keith, 241
Herbert, see Haas, Herbert
Hill, Carol, 209
Hinsdale, Ira, 209, 249
Hirota, Koki, 134
Hitler, Adolph, 105, 106, 121, 123, 134, 136, 148, 168-169, 173, 211, 259, 303
Hitz, John (Pflegevater), 183
Hoffman, Malvina, 192
Holmes, Edward L. (Ned), 10, 58, 147, 267, 273
Holt, Rush, 221
Hoover, Herbert, 55-56
    Mrs Herbert, 55
Hopkins, Harry, 88, 145
Howe, Samuel Gridley, 223
Hugo, Victor, 165
Hunt, Frazier, 122
Hunter, Major, 235-236

Irwin, Robert (Bob), 220, 233
Ishi, Mr, 275
Ishimoto, Baroness, 201
Iwahashi, Takeo, 84-86, 226, 227, 299

Jackson, Pilkington, 117
Jastrow, Joseph, 246
Jeffers, Robinson, 42-43
Johnson, Dr Samuel, 14
Jones, Alice, 258-260, 263, 265
    Bryson, 258, 261, 263, 265
    Stanley, 245
Julian, M. J., 202

Index

Kaneko, Capt., 275, 276, 286, 296-297, 298, 301, 304
Keith, Ian, 228
Keller, Helen, *see* especially entries under Macy, Anne Sullivan, and Thomson, Polly
Kent, 221, 222
Khayyam, Omar, 21, 73-74
Koyama, Homer, 263
Kraemer-Bach, Mme Marcelle, 158, 177, 238

La Follette, Philip, 215
 Robert M., 220, 233
 Suzanne, 221
La Fontaine, 73
La Guardia, Fiorello, 227, 228
Lansing, Robert M., 97
Laurens, Jean-Paul, 168
Lawes, Mrs Lewis, 203
Lawrence, Thomas E., 150
Leigh, Mr, 247-248
Lenin, 87, 137, 192, 210, 250
Leonardo da Vinci, 180-181
Lewis, John L., 200
 Joseph E., 21, 160, 246
 Mrs Joseph E., 246, 251, 254
Liliuokalani, Queen, 288, 290
Livingstone, David, 114-117
Lockhart, John, 109
Loughran, Martha, 251, 253
Lovat-Fraser, Mr, 154
Love, Dr James Kerr, 24, 37-38, 39, 40, 41, 56, 120, 121, 124, 126
 Mrs James Kerr, 24, 37, 39, 41, 56, 120
Lubbock, Peter, 200-201
Lucas, E. V., 4, 21, 82-83
Lund, Charlotte, 246

MacDonald, Mrs, 164, 175, 176
MacKenzie, Mrs, 46
Maclaren, Ian (Dr Watson), 109-110
MacLeary, Bonnie, 243
Maeno, Mrs, 238-239
Macy, Anne Sullivan, Helen Keller's longing for, 1, 8, 15, 26-28, 33, 51, 69, 74-76, 90, 147, 154-155, 184, 190-191, 193-194, 199, 203, 210, 212, 225, 233-234, 243, 261, 266-267, 305-308; Helen Keller's dreams about, 6, 77-78; visits and travels, 7, 12, 17, 30, 39, 40, 49, 54, 55, 56, 67, 97-98, 111-112, 119, 125, 129, 143, 151, 164, 171, 257, 260, 273, 277-280; death, 10, 32, 41, 103, 127, 187, 219, 230, 237, 277-280; article on, by Dr Love, 38, 124; esteemed by Alexander Woollcott, 60, Maria Montessori, 66, A. G. Bell and Mark Twain, 70; Gutzon Borglum, 161, Schiaparelli, 175, Edward Bok, 217; compared with Mme de la Nux, 163, with Rodin, 166; at college with Helen Keller, 71; illness and last days, 85, 138-139, 208, 231, 248, 249, 251, 278; with Tagore, 89; reading, 140-141, 284; Dr Berens' care of, 149f.; feeling for Ireland, 186; delight in spring, 197, in dogs, 198; attitude towards Helen Keller's independence, 209; inspiration of, 216, 223-224, 274, 308; and John D. Wright, 229; at the *N. Y. Times*, 236; and Ethel Freeman, 240; cast of hand of, 243; bird reminds Helen Keller of, 244; at Wrentham, 246; at the Jones', 258
 John, 141, 219
Mann, Thomas, 122, 303
Margaret Rose, Princess, 22
Mark, Somers, 41
Marx, Karl, 118
Mary, Queen, 49-50, 59
Maule, Harry E., 241-242
 Mrs Harry E., 241
Maurois, André, 28, 46
Maxton, James, 147, 151, 152-154
 Mrs James, 151, 152, 153
Mears, F. C., 116
Melchett, Lord, 126
Mellon, Andrew, 97
Menten, Mr, 171, 172-173
Michelangelo, 167
Migel, M. C., 9, 86, 197, 198, 214-215, 226, 229, 245, 254, 294
 Mrs M. C., 229
 Richard, 257

[*311*]

Index

Mitani, Mr, 294
Montessori, Maria, 66
Montrose, Duke and Duchess of, 39
Moore, L. E., 8, 146, 149
Moore, Mrs William, 284
Morgan, Marion, 236, 237, 254
Morley, John, 83, 95
Morton, H. V., 21
Muir, Charles Augustus, 9, 135, 137, 138, 140, 141, 142, 147, 148, 149
    Jean, 9, 135, 137, 139, 140, 141, 143, 147
Murray, Gilbert, 53
Mussolini, Benito, 134, 259, 303

Nelson, William Rockhill, 260-261
Newton, Sir Isaac, 150
Norris, George, 227
Nuffield, Lord, 38
Nux, Lilie de la, 190, 208, 246, 251, 254
    M. de la, 162
    Mme de la, 162, 163

Ossietzky, Carl von, 68-69

Paine, Thomas, 8, 106-107, 144, 157, 158, 246, 248
Palmer, Mr, 291
Paul, Prince, 16
Pearson, Sir Arthur, 207-208
Pepys, Samuel, 22, 249
Perkins, Frances, 88
Pfeiffer, G. A., 274
Phillips, Wendell, 100
Pickford, Mary, 72
Pitcher, R., 71
Pitrois, Yvonne, 165
Platt, George Foster, 72
Poindexter, Helen, 290, 292
    James Boyd, 288, 292, 294
Polly, *see* Thomson, Polly

Radek, Karl, 145-146
Rait, Sir Robert, 40
Ratcliffe, Mr, 22
Ravarat, M., 176-177
    Mme, 176
Raymond, Robert, 198-199
Reith, Sir John, 109
Rhoades, Nina, 159, 249-250
Richards, Judge E. A., 190, 224, 225

Ridge, Dr and Mrs Frank, 263-264
Ripon, Archbishop of, 71
Rockefeller, John D., Jr, 38
Rodin, Auguste, 161, 164, 166
    Mme, 167
Rogers, H. H., 14, 15
    Will, 96
Romaine, Jules, 158
Roosevelt, Franklin Delano, 97, 102, 192, 196, 270; and South America, 35, 79, 248; inauguration, 129-131; and Supreme Court, 184-185, 215, 256-257; letter to Helen Keller, 268-269
Rowley, Mr, 22
Rutledge, Archibald, 20

Sabin, Florence, 192
Sardi, 237
Sargent, Margherita, 228
Satterthwaite, Mrs, 289
Saybolt, William, 190, 223, 224, 233, 252
    Mrs William (Barney), 209, 224, 233, 234, 249, 251, 253, 254
Scheffer, Paul, 122
Schiaparelli, Elsa, 164, 175-176
Schramm, Otto, 87, 148, 210, 232, 242; letter to, 103-106
Schreiner, Olive, 284
Schwimmer, Rosika, 246, 248
Scott, Mrs E. F., 43, 44, 45, 47
    Walter, 257
    Sir Walter, 108, 109
Shaw, George Bernard, 40, 67-68
Sheean, Vincent, 93
Silvestre, M., 188
Simpson, Mrs Wallis Warfield, 52
Slade, Miss, 171, 178
Smith, Constance, 218, 219
    Katharine, 218, 219
    Dr Philip, 218-220
    Mrs Philip, 218-220
Socrates, 54
Sokolnikoff, Gregory Y., 145
Sperry, Elsie, 271, 273
Squire, Sir John, 151, 182
Stalin, Joseph, 145, 192
Street, Charles H., 232
Stevenson, Robert Louis, 57, 118, 292
Stewart, Meum, 139
Sugimoto, Etsu, 253

Index

Sun Yat-sen, 93, 94
Swedenborg, Emanuel, 119, 307
Swinburne, Algernon Charles, 208

Tagore, Sir Rabindranath, 89-90
Taylor, Mrs E. M., 110
Teacher, *see* Macy, Anne Sullivan
Terauchi, H., 134
Thompson, James, 138
Thomson, David, 30, 50, 90, 131
  Effie, 30, 132
  John, 30, 42, 101, 117-118, 132
  Polly, with Helen Keller, on SS *Deutschland*, 1, 2, 3, 6; in London, 7, 8, 9, 12, 14, 15, 18, 19, 20, 21, 22, 143, 144, 146, 147, 149, 151, 152, 153, 155; in Surrey, 13; between Glasgow and London, 26, 135; in Glasgow, Scotland, 29, 30, 32, 33, 34, 35, 36, 48, 52, 54, 57, 59, 62, 66, 68, 76, 81, 86, 89, 96, 102, 106, 108, 127, 128, 129, 131, 133; at West Kilbride, 39, 41, 120; on the way to Dundee, 43; at Dundee, 44, 45; at Buckingham Palace, 49; at the White House, 55; at Lady Astor's, 67; in Hollywood, 72, 131-132; in dream, 77, 78; at Stirling, 82, 99; in Washington, 88, 218-219; at Haddo House, 97; in the Orkneys, 111, 114; at Skibo Castle, 125; in Essex, 137, 138-139; en route to Paris, 156; in Paris, 158, 159, 160, 163, 168, 169, 170, 174, 176, 177, 178; at Cherbourg, 164; en route to Havre and in Havre, 179; on SS *Champlain*, 180, 184, 185, 188, 189; on Long Island, 187, 195, 196, 198, 200, 203, 205, 208, 219, 222, 223, 224, 225, 226, 229, 231, 232, 233, 234, 239, 240, 241, 242, 243, 244, 248, 252, 253, 254; in New York City, 193, 199, 202, 204, 209, 212, 213, 227, 228, 236, 237, 246, 249, 251, 254, 255; en route to Philadelphia, 215; in Philadelphia, 215-217; en route from Washington, D. C., 222; in Chicago, 257; in Kansas City, 258, 259, 260, 263; in Denver, 265; en route from Denver to the Coast, 266; in San Francisco, 267, 268, 269, 270, 271, 273; in Honolulu, 287, 288, 289, 291, 292; on board the *Asama Maru*, 274, 275, 277, 280, 281, 284, 293, 294, 295, 297, 298, 299, 300, 301, 302, 304, 305, 308
  Robert, 30, 42, 80, 90, 117, 132, 133
  Robert J. (Bert), 29, 32, 73, 111, 132
  Mrs Robert J., 29, 32, 35-36, 107, 128
  Margaret, 43
Todd, Commander, 287
Tokugawa, Prince, 300
Tolstoy, Leo, 122, 136
Trotsky, Leon, 103, 145
Trudo, Mrs, 257
Turgenev, Ivan S., 207
Twain, Mark, 70-71, 145, 302

Van Doren, Carl, 52
Villard, Oswald Garrison, 68
Von Schirach, Baldur, 121

Wagner, Robert F., 88
Walker, Mr, 88
Waln, Nora, 93
Walsh, D. I., 196, 220
Walz, Mrs E. A., 215, 216, 217, 218
  Edward, 217-218
Washington, Booker T., 211
  George, 102, 205-206
Wasilewski, Mr and Mrs Jan, 228
Wilcox, Elsie, 288
Wilhelmina, Queen, 172
Wilkie, Sir David, 109
Windlestraw, George, 33
Witherspoon, John, 109
Wolf, M., 157, 159, 163, 169, 170, 171, 173, 174, 178
Woollcott, Alexander, 60 61, 212-213, 223, 225, 251
Wood, Sir Kingsley, 11, 151
Wright, Harold Bell, 247
  John, 229

Young, Gavin, 56
  Marjorie, 56